MW01526219

Guelph Public Library

971.10092 KIMUR
Kimura, Reggie, author
The life of one Cherry Charlie :
philosopher, poet, and pool player

SEP - - 2015

The Life of One Cherry Charlie

Philosopher, Poet and Pool Player

Reggie Kimura

971.1
0092
KIMUR

The Life of One Cherry Charlie

Copyright © 2013 by Reginald Kimura

ISBN-13: 978-1491084915

ISBN-10: 149108491X

All rights reserved. No part of this book may be reproduced or transmitted in any form or by any means without written permission of the author.

This book follows US spelling.

Sensei

Father of humanity, true human being

You cherish the Family of Myo Ho

Through our deluded lives

You have awakened "the promise"

that the 21st Century

will be the century of life

Reg Kimura

3 3281 01828 412 2

Table of Contents

+312

Bathtubs

December 11, 1927 in Victoria B.C. My how time flies -- transient life. Seventy-seven years -- a twinkling of an eye. I recall between the age of eight months and 18 months that the big fuss was who and how I was to be bathed.

Both my grandparents were born in Japan and mother was born in Vancouver. B.C. If cleanliness is Godliness then bathing was a religious ritual. I remember it always took place on the kitchen table. Earliest recollection, the tub was an ordinary basin and later a small dark wooden barrel cut to size. I wasn't able to talk but sensed that everybody was arguing who was going to bath me. Usually it was grandfather. According to my oldest uncle Michi, grandfather, including everybody else, spoiled me. He told me quite often that grandfather treated me like a prince and his own children with harsh discipline.

Apparently grandfather was a drunk and gambler. He was a good tailor and had his own store, quite successful in business, but squandered his money. My mother used to tell me she prayed that none of her children would drink and for whatever reason her wish was granted. If I drink a half a glass of beer my face will turn red and I either get sick and vomit or feel good and go to sleep. I have three brothers and two of them think they are macho and try to drink a lot but they can only handle a couple of beers. I do not know if my uncles are alcoholic but they sure can drink. On special occasions both could drink beer and whiskey all day, keep drinking into the night, and still be sober.

I guess we took after dad. He couldn't handle it and didn't like any form of booze. My father was a good man. He told me once he placed a $50 bet on a fan tan table in a Chinese gambling and almost had a nervous breakdown. After that he never gambled.

Another interesting incident happened when I was pre-speaking age, somehow I managed to get a small box of matches and I lay underneath a bed striking the matches, fascinated by the flame and unaware of burning the mattress and creating smoke. My grandmother and mother smelled the smoke and were frantic until they found me under the bed. In a soothing voice they conveyed the message not to play with matches and fire. I think they were puzzled at how I got hold of a box of matches and I can't remember either.

So I must have spent a regimented and ritualistic life until the time came to mumble and say some words. When anybody wanted to know the time I would run outside to look at the Town Clock, then show them where the hands of the clock were with my arms so they had a rough idea what time it was.

Introduced to sport at an early age. My youngest Uncle Yo, and sometimes Uncle Hank, would sit me on a couch and place me between his knees so I couldn't escape and kind of force me to box. It was tiring. Uncle Hank created hoops, probably from coat hangers and placed them all over the house, above the woodshed door, outside and inside the kitchen door, hallway door, hoops galore. He would use a tennis ball to play basketball and try to shoot it through the hoop and I would throw the tennis ball all over the place trying to put it through the hoop. Sometimes Hank would lift me up so I could dunk the ball. No wonder Hank became a good basketball player.

In front of the house, across the street, it looked like a fair size empty lot. My Uncles and his friends would play catch and hit some baseballs to each other. At an early age they tried to teach me how to play catch and with a little toy bat hit a tennis ball. The oldest, Uncle Michi pitched and Hank played shortstop for the Victoria Senior team. They also played football, rugby style in High School with the Patrick brothers. My Uncles told me how great the Patricks' were in sports and later they ended up as big hockey stars for the New York Rangers. Michi in later years played mostly golf and badminton and Hank continued to play basketball and some baseball.

When we all moved to Vancouver, Hank was a star in the Japanese Canadian Basketball league. He was considered quite tall for a person of Japanese ancestry, about five foot ten. If it weren't for seasonal work during baseball season, Hank would have been a great pitcher. He was able to pitch one or two games for the Asahi baseball team. The story goes he had a fast ball like Bob Feller, a great pitcher with the Cleveland Indians. Even in the late 30s and early 40s, Major League scouts were interested in some of the Asahi players. Roy Yamamura for the Yankees and Kaz Suga who later played for the Montreal Royals, Jackie Robinson, the first Black player to break into the Major Leagues, played for the Royals, farm club of the Brooklyn Dodgers.

However, I felt real good watching uncle play basketball. I don't think he had great running speed but the way he handled the ball was like magic, very smooth and deceptive. One of his friends told me in a practice he saw Hank shooting from the outer corner perimeter court, moving in a semi-circle to the other corner and never missing a shot. I saw my uncle make an incredible shot in practice from mid-court. He flexed his wrist without moving his arm and scored a basket. He had powerful wrists.

My uncle's friends used to tell me they never lost money betting on him in arm wrestling. When they worked in logging camps, strong men would come from other camps and all over to challenge Hank in arm wrestling. Many of the Caucasians were surprised and shocked when their big arm Swedish or Irish friends couldn't beat my Uncle Hank in arm wrestling. He once told me when he held his wrist in a certain way, nobody could bring his arm down and when he twisted their wrist in a certain way it would weaken their arm and made it easy for him to win.

Even my Dad who had tremendous strength was puzzled that he could not beat Hank in arm wrestling. Dad could lift the back end of a Model T Ford. I saw him put two sacks of rice on his shoulder weighing 100 pounds each and do the judo split ten or twelve times in a row, training in order to throw a two hundred pound man over his shoulder without wavering.

In Victoria BC dad taught the RCMP Judo. He would line them up and one at a time demonstrate the Judo technique. For him it was as easy as tossing a broomstick around. Those tall RCMP boys must have thought Dad was a superman. Although Dad did mention one person, Bob, who was not as tall as the other policemen, but had natural strength, good balance and knew wrestling. He became very difficult to throw or toss after a few lessons. When Bob learned all the judo technique he became a formidable opponent. Dad always used to say, give him a naturally strong and powerful person and he could make him into a black belt in six months. Most people take three to five years to develop the kind of strength and power needed in order to become a black belt.

It was interesting to hear when Father told me Uncle Hank was the most difficult person to throw. Every time he caught Hank in a position to throw him, Hank would just drape over Dad's body like a wet blanket. Dad mentioned he was like sticky glue and it was difficult, very difficult to throw him cleanly. Hank used to say just before contact to relax the body, especially in hockey and football, to avoid injury.

Dad was a good acrobat. I've seen photos of him doing handstands on the railing of a high bridge and another where he held a vertical pole, his arm in a V shape and body straight out parallel to the ground, high above on the bridge. Barnum and Bailey, the Circus people wanted my Dad to perform on the trapeze. My Dad wanted to join and travel with the Circus but my Mother was against it. She didn't like the idea of Dad being half-naked, showing off his body.

Mac Miya, a well-known body builder, has his own Gym in Toronto and trained many body builders. Mac was amazed at my Dad's body. He kept saying all of Dad's muscles had definition, meaning that Dad developed every muscle proportionally. Mack would name all the muscles like a Doctor using Latin medical terms. Mac and Dad worked in the same place and Mac would brag about how big his muscles were. Dad agreed but would tease Mac by saying even though his whole body was developed, his neck was small and still underdeveloped. Mac challenged Dad that he could put him to sleep with a judo choke and Dad said he couldn't because the training in Judo developed his neck muscle. Also, Dad knew how to position his neck and shoulder muscles to protect himself. Mac tried to choke Dad but couldn't put him to sleep. Father showed me the red welts around his neck which some of it bled a bit. Because of Mac's tremendous strength the cloth of the collar dug into his skin. Father laughed it off saying that Mac finally admitted his neck was the weak link in his body and wouldn't let Dad do a Judo choke on his neck even with only one hand. I didn't see this happen even though I was working there part time.

It would have been nerve wracking to watch that choking contest. After Father got married twenty years ago he stopped training in Judo and was much older and not in real good physical condition. On the other hand, Mac was young and strong. Later Mac, in the all-weight division, won the World Record One Hand Clean and Jerk 300 pounds over his head. It's an amazing feat considering Mac is only 5'5" tall and weighed approximately 170 pounds at that time. My Dad was 5'3" and in his prime weighed 145 pounds. When I was a little boy I saw Dad in a couple of fights. Little man throwing a big man around. Things happen so fast that it was over in seconds. No time for emotions; I would just stare and wonder why the big man is laying on the ground.

After my grandparents died grandma first and shortly afterwards, grandpa, our family all moved to Vancouver. I guess we lived on Cordova Street. Across the street was the Powell Ground where the famous Asahi baseball team played. To the West corner block was a Catholic Church. My Mother was an atheist and thought all religion was the same and Father believed in all religion and thought all religion was the same. My Mother was a great believer in education so she sent me to the Catholic school Kindergarten that was the closest to our house. I was the eldest. My sister Doreen attended later, and as the family grew, all my brothers and sisters became Catholics. If it had been a Hindu temple with a kindergarten, we would all have been Hindus.

I was baptized, indoctrinated, ritualized and participated in all the sacraments including being an altar boy. During that time, two things come to my mind -- lots of spanking done by the nuns, even to the girls and I'm pretty sure I was never spanked. The other one was about the story of a statue of the Virgin Mary somewhere else. Blood was flowing from the palm of her hand so I prayed and prayed for the blood to flow from the palm of our statue. After a few months I sort of felt something was wrong so I quit praying for blood.

Another incident I remember well was Mom was doing laundry in the backroom bathroom on the second floor. My sister Doreen was standing on a chair, leaning over the windowsill, and suddenly it seemed like she disappeared into thin air. I said, "Mom, Mom" and pointed towards the window. Mother, without hesitation, dashed downstairs to the back yard. Doreen must have flipped over and landed on her bum, sitting in an upright position on the soft garden soil. Outside of just whimpering she had no injury and was in perfect physical condition. I believe for two weeks or more my sister was the center of attraction and the talk was about her miraculous fall.

My sister was always falling. About a year earlier in Victoria, we moved to a logging camp where my Dad worked. Doreen fell into a well so I ran to Mother saying ba-ba-ba-ba which was baby talk for water. Mother instinctively ran to the well and jumped in. She shouted to me to lower the bucket then go for help. I can't remember the instruction she gave me but I found a man, probably the cook, and he helped Mom and Doreen out of the well. I don't think Mother's jump into the well was that deep, probably less than ten feet, but to me the well looked like a bottomless pit.

Another time at the camp, for whatever reason, Mother made me angry so I threatened her by saying, "I'm going to run away from home." It didn't seem to bother her and she just ignored me. This made me furious and, sticking to my promise, I started to walk along a dirt road away from home. After a while I came to a section of the forest where all the trees were burnt and I couldn't help but notice the landscape looked black and eerie. I knew from hearsay that thunder and lightning caused forest fires and while walking I began to feel spooky about the surroundings. Sensing it was getting dark, I thought it would be crazy to spend the night sleeping on ashes so I turned around and went back home, behaving like nothing had happened. I didn't want to admit the failure of running away from home.

Doreen, later in life, became a cardiac nurse, lived in Calgary and worked for the Foot Hill Hospital. Dreams come true; she enjoyed skiing and falling. Her worst fall was the night her vehicle went off the road, down the side of the mountain, into a heavy growth of bushes supported by two trees that prevented her car from plunging down the abyss. At night, pitch black, seriously injured, she had a near death experience and a vision of the person who actually did call for help and saved her life. In some ways, Doreen led a troubled life due to her relationship with Mom, which was quite hectic. Now in her senior years she's found some sort of spirituality for happiness and peace.

After Cordova Street we moved four more times. The second place was Atlantic Street. It was like living in Italy. Most of the families were Italians. Atlantic Street was only one long block. Behind it on the north side was the Italian community and to the south, across the street, lay the CNR flats, probably half a mile wide. Near the middle of the flat were the railway tracks and boxcars. Passenger and freight trains were running quite frequently. To the right was the CN Station and to the left was the city dump, mountains of garbage. It was far enough away that we never smelled the stink.

Our neighbor was Italian and mom learned how to cook pasta sauce. She was an excellent cook when it came to preparing quick meals. She never did any elaborate Japanese meals that took half a day or more to prepare, although she did make some Japanese meals that did not take too long. Dad sometimes worked in a restaurant as a waiter and most weekends he would cook Chinese or Japanese food. I thought it was okay but Mom really liked his cooking.

Meat was a rare treat and I couldn't get enough of Mom's tomato mushroom meat sauce. Loved those wild mushrooms. We would go out to the flats and the Italians showed me where to find them. Underneath clumps of dried up grass were nipple shaped wild mushrooms. They taught me the difference between poison mushrooms and edible ones. Everybody loves Treasure Hunts.

Most of the Italian families had a cow and some chickens in the backyard shed. Everyday somebody would round them up and take them across the flats for grazing and return late in the afternoon.

Once I was standing near the edge of the flat watching the cows being led back to their owners. They seemed so slow moving but one cow came out of the herd and started charging towards me so I ran and scampered up the stairs of the porch. The cow stopped in front of the sidewalk and then slowly went back to the herd. One of the neighbors yelled out to me "you got to watch out for the cows." It puzzled me; a docile domesticated cow would try to hurt me.

Talk about a treasure hunt. Periodically a man coming from the CN tracks would have two watermelons underneath his arm. He tells people about a boxcar full of watermelon. I went there with an older boy and some man cut a melon in half so I could carry it home. Other times it would be bananas or sacks of nuts or fruits or whatever. Come to think about it now, it wasn't a treasure hunt it was plunder.

Whenever Uncle Hank came around he would find some kid in the neighborhood to put on the gloves with me. I hated boxing. He would always find a kid older bigger and heavier. I was fortunate that I found them clumsier and slower but it was strenuous. It didn't take me too long to learn to end the match quickly. Aim for the nose. A nosebleed always ends the match.

It's interesting to note how much a preschool kid learns about life. The flat was filled with interesting things. Swamps, ponds, tadpoles, frogs, snakes, rats. Sometimes we captured some tadpoles and raise them in a container filled with water to see how they gradually became frogs. Hey Reg, watch this, and some kid would throw a rock into the city dump with all its mountains of tin cans and garbage and the whole mountain would move with thousands of rats scurrying around. Scary especially when I saw it for the first time. Another fearful moment a few years later when I was 11 years old and three of us hitched a ride on a Box Car before it picked up speed. The question was how are we going to get off? We didn't want to go ten miles or even one hundred miles away before it stopped. It was our first time but somehow we knew how to jump off a moving train. After a few miles we came across level ground so we all jumped off. Nobody was seriously injured.

In the fall we picked bull rushes and took some oil rags from a small compartment near the back wheel of a boxcar and used it as a torch. In the darkness of the evening we would have pow wows and safaris. I guess as a kid a lot of our adventures were based on imagination.

In winter the swampland would freeze and there would be pockets of ice. We would all go out to skate and play hockey. Most of us never had ice skates so we tried to skate with our rubber boots. One day, trying to play hockey, I slipped and my head, fell on a log, cutting a deep gash along the line of my eyebrow. I felt real dizzy so I went home. Good thing my dad was at home. He pulled out all the slivers and stitched my cut. To this day the eyebrows camouflage the scar. Another time my little finger got jammed by a door. It was almost severed but Dad put it together and stitched it. Even now it has a nice clean scar.

Vancouver was not a great Hockey Town in those days but as kids we tried everything. A few years later when I lived on Powell Street we played hockey on roller skates. Playing on cement was punishing especially if you fell down. It felt like being rubbed with sandpaper. We would wait for rain and when the rain stopped we'd rush down to the Can Company where they had a wide driveway with a smooth surface of asphalt. Then we would put on our roller-skates and play hockey. It was just fun, sliding in puddles of water without damaging our skin.

Pender Street - Our Second Home

Shortly (I began) going to Strathcona Public School as a first grader the family lived across from the school in a corner building of Pender and .... The front was a small variety store with a kitchen behind it. Adjoining the back of the kitchen was a woodshed converted into a Japanese bathhouse by my Dad. The bathtub was made from wood with a steel drum near the bottom and a platform over it. Making a fire in the steel drum heated the water quickly. I was frightened when Mom and Dad were quarreling over the bathtub and Dad yelling and hollering went into the bathhouse with a big axe and it sounded like he was chopping up and wrecking the whole place but he was only pretending and just lowered the height of the tub so the kids could easily go in and out of the tub.

Mother often took me to the movies. Dad was upset one time and threw a jar of candies behind me as we were leaving the store. The sound of the exploding jar, broken glass and candies all over the floor shocked me. It really disturbed me when my parents fought. Mom told me to wait outside and she went back into the store. She must have cooled Dad off because she came out and said, "Come, we're going to the movies." I was both relieved and respectful of my Mom. Mom loved to see drama and musicals. Dad only like the musical when Eleanor Powell played the leading role, saying that she looked like Mom. Most of the time I was bored with the movies Mom took me to.

I recall one movie I think it was Hedy Lamarr in a love scene and she had a pearl necklace in her hand at the moment of ecstasy the pearls started to drop on the floor, bouncing and rolling all over the floor. After the movie, Mom mentioned the scene and said I was too young but when older I would understand.

It must have been in the morning on weekends I used to make tea for Mom and Dad. It was like breakfast in bed. Lifting the kettle and it must have tilted because boiling hot water scalded the inside of my left arm around the elbow. It took over forty years before all the burnt mark disappeared. My parents were horrified and realized maybe I was still too young to be boiling water as a five year old. Strangely, I thought the whole incident was nothing and never even gave it a second thought.

What was scary was one evening I was sitting on a chair in the kitchen when Mom came in and said, "Robbers -- go upstairs and hide. I ran upstairs where the bedrooms were and hid underneath a bed. I was shaking. As a kid we played cops and robbers but the real thing shook me up. After a while, Mom called me downstairs and held me in her arms saying everything was okay. I could hear Uncle Hank talking to the police and after they left, Uncle came into the kitchen smiling as if everything was okay and said the holdup was nothing, not a problem. This helped me to calm down.

He was in the store with his father and it was the first time I saw a black boy. Uncle Yo said I should put on the gloves with him. Many times, Uncle Yo mentioned how good and fast the blacks were in boxing. His black skin intimidated me but he had a friendly face and for a change he was not a bigger opponent but about my size. The match never took place. I guess they moved out of the neighborhood.

*****

It was mostly good times going to Public School. The reason was I never had to study or do homework at home. My marks on Exams were fairly good and classes were interesting just listening and learning from the teacher. Throughout the school years writing was very difficult. Even scribbling a few words on a postcard required great effort on my part. By the time graduating senior high school, the longest essay written was 87 words. A few years later I became a first year drop out at U of T. Couldn't handle the 1000 word essays and long hours of study. Mother was probably disappointed but accepted the fact about my weak health and this was a good excuse on my part.

Many people have different abilities and talents. Reading books on eastern religion and philosophies was like recalling something I already knew. Most of the European philosophers were quite familiar with eastern thought and I feel they had a similar profound thoughtful experience. In my arrogance I thought to stump the lecturer by asking some profound metaphysical questions. The opportunity came of two separate occasions and both times he replied, "for that question I would give you a Ph.D". I was surprised that he developed a keen awareness of the noumena realm without being familiar with Eastern thought. Of course the principles of humanities and the Cosmos are the same for both East and West.

The wonder of the mind in childhood and early teens. Full of life force and fun and games. It's only in the later years I realized the reality, the oneness of noumena and phenomena. As a kid, everything was phenomena.

After school, the curtain rises and the theatrics begin, ritual routine of fun and games and the rhythm of life. Suddenly one day every kid would have a bag or small box full of marbles. Games of follow or circles rain or shine, dirt or mud, grass or concrete, the clicking of marbles. Win or lose, some kid would go home with an extra pocket full of marbles. Beautiful marbles, different sizes, different colors and patterns. Few kids power trippery would have a monster steel ball that would scar and deface and ruin a marble's life. Instinct or by the Order of the Universe the marbles disappear and are replaced by a larger rubber ball attached to an elastic band tied to a flat wooden bat or racket called yo sometimes it's yo-yo depending on the sponsor that gives out the prizes.

All of a sudden, Mungo Sungo the magic and imagination of kids. It's a Chinese game and at Strathcona public school, approximately 600 Chinese pupils attended, add another 800 kids to "the school of many nationalities with one flag" the motto --- and every boy in Strathcona played Mungo Sungo. It's like the birdie used in badminton only it's made with washers and crepe paper used to wrap fruit and the paper comes in different colors -- purple, orange, yellow, white, etc. Part of the paper is cut into strips and pushed through the hole in the washer and the uncut part is wrapped over the washer, the bottom being flat and an elastic band tied to the neck to keep the strip of paper and washer together. Kids were innovative. Some would use one big washer, others would use 2 or even 3 or 4 washers, not too tightly bound, a little loose so when it was kicked and bounces, it made a clicking sound.

All the birds looked different. Some would use different color papers and have the strips of paper short so the bird would look short and fluffy. Others would use one or two heavy washers and have long strips of paper that looked like a colorful pony tail. Some birds would only have 1 or 2 or 3 long strips of crepe paper. In those days we all wore Lechie boots with steel toes and half-moon made of metal added on to the heel by a shoe maker. As kids we liked the clicking sound walking on the hard surface of the sidewalk. I have to give this a thought; none of us did any tap dancing.

We would use the inner flat side of the boot to kick the Mungo Sungo and keep bouncing the bird up and down just like if we were using the palm of our hand, bouncing an object up and down. Eventually most of the kids got really good and were able to keep the bird bouncing in the air without it touching the ground 3 or 4 hundred times. Sometimes we would form a circle with 5 or 6 kids and kick the bird back and forth and the odd time we would kick the bird over our shoulder and kick it back out front with the outer flat side of the boot. We enjoyed showing off especially if it succeeded.

The cracking of horse chestnut. It was exciting to go to big homes around Stanley Park and English Bay.

If the tree was on the side of a slope it was much easier because we could climb it from the top side. We were always looking for a big chestnut. If we spotted some, we would go out on the limb and shake the branch. It was a great feeling, high above the tree looking over the street and houses and parks. Felt free like Tarzan but sooner or later the owner would spoil it and kick us out. They weren't upset over a few chestnuts but were afraid for our safety. When we got home we had chestnuts 2 and three years old harden and dry out. Sometimes we would roast some, others we would soak it in brine. We tried all sorts of things hoping to find a magical potion that would make the chestnut uncrackable. A hole is made in the center of the nut and a knot is made on one end of a string. The other end of the string we put through the chestnut and let the chestnut slide down the other end where the knot prevented the chestnut from dropping off. Usually we used shoe-string.

The holder would wrap the end of the string around a couple of fingers and let the chest-nut dangle on the other end of the string. The striker would hold his string and chestnut in similar fashion and swing it downward, cracking the holder's chestnut. If the swinger misses the holder's chestnut then the holder becomes the striker. They keep alternating in this fashion until one of the chestnuts breaks. It's a gunslinger's game. Every kid keeps a record of wins. If you beat a kid that has 10 wins you add on 10 wins to your own chestnut. In this way a chestnut kill could go into the hundreds. My biggest thrill was to find the greatest leverage on the string, swing it with great force downward and to shatter the holder's chestnut. Once I hit the holder's chestnut so good and hard, my own chestnut shattered. The hit was so great it shocked me but still felt good about losing.

*****

Growing up in Vancouver as a kid was like living in Disney World. So many exciting things to see and do. I could hardly wait to get up in the mornings. Vancouver is a seaport and a lot of our activities were centered around the ocean.

The location of our third home was Powell Street just east of Downtown Lil Tokyo. Kids on the same block usually hung out together. Every block had a group of kids that formed a little gang. The ages ranged from five to 14 years of age. I don't know if it was because of our Japanese ancestry that it was quite hierarchical in nature. The older ones always protected the younger ones we followed.

I remember the first time some of us went fishing down at the docks. They showed me how to fish. All that was needed was a fishing rod made from a branch of a tree and a line with ten or 12 hooks attached to it, including a sinker, some earthworms or sea worms and that was it. Nothing fancy.

We would wake up at 5-o clock in the morning on a Saturday and less than 15 minutes we would be at the docks throwing our line into the water. We fished for shiners. They are shaped like bass but a little smaller about six inches in length and very shiny with a silvery color. It was really fun. It didn't take too long to have a nibble and when you pulled the line out of the water, one or two shiners would be on the hook. At times you could have six or seven shiners wiggling on the line. Never a dull moment. After we got three or four buckets of shiners and it was still early, the older boys would try to catch Dogfish.

They looked like sharks, the mouth underneath the head and quite big, about two to three feet in length. Apparently they are good scavengers. The older boys used a heavier line, a bigger hook and sinker and would use one of the shiners as bait. They would swing it around like a lasso and throw it as far as possible towards the Cannery Building. Fish canneries dump a lot of fish waste and it attracts Dogfish. It's not always easy to catch a Dogfish. But when somebody does, everybody gets excited. The wheeling and pulling in the fish and when they finally land it on the dock, jumping and flopping around, it's an amazing sight. A few years later when I was older, I caught my first Dogfish. It was such a big thrill it made me feel like a great shark hunter. No wonder people like fishing.

Anyway, when it was time for the Fish Market in Lil Tokyo to open, we would take the buckets of shiners and sell them. We used to get 25 cents a bucket.

Wow, the things a kid could do with 10 or 15 cents. Take in action movies for a nickel and watch movies like the Lone Ranger, Tom Mix or the Dead End Kids... We bought huge amounts of peanuts and popcorn and still had a few pennies left over. I remember with the left over pennies buying chocolate coated hard hats, very tasty and seemed to last forever in the mouth.

Another great adventure was like a Treasure Hunt. We went to different docks sometimes climbing over chain link fence to see the big ships from all over the world

The sailors were always happy to see us and depending which country they came from they would give us bunches of bananas or sacks of peanuts, coconuts and even fruits. It was the security guards that gave us the hard times, always throwing us out of the ship-yard.

Those Japanese ships. The sailors would even welcome us aboard the ship where the security people couldn't see and bother us. We always ran around on top of the deck and it felt like the top of the world. They always fed us Japanese food, gave us gifts and always asked how they could meet our older sisters.

Once we built a raft about ten feet by 15 feet. We used logs to keep it afloat and two by fours to hold it together and cedar shake as flooring. One raft we erected a mast with a small sail and a place to have a fire. Like adventurous pirates we set out to the open seas. We paddled the raft away from the shore and had a smoky fire burning. It wasn't too long afterwards we felt the current pulling us from the inlet towards the open ocean. The current was quite strong and before we could worry about it we heard the siren of the Coast Guard. Through the light fog I could only see the front of the boat.

The siren went silent and it looked like a ghost ship, very small at first, it became bigger and bigger as it came towards us. It must have been travelling fast; in no time it was on top of us. Then the siren started to wail and the ship put on the brakes causing huge waves rocking our raft enough that one kid fell into the water. Then a loud voice from the horn gave us instruction and towed us back to shore. After the lecture and warning we promised not to do it again and they let us go.

This escapade did not stop us from going out to the middle of the inlet to the warning bell. We always used someone's rowboat thinking it's much safer to fight the current. We heard stories that the fish were much bigger out there. The warning bell was constructed in shallow water where logs anchored the bottom and the part above the water painted red.

It was only the two of us the first time. The rowboat was gently rocking and hardly a splash of water against the upright posts. It was true, the bass and tommy cod swimming around the post below the surface were big. We couldn't catch anything that day. The very next time we went there we used sea worms as bait instead of earthworms. That did the trick. I caught three bass and my friend caught a bass and a tommy cod. These fish were almost twice the size of the ones near the shore.

Nobody goes fishing in the month of December but we tried anyway. To our surprise we caught an Octopus. It was a baby one. The size of the head was about the size of a 5-pin bowling ball. We threw it back into the water. Wow, it was still an octopus no other kid ever caught one that we knew of.

As kids we were quite busy but whenever we had some spare time some of us would row out to the warning bell. After catching a fish or two it always made me feel like a great shark or whale hunter. One time that feeling didn't last too long. We saw a seal about 300 feet away. Then it disappeared and resurfaced again closer to us. It came closer and closer. The last time it bobbled its head above water it was only thirty feet away. Did we ever panic. We paddled like crazy toward the shore thinking the seal might ram or tip our boat over. After reaching the shore I lost that feeling of a big whale hunter.

Once I went with Dad's half-brother and his friend across the inlet to the north shore to look for King Crabs. Was it ever adventurous! My uncle showed me how to pick up the crabs without getting swiped by the claws. Very few were on the surface of the wet sand. Most of them were half buried or almost buried. Later on for supper my Father cooked the crabs. Boy did everybody like the taste of those King Crabs. Unfortunately the King Crabs on our side of the shore were condemned by the Government as unfit for human consumption due to the city waste dumped into the inlet.

Pender Street - Part Two

In the hot summer months we did an awful lot of swimming. Every kid knew how to get a tan without getting a sunburn and every kid at least in our neighborhood knew how to swim. Our tan got so dark that the line of the bathing trunks on the skin lasted through fall, winter and spring until we were ready to go swimming again. I remember teaching two-year-olds to swim. Hold their hands and let them paddle with the feet. When they got fairly good at paddling we let them do the torpedo, which they would paddle with their feet, head face down in the water and arms extended, palms together shaped like a torpedo. As they kept improving, the next step was the dog paddle. Feet kicking, head above water and arms below in the water paddling like a dog. After that, breast stroke came naturally.

We all liked Tarzan and liked the way he swam. His style was for speed. We called it the Australian crawl. Both arms and legs paddling face down and head in the water and once in a while, tilt our head to breathe. We used to race each other at first the width of the pool and later in the year, the length of the pool. The water in the pool was ocean water and a curve wall separated it from the ocean. I don't think the length of the pool was as long as a football field. Anyway it was big enough and by the time I was eight years old, swimming the length of the pool back and forth a few times was routine.

Another great event was when some older boys would swim and escort us out into the ocean. About 200 yards from the shore were small sail boats anchored side by side. It seemed like the middle of the ocean and it felt great lying on our backs, mouth full of salt water and spewing it out like the whales. Other times we would go deep into the water to see how long and far we could swim underwater, then with all our might we would break the surface of the water gasping for air and trying to jump out of the water like the Dolphins.

After swimming, everybody would be famished. The greatest fear for any kid was to get cramps while swimming and the best way to avoid cramps was not to eat several hours before a swim.

I don't know what it is but the food as a kid tasted so much better. Near the beach was a fish and chip stand. The potatoes were peeled and cut up fresh and then deep-fried. With a bit of salt, pepper and malt vinegar it was better than any fried rice and I love rice. What a treat it was on rare occasions when we had some spare nickels to buy fish with the chips. The portion of fish in the batter was much more in the Good Ole Days and sharing the fish with our buddies made it even better.

After eating we would be in a good mood, talking and laughing about what we did. We still lay on the beach relaxing and enjoying the sun, giving our dark skin a chance to get even darker.

Finally we decided how to go home, at least back to our neighborhood. Sometimes we all walked home. Other times we ran home as a race.

The distance from the beach to our neighborhood was a little less than four miles. We all took our own shortcuts and routes. Some days a couple of guys would take a streetcar and the rest of us would race it home. Running and taking shortcuts was much faster than the old fashion streetcars.

Once I was out of the house I was on my own. My parents never asked where I was or what I did. The only rule we had to obey was the cannon rule. In Vancouver, 9-o clock sharp the cannons go off and the roar is heard all over Vancouver. Which means all the kids scamper home and the streets become silent.

Summertime Vancouver is hot and very humid. Inside the frame house the heat is unbearable. Many a night I slept on the bare floor, the coolest spot in the house. No wonder we could hardly wait to go to the beach every day.

Most mothers let the kids go camping if a 14 or 15 year old was a chaperone. North Vancouver Lynn Valley was the favorite spot. We'd leave Friday and come back on Sunday.

Sitting around a campfire at night watching the sparks fly and flames darting about in the darkness was always a neat experience. We enjoyed cooking like baking potatoes in the ashes -- wieners and marshmallows on a stick. Cooking canned goods it wasn't like Mom's home cooking but we enjoyed eating in the great outdoors. The new or renewed experience of sleeping under the stars. No question, no answers, just the wonder of the stars and vastness of the Universe. I felt secure and at home.

The older boys seemed more interested in spotting lovers, like peeping Toms. The younger ones like myself would try fishing or hunting for mountain lions and bears. We never caught any fish or even saw any of the big game animals. The make believe of playing the big hunter was still a lot of fun.

*****

Once I spotted the Suspension Bridge across the Canyon. We managed to hike up the canyon, followed a trail to the bridge. The Suspension Bridge was made from only rope and wooden planks. The railing was a single large long rope across the canyon on both sides of the wooden plank flooring. The wooden planks were tied together with rope. I decided to test the safety of bridge and went out about 30 feet on to the bridge. Some planks were missing and a lot seemed very loose. Hanging on to the railing and trying to find good footing on the wooden planks caused a slight vibration that swayed the middle of the bridge. When another kid got on the bridge a loose plank fell and watching it go down was a mesmerizing sight. As a kid the bridge seemed like it was a mile high and a mile long. The disturbance created by us made the center of the bridge rock a lot more. We both realized the risk and danger so we hurried back and just before we jumped off the bridge, back on solid ground, we heard an angry voice: "Can't you kids read the sign Off Limits" It's Off Limits. I don't want to see you kids around here again." We back tracked on the top ridge of the canyon and went down to the bottom of the ravine from the place we came up. Seventy years later I was able to walk on the bridge with other people. It was rebuilt with steel cables and solid. Couldn't sway the bridge a bit. I thought was I that crazy as a kid? Living in Toronto, I always missed the ocean and mountains of Vancouver. Camping out as a child was always a happy time, being close to nature and feeling the sense of independence and freedom.

*****

It's mind boggling how many games we played as youngsters. Kick the can, cats and dogs. Cowboy and Indians. Eastern and Western style sword fighting and the list goes on and on. One interesting game was called peg. We would cut a broomstick about two feet long and use it as a bat. Then we cut another section about six to eight inches long, one end shaped into a pointed spear. The peg is placed on the ground slanted about 45 degrees, resting on a small piece of two by four with the pointed end upwards. Then hit the peg near the top end where it somersaults into the air about shoulder height and then with the bat keep hitting and bouncing the peg, three or four times in midair, and then whack it as far as possible.

Most of the kids around the age of 10 or more really enjoyed the rough and tumble physical aspect of the games. One of the most physical and enjoyable games was "ship on sailor." Group of kids, as many as twelve to twenty, would form two teams. Toss a coin and the loser becomes the ship and the winners are the sailors. On the ship side, the youngest kid stands with his back against a wall. The first kid bends over and puts his head between his legs and then the rest of the team follows in the same manner and all you see is a row of backs. The first sailor will yell "ship on sailor coming on" running to gain momentum to be able to leap as far as possible on somebody's back. The next person would follow shouting "ship on sailor coming on" and land right behind the first jumper. The third kid would do the same and land behind the second jumper.

Some kids would jump like a cowboy on a horse and others would leap like a frog. The sailors or the jumping team had to be careful not to fall on the ground or otherwise the whole team is disqualified and the other team would have the opportunity to do the jumping. When three or four sailors jump successfully the rest of the kids would start jumping higher to land on top of them. It gets interesting when the bodies begin to pile up and the weight of the jumpers could sink the ship. The last sailor has the greatest thrill "shouting "ship on sailor coming on!" and landing on top of the bodies as hard as he could hoping to cave or sink the ship, like the last straw that broke the camel's back. Sometimes the ship would hold and usually the sailors would slide off and fall to the ground. Win or lose, as kids it was gleeful and joyful times playing "ship on sailor."

Another rough game was piggyback fight. The younger smaller kids called the piggies would be on the back of the older boys. The piggy would partially wrap his leg around the waist and the carrier would hold both the piggy's legs with his forearm pressed against his side and grip the ankle area. The piggy would have both arms and hands free to fight and pull the other piggy off his horse so to speak. At times it gets heated with competition and gets out of hand when the horses bump and jostle each other and even try to knock both rider and carrier to the ground.

We were so preoccupied playing boys' games that I discounted the activities of the other half of the species, girls. They would bounce a small rubber ball and swipe up jacks or draw up squares on a sidewalk. I think it was a game of hop skip and jump. Outside of that they did an awful lot of skipping. Two girls holding a skipping rope or sometimes they would have two skipping ropes one in each hand, twirling it where the skipper had to skip and jump both ropes. The odd time some boy would muscle in trying to skip two ropes and get his feet all tangled up. Then the girls would giggle and laugh at him. Only once did I get involved with three other girls to make a foursome. It had something to do with filling up a bottle cap with dirt and flicking it with the middle finger on the ground that had been smoothed out and then with the thumb as a fulcrum make a semi-circle to claim territorial rights or maybe it was something else. All I can remember is the flicking and the fulcrum.

Like most kids I saw and experienced all sorts of violence. The worst was Mom and Dad fighting. It really made me feel distraught and helpless.

In our classroom were many Chinese and Japanese pupils with a small number of other ethnic groups. Even with the war between China and Japan in the classroom, we all knew each other and got along fine. Can't recall any derogatory remarks of racism made among the classmates. It wasn't that bad outside of the classroom either except for this one event. A Chinese kid had to fight a Japanese kid at least once a week. Peer pressure. "Hey Reg, there's a Chinese kid, Stanley, wants to fight you." Apparently, Stanley won a few fights against Japanese boys and was looking for another fight. After school my chums grab my arms and steered me towards Stanley who was surrounded by his buddies egging him on to fight me. It was a small mob scene and we had no choice but to get into a scrap. It was a relief to be able to box with someone my own size for a change instead of my uncle always picking a bigger older boy for me to box with. After landing a few punches to his face, red welts begin to show on his cheeks, near the eyes and forehead. It didn't make one feel good knowing it would swell and turn black and blue later. Saved by the bell! Miss Effort, the teacher, from the second story window shouted and screamed out loud "Reg! Stop fighting. You kids -- get (going)." The crowd scattered. Walking home with my buddies, they made complimentary remarks about how great my fisticuffs were. I only had one other fight without gloves and that was with a Japanese kid.

Strathcona Public School was very proud of Jim MacFarland who won the World Championship in boxing. He fought in a lighter weight division. Boxing was not my bag but the Heavy Weight Division excited me, especially Joe Louis when he fought Primo Carnero. I remember looking at a picture in a newspaper showing the two standing back to back. It looked like David and Goliath. I think the fight lasted one round and the feeling was "Wow!" Louis had those great knockout punches.

The Japanese kids in a sense were fortunate because every time a Caucasian kid wanted to fight one of us he would say, "I'll fight you if you don't use Judo." And of course we would say, "I'm going to use Judo." And that was the end of it. It was always a good laugh especially for some of us who never trained in Judo.

One of the most exciting and dramatic fights was between Wally the kid from our public school and his two older brothers who were adults and members of the notorious Gorgia gang and Tad Ban who came recently from Japan to study English at our school. Tad was a naturally skilled judo man. At least a hundred kids shoulder to shoulder were straining their necks, leaning over a fence, looking down the street at Wally and his two brothers coming towards the school. I was close to Ban and he had a very serious face pacing back and forth and at times walking around in a small circle. There was a commotion that kind of signaled the threesome was getting close. I followed Ban out of the schoolyard and he walked towards the threesome. I stayed on the corner and Ban crossed the street to meet them. I thought I had a good view but it happened so suddenly -- arms, legs, bodies flying and then lying motionless on the ground. The fight was over in seconds and the whole school cheered with approval. Ban trotted across the street and went the opposite way. Little W and his brothers started to get up slowly

I don't know whether it happened before or after this incident, little W and some of his friends broke into his and our school and stole all the silver cups and trophies. Strathcona Public School won a lot of championship trophies in sports.

I enjoyed snowball fights. One day in Vancouver the weather was damp cold and clammy. Making snowballs by squeezing the water out of the slushy snow made it hard and icy. There was a lineup of 20 to 25 kids each having a dozen snowballs ready and waiting for Fu Chu a big Chinese boy, heavy around the waist and supposedly a little retarded. It's bad enough pelting someone with icy snowball but when some of them were putting rocks inside the snowball it made me cringe. The squad was made up of different ethnic groups including a few Chinese. It wasn't a racial issue, it was just a cruel aspect of kids' behavior caught up in a mob mentality, victimizing the weak. I had to walk away. Later there was a big outcry by the teaching staff and it probably stopped anything like this ever happening again.

One time just before noon all the students were told to go home and stay home because of the fighting between the Longshoremen and the police. It was already too late by the time I reached Hasting Street. It was one of the main streets I had to cross to get home. A small crowd stands along the sidewalk, watching the fight. Across the street a man wearing a faded denim shirt and jeans leaning against a grassy embankment, aiming and firing his rifle. It seemed the fighting was moving towards downtown so I walked the opposite way to the next block to avoid stray bullets, crossed the street, and went home. I heard stories of brutality committed both by the longshoremen and the police.

Terry H was not part of our regular gang but a friend I went to see occasionally. He phoned me saying he had a fight with the kid across the street. He showed me a bullet hole that went through the front window of the house including some bullet marks on the veranda. What was wicked, the marks were made from a 22 caliber rifle. Some kids had BB guns but a 22 rifle was unheard of. I assume the parents settled the matter because the shooting stopped.

It was shortly after the gunfight I had my second and last fight with bare knuckles. Terry's friend who was eleven years old was a year younger than we were. His face was all black and blue with bumps on his forehead and cheeks. He was beaten up by a 15-year-old kid from across the street. Terry was shouting, "Manabu come on outside and fight." Eventually he came outside from the house onto the road. He charged towards me with his arm outstretched trying to grab me. Realizing he was too big to wrestle with, I side stepped and punched him on the side of his face. Then turned my back zig-zagging and ran about ten feet, zig zagging, stopped, turned and hit him again on the face. This happened about seven or eight times. Most of his face became red by my punches. The last punch must have caught him near the eye because he stopped and put his hands over his face and stopped chasing me. At least it was over with. Terry seemed happy and Nobu looked satisfied. As a kid, I thought I did the right thing. Probably reacting to the Law of the Jungle. Eye for eye -- tooth for tooth.

When I went home Mother noticed a slight bruise under my eye and asked me, "What happened? You been fighting?" "You should never lose a fight." I didn't realize there was a mark on my face. I went to a mirror and the bruise was hardly noticeable. Mom was going on and on, "It's nothing Mom, you should see the other kid and he was much bigger. " that ended my side of the conversation/ Never talk back, or argue with Mom especially when she's pissed off.

Next evening, entering into the kitchen, my Mother's face was beaming. She told the women sitting across from the kitchen table, "This is my son." The woman was astonished, "is this the boy, this little boy, which gave my son a beating?" She must have been ashamed of complaining to my Mother, thinking that I was some kind of a big monster. Before the women left she said, "I'm going to tie my son to a post and give him a whipping for losing a fight to such a small boy. My Mom told me her son's whole face was black and blue and swollen. The woman found out where we lived and came over to complain to my parents. Mom's face was still beaming.

Mothers are strange. Once Yoshi, a hot-tempered bully kid in our neighborhood chased me, threatening to beat me up. I stopped in front of my house and was ready for a good scrap. He picked up a board lying near a fence with a spike sticking out of the other end. There we were. Yoshi poised to swing the board, hoping to puncture me with the spike, and I'm in a boxer stance. We both took lessons in Kendo, which made us motionless, each waiting for the other to make a move. I don't know how long we were in that stance when I became aware of my Mother standing behind Yoshi with an armful of groceries. She didn't say a word. This wasn't like a Kendo style movement of just going forward and backward, it was more like a knife fight, moving ever so slightly in a circular motion. This circular movement enabled Yoshi's peripheral vision to catch someone standing beside him. He looked and realized it was my Mother, dropped his weapon and ran away. Later my Mom told me she was very proud of me for standing up to Yoshi. She could have stopped this potentially dangerous situation but waited to see what I would do. It didn't seem right to me.

Yoshi, in his anger, was not afraid of physical violence but was afraid of his own imagination, especially ghosts. To get home, he had to walk through an outdoor sheltered hallway about 100 feet long. At night he would ask us to escort him home. He was afraid of the fireball, which everybody assumed was the soul of the dead. Some of us believed in it, others didn't. It was routine every night: we would stand around at the entranceway and some of us would escort him to his door. Other times we wouldn't baby sit him to his door and he would be huff and puff as if having a panic attack and then dash down the hallway to get home. We would all scream "Fire ball! Fire ball!" sometimes he was halfway down and at times almost to his door but he would turn and run all the way back to us. Some kid would tell him scary stories. Like, if he feels a hot hand grabbing his neck from behind it will be the fireball or if the fireball is in front of the door, don't open it; otherwise he would become blind. Some of the guys think the fireball is all bull and others would swear it's the truth. Eventually, after 7 or 8 tries, he'll manage to get home. We didn't like his bullying but we made up by laughing and talking about Yoshi's fear of Ghosts.

Powell Street

Living on Powell Street was like living in Little Tokyo. All my friends were of Japanese background. The only difference was we all spoke English. At home, my Mother was born in Vancouver and she was quite fluent in reading and writing both Japanese and English. We all spoke English at home and broken English when our Dad was around.

It was a new experience, going to Japanese School. Most kids started when they were six years old. My Dad wanted me to go early but Mom said there's no hurry. Most of the kids were a few years younger as a six-year-old, age wise, but I didn't particularly look out of place among them as an eight year old.

What was different from public school, the desk and seating were longer where they sat down, boy-girl, boy-girl. It was my first close encounter with a girl. Even at that age I found some girls very attractive and others just so and so. My desk mate was Miss Y.K. I thought I was the luckiest guy in the class. Girls seem different but were so loveable, especially Y.K with her big eyes, the smile, her hair, her mannerism. I was smitten.

Thoughts of walking her home, holding her hands cuddling, even kissing her, awakened my sexuality without the urge for sex. I loved to show off, to be able to protect and care for her. I guess it's Nature's "Prelude to Procreation." Y.K. made going to Japanese school really worthwhile. She was my object of love and fascination.

After the classes in Public School ended about 3 o'clock, we would all go home and have a late afternoon snack. It was usually a handful of rice crackers, peanuts, candies or fruits. We would take it with us and munch on it while heading towards Japanese School. Most of us like to get to school early so we could play in the yard or auditorium. What was interesting and amusing was younger kids would come to me and offer me snacks. I kept refusing, not that I wasn't hungry but the reason was I always stopped by my friend's store on the way to school. A. Hayashi family run a rice cracker place and he would always give me a handful of rice crackers. His dad really made tasty rice crackers. Sometimes we would throw the crackers up in the air and catch it with our open mouths. Akio was a good-natured person and I enjoyed playing baseball with him. He was an excellent short stop - - good with his glove, catching ground balls and good with his mouth catching rice crackers.

One day this kid came up to me and offered snacks and a gift. I said, "How come you want to give me a gift?" He said he didn't like bullies and wanted protection. This was something new to me and caught me by surprise. I liked him so I said if anybody bothers you just let me know. He kept insisting for me to accept his gift in such a polite way it was hard to refuse. Besides the gift, every day after that he brought me snacks -- rice crackers, cookies, candies, etc. It's surprising to hear many kids had bodyguards. Quick calculation, my birthday was a few months away. It would make me nine years old. The older boys who were in the upper grade would be around eleven or twelve years of age. I sort of felt relieved, figuring to be able to handle twelve-year-old toughies.

Sooner or later it happened. My little friend with a stressed look said somebody was bothering him. The other boy was shorter, smaller, well-built and seemed very physical. I told him in a very commanding and firm voice, not to bother my friend. Recollecting this incident reminds me of our reptilian brain. Tribal consciousness -- warlord mentality is not only a Japanese trait but a human condition applicable to all races of people.

The next day, the other kid brought his bodyguard. It raised a bit of concern because it was T. Hatashita and as they approached me, thank heaven, he said, "Hey Reg -- how are you?" He said to the kid, "Is this the guy you want me to beat up? Are you crazy? He's a good friend. Beat it!" and kicked his rear end with the side of his foot. We shook hands and, like adults, talked shop. "How's your Kendo class?" "My teacher, Sensei Matsushita is 3rd degree Black Belt -- lightning speed." "Any Judo tournaments coming up?" Mutual respect, we parted still good friends.

It was the summer before three of us from our neighborhood were walking along an alleyway. Some kids were standing around watching a boxing match. The place was behind T. Hatashita's home where the small crowd was enjoying the fight. When it was over, T. Hatashita said, "Reg, why don't you box with my friend? He's not bad and I hear you're pretty good in boxing.

Kids like to see a boxing match. Egged on by my two buddies -- they even put the gloves on me and -- and swept away by everybody's excitement, I found myself boxing a stranger. The mongoose and the cobra-- stick my face and nose right in front of his glove. And before he could react and punch, the head would be somewhere else. Just try to figure out why some guys are quicker and faster than others. We all knew that big muscles and muscle bound guys moved slower. T. Hatashita was REALLY impressed with my ability to box. I heard stories about how good he was in judo. In fact, all his brothers were famous Judo men. After the war, many of the Japanese Canadians moved eastward, especially to Toronto. It must have been in the late fifties. T. Hatashita.'s eldest brother Frank started the first Judo club in Toronto. It surprised me, the aura of honor and purity of marital art training that Dad, of all people, told Frank Hatashita it was Okay to make money teaching Judo. In the old days, nobody made Martial Arts a money making business.

T. Hatashita, with his sloping neck and shoulders was a sign of strength and power. The thought crossed my mind if there was no choice but to fight a Judo man like T. Hatashita. Jump time now -- we know among all the different schools and styles of fighting in martial arts, the grapplers usually win although I've seen a puncher beat a Judo man in a real fight at Powell St grounds. Rule of thumb is to try to avoid a Judo man's grip; if he holds you don't react and try to hold back, otherwise you are at his mercy. Whatever happens, keep punching. If he grabs one arm, keep punching with the other arm. If he throws you on the ground, keep punching with both hands to his face. Flying through the air, grab with one hand and punch with the other. No matter what, keep punching. All it takes is one good shot. If he's stunned, then he's at your mercy. A quick follow through with a flurry of punches and he'll stagger and feel groggy and will show signs he's had enough. Anyway, it was awfully nice feeling. T. Hatashita was a friend rather than a foe.

Train in Judo? Follow in my Dad's footsteps? No way, he insisted I take Kendo "the way of the sword." Dad was a firm believer in "Bushido" the honor code of the Samurai Warrior. He firmly believed it was barbaric and uncivilized to die by a bullet or rope. For him, to get his head chopped off by a sacred and magnificent sword was a divine act.

Westernized and seeing many action movies like cowboys and Indians, cops and robbers, and men fighting with cannons, guns and swords, it didn't really matter to me how people died. Death was still death and most people do not want to die.

The Dojo where we trained in Kendo was located across the street from our house on Powell Street. Five kids from our block joined at the same time. The majority of kids came from other areas of the city. Month after month we only practiced Kata with Ki-eye. Kata is a series or combination of structured form of movement used in two-handed sword fighting. In all martial arts, Kata is a very important part of training. The more perfect the Kata the faster the movement becomes. Speed is vital in any martial art. In Kendo, the series of Kata movements is in three target areas. The right wrist and forearm (KOTE) the head (MEN) and the ribs in the right side of the body (DO). The Samurai sword has one cutting edge held with two hands it strikes and cuts downwards with tremendous force for KOTE! MEN! and for DO! It cuts downward at a slight angle. Another target area is the throat (Tsuki) as a kid we were not allowed to spear.

The helmet is made of metal and padded cloth. The face is protected by steel bars parallel with the eyes, spaced about an inch apart, slightly egg shaped from the top of the forehead to the chin. The rest is padding which covers the top of the head, not the back and continues on the side of the face onto the shoulders and around the front of the neck.

The throat area looks like a wide necktie with two slits on either side separates it from the shoulder pads. If the spearing is off target, it could easily slip between the flaps and cause serious neck injury. The helmet could only be worn by pushing the face in, and in taking it off it is pulled away from the face.

The first thing to wear is a robe the length between the ankle and the knee. The whole front is open so to close it we overlap and belted it at the waist. Then we wear a well-padded skirt the length somewhere between the knees and waist and it covers the front and the sides. The front has three flaps. The center flap is the widest. The robe and protective skirt gives our thighs legs and feet complete freedom of movement. The chest armor is slightly rounded to make a better fit around the chest and the waist just overlapping the skirt. It looks like a pattern of a suit jacket without the arms and covers both sides of the rib cage. Complete freedom of movement for the head, neck, upper arms and legs. Come to think about it, wearing the Kendo outfit, one could perform in Judo and Karate without restriction in movement.

When we go into the Dojo from our dressing room, the discipline and ritual begins. We all kneel down in a straight line. The teacher barks out and we tie a bandanna around the forehead and slip on the helmet and strap it. Next come the gloves. They look like 3 to 4 ounce boxing gloves without the thick padding and the length of the sleeve is just below the elbow. The sleeve has some padding to protect the Ko-te target area. In Kendo training it's always a frontal attack. The movement is forward or backward. The outfit only protects the front and sides and the section in the back is exposed from the head down to the padded skirt.

After months of training in Kata of Kote/Men/Do/, striking and cutting through thin air to an imaginary target, teacher finally pairs us off for more Kata training. One partner would hold the sword in dual stance, motionless like a statue and his partner would go through the Kata and Ki-eye Ko-te!men!do! hitting the three target spots in quick succession. This is done a number of times and then the partners alternate. The process of Kata continues in one voice loud and clear Ko-te! Men! Do! The teacher's eyes spot everything and barks out orders -- to whomever: "Right hand lower! Back foot closer to the front foot! Tip of the sword higher! Shoulders square! Head up! Elbow lower! Back straight! Striving for perfection is never easy and never ends.

Tradition or hearsay training in Kendo improves mental and physical ability. As kids we were motivated by the spirit of competition. Win or lose, improving the skill of swordsmanship made us feel like somebody. The greatest motivator was fun time and camaraderie. Just being part of a group added to self-worth.

Naturally most of my close friends were from the neighborhood. Some of them started to complain about a big and strong kid who punished them during Kata training. Apparently he trained in Judo and decided to learn a bit of Kendo for a year. My buddies had welts, bumps and bruises around the elbow and biceps and moaned about the head hurting. It was easy to show them how not to take a direct hit in order to minimize the pain. The teacher mentioned to keep the chin up so the top part of the metal facemask would take the brunt of the blow to the head instead of the padded cloth covering the top of the head. The very first time the strong big chested kid was my Kata partner, motionless in dual stance, right hand gripping the hilt touching the top of the protector guard, the left hand holds the other end of the handle. The tip of the sword, close to eye level, right foot flat on the floor, left foot behind heel slightly raised. He did not have the speed like some of us but had tremendous force. His Kata of KOTE! MEN! DO! Numbed my forearm, jarred my head and Do! was just a loud noise. The chest armor is well constructed with wood -bamboo-leather. I couldn't believe a kid just a little bigger than me had so much power. However, if he's off target in DO! And hits the elbow or biceps muscle it causes great pain. The trick is to twist the wrist slightly behind the sword. His KOTE! Will glance off the protector guard of the sword or glance off the padded elbow length glove.

No wonder some of my friends had a painful head. A forceful blow on the forearm made them cringe, which lowered the chin and a quick follow up to the head with MEN! The sword hits the soft top spot rather than the metal of the helmet. For the side rib area, keep the right arm straight and closer to the other arm slightly raised to expose a larger target area of the armor. DO! If he's off target he will not hit the elbow and hit only the biceps muscle, which of course is less painful.

My friends were upset. Some wanted to gang up on him; others wanted an older boy from the neighborhood to beat him up. The smallest boy came up with the best plan. Even today when I recall his devious plan it makes me chuckle. After Kendo class is over we all go into a crowded dressing room to change into street clothing. The idea was to switch off the light and somebody from behind hit his head with a Kendo stick or with the steel part of the helmet. The Kendo sword is made up of five or six flat bamboo sticks tied together forming a round hollow rod tapered slightly at the end. The end is capped with a small leather cup and a leather sheath 10 to 12 inches long covers the handle. The diameter of the sword is approximately one and a half to two inches. Small protector guard separates the blade and the handle. The hollow Kendo sword really makes a loud cracking and snapping sound when it strikes the metal facemask or the side of the chest armor. Outside on the street and close to the neighborhood from the Dojo, one could hear the clashing of the bamboo Kendo sword and the yelling of Ki-eye piercing the night air. No matter how cold and barren the night, sparks were flying in the Dojo.

The timing was right. The lights went off with a short swing, the steel face of the helmet aimed at the side of the face around the jaw area. This move was premeditated; didn't want to injure the eye or hit the temple. The worst -- a broken jaw -- which is nothing. We all scampered out of the room in the dark. He missed classes for over a week -- perfect hit. Damage on the side of his face was from the cheekbone to his jaw. He was leery about us but couldn't prove anything. My friends kept smiling at him which added to his suspicions. No lecture or scolding by the teacher, no complaints by his parents of this incident. He must have kept it to himself. Took it on the chin like a man. I liked that. I would have liked to be his friend if he hadn't lived so far away. Shortly afterwards he quit Kendo and went back to Judo training.

All my friends were happy and decided to give me a new name. They started to call me Rip except Roy E preferred the name 'Rippo.'

If you're quicker than the average kid, it's easy to take advantage of them in sports. Playing soccer, the ball rolled right beside me in front of the goal. The goalie came out to stop me, excited by the opportunity to score, just kicked the ball and it hit the goaltender. Thinking about it later, all one has to do is side step the goalie with the ball and have a clear and easy shot to score. Lying in bed thinking and visualizing the anticipated movement of myself and other players helped me to perform better. Scoring goals in soccer became much easier.

Near the end of the Kendo class we would duel with the teacher one on one, the rest kneeled on the floor watching until it was their turn. The teacher had the knack of making us exert ourselves. Near the end he would tsu-ki and spear the throat padding, pushing us backward. The teacher would do this until we had our backs to the wall; trying to come away from the wall he would tsu-ki and knock us back to the wall again. This would happen 5, 6, 7 times and it felt like a stand up rocking chair. One night walking home, the thoughts came to me. The next time he spears my throat, knock his sword sideways and spear him back.

Next night I could hardly wait for the one on one sessions with the teacher. I remembered clearly how he knocked my sword sideways and speared my throat knocking me backward and before I could recover, he would push my throat padding with the end of the sword and kept doing this until my body was against the wall. Coming off the wall he would pin me back against the wall again with his sword and my only thought was to knock his sword sideways and spear him. I couldn't do it every time he pinned me against the wall and step backward I tried to hit his sword aside when it was coming towards me but I couldn't. My arms seemed to be chained by an invisible force and after four or five times rocking back and forth, my thoughts were saying don't stop this spearing teacher, I'm going to knock it aside and on the sixth or seventh try, my arm reacted and hit the teacher's sword aside and tried to spear his throat. Behind the steel mask, teacher Matsushita was smiling and I could see his big white shiny teeth. He must have been as surprised and pleased as I was.

The older boys occasionally went out of town to compete in tournaments. Finally one day the teacher said that our young bunch were going to Stevenson B.C. to participate in a tournament. We were all excited just travelling to another town, never mind competing with kids from Stevenston. I believed I choked a bit. I did well but knew I could have done better. The Japanese people in Stevenston came mostly from Wakayama Japan. My Dad was from there and they all spoke with a dialect. It was the first time Dad spoke funny Japanese. He seemed to be among friends. Later Dad told me the teacher of Stevenston would have awarded me as the best performer in the tournament if my follow through were stronger.

My teacher was smiling ear to ear after my exhibition match with a 16 year old girl. Besides the regular protective gear, they strapped on a padded shin guard around my calves. It was the first time I encountered a person who trained in Naginata. The real weapon was a pole much longer than a sword with a blade like a spear on one end. She handled it like a quarterstaff used in the old Robin Hood days. She attempted to hit me on the head with one end of the stick which was easy enough to ward off with my sword but at the same time, swung with the other end "wham!" and hit my calves or swung one end of the pole to hit my leg and "bang" hits me on the head with the other end. It was confusing like trying to fight two Kendoists at the same time. The first few blows she had me at her mercy.

It's a cardinal rule in Kendo to understand space. You know if the opponent's sword enters your space, it's a tip that the sword is already in motion to strike your target area. This gauging is done by the tip of the swords. The tips of the two swords are usually three to four inches apart. Sometimes it just touches which is a warning sign. If it crosses over two or three inches, someone is in the process of striking. You either strike first or step back. If you step back it's much easier to ward off the striking sword. If you don't step back you will be at the mercy of the lightning speed of the striker. Speed wins.

The dance of space couldn't be done with this girl. Just guessing her space and the point of no return (takes the offensive strike first?)

Unusual experience similar to the second wind in running. We used to have relay races around the block. The challenge was to run at top speed all around the block. By the time we got to the middle of the second block the body was exhausted and mentally determined to keep running hard; the body wouldn't listen and begins to slow down. By the time we ran on the third block, the body felt like lead and the lungs are bursting in pain. We all knew on rare occasion Boom! It happens. The second wind kicks in. Surge of energy, effortless running, and absolute freedom -- exhilarating.

Enter her space, control violence, fury of a charging lion, and ends in locking horns. The point of contact is part of the handle between our right and left hand. Push or be pushed. In Kendo, balance is the key to victory. Feeling the pressure of her push -- side step and push with the handle part of the sword -- perfect Kata poised to strike opponent off balance -- stumbling then the second wind kicked in. This time it wasn't the complete lung functioning at full capacity. I believe it was the full brain operating with zillions of cells touching the Timeless moment. Her tumbling was in slow motion. Everything was silent. Never heard my own Ki-eye, only the snapping of the Kendo stick striking the target area three or four or five times. By the time she regained her balance and composure my body was out of her space. Feeling her space once more entering it, strike first. The mind is focused still in the zone. Locked in with a clinch = Kata of balance, side step and push again. Time stood still while she's falling.

One, two, three sharp blows all hitting the target area four, five as she hits the ground. Back to my space, poised and ready for another attack. Teacher steps in to end the match. We both bowed to each other the ceremonial end to a contest. Went back to the position of our group all in a line seated on the floor. Heads all upright, backs straight, upper legs and knees in a slight open position, the ankles and feet on the floor as a cushion to sit on. For me it was the Kata of rest at ease, relaxed with a real sense of emotion of wellbeing. Calmness that surpasses understanding.

In sports this frame of mind is called the Zone. Golfers, jockeys, soccer players, etc., all experience the Zone. Football quarterbacks stepping back to pass -- 3 seconds seem like five minutes -- baseball hitters see the 100-mile fast ball coming in like a grapefruit instead of an aspirin. Michael Jordan, for the NBA Championship, the final shot, jumps in the air -- snapshot of eternal time. The moment of truth -- swoosh -- the winning basket. I feel this second consciousness or altered state happens in all human endeavor when our brain and consciousness hits the single moment to moment now time. The eternal present.

Later my Dad mentioned that Sensei Matsushita was going to give me a Brown Belt. Wow! At thirteen to receive a Brown Belt was unheard of. Usually people were 16 or older to receive a Brown Belt. Kendo picnic was another exciting event. We would all dress in Kendo gear and pick sides. The whites wore a white ribbon on their helmets. The reds wore red ribbons. Each person had a tiny box tied to the top of their helmets.

If someone breaks the little box with a Kendo sword it showers out either red or white confetti and the person is eliminated from the battle. As the battle progresses some kid would raise their arms and cover and protect the box on the head with the handle of the sword. Then anything goes, a free for all begins. Then the kid covering his head is knocked down on the ground and his box is broken either by the sword or by a fist. Sometimes three or four persons would gang up on one person. Judo throws punches, swords flashing; it's a melee. Being on the losing side eventually have to face five or six guys. Couldn't win; one or two will rush in and grab my arms and the rest is history. Thought about how to handle a bunch of guys like in the Samurai movies, one against the many, but never thought how terrible a real battle with blood all over and people dying is.

Kata with a real sword is awesome. Men! The edge of the sword would stop just a hair away from the head. In later years, people saw a TV program where a master placed a grape on a person's bare stomach and, with a stroke of the sword, split it in half without scratching the skin. It's hard to believe. Not only were we not able to touch the sword, we couldn't even see it up close. It's sharper than a razor. No wonder Dad thought it was sacred. I could hardly wait to grow up and use a real sword for Kata. The entourage from Japan was impressive in Kata but the Master 5th Degree Black Belt in Kendo was something else.

Stunning Duel between our teacher Matsushita -- a 3rd Degree Black Belt and the Master. Clash of the Titans, like two ferocious Bull Moose butting heads and antlers. The (tummy?) being the head and the hilt of the two handed sword, the antlers. Locked in with hilt to hilt positioned in front of the solar plexus, the center of energy and balance. Master shifts ever so slightly and then a quick push with both hands using the full force of the hilt as a battery ram. Teacher loses balance, thrown backwards. His toes trying to grip the floor, the heels digging in to regain balance each step backward, feet pound the floor Boom! Boom! Boom! The noise of Booming tails off and finally Wham! My teacher falls flat on his back arms spread-eagled. Never heard the Dojo shake and rattle so much. Even in judo when a Master throws and slams a good teacher on the mat the building shakes much more and the sound is much louder.

The only other time watching an exhibit by a 5th degree Black Belt Kendo Master was in the Toronto Japanese Cultural Centre. My Irish friend Willie H. trained and fought in boxing. He knew all about balance, timing and speed and showed me how to punch correctly. Thank heavens I was already too old and over the hill to train in boxing. The crowd was around the gym watching the Master perform Kata in the open area.

When he faced us he leapt and sprang forward with a Ki-eye that sounded like the roar of a lion. Kote! Men! Do! The point of the Kendo sword only a few feet away from our head. Willie H. flinched and took a step back. He calculated that the Master was about 40 feet away when he started the Kata and within a second was on top of us.

As friends, we get together quite often and talk and argue about religion, politics, nutrition and conspiracy theories. Very controversial subjects, so the arguments never stop. Willie is quite a stubborn Christian fundamentalist captivated by some self-interest groups that teach limited and partial truth as the whole absolute truth. Mountains of assumptions based on emotions or feelings may be true or untrue. Illusions of thoughts, incorrect views, make people suffer over subjective reality. I myself, brought up as a Roman Catholic, was devoted to the Church's teaching until the early twenties and began to lean towards Eastern thought especially the branch of Yoga that teaches the method of reasoning. It's amazing from what is axiomatic (self-evident truth) reason out a whole philosophical system explaining the why and hows of the existence of the Universe and life. The axiom is "something real (absolute) or relative (phenomena-creation) cannot be caused, created or proceeded from nothing (denial of existence) and the corollary "nothing will always be nothing" and "something real or relative will always be something real or relative." Every philosophical thought whether reasoning the physical or spiritual is deduced back to the self-evident truth. If the thought cannot be deduced back to what is axiomatic, it is incorrect, an illusion of thought. Sometimes it's interesting to trace an illusion of thought to its illogical conclusion.

Through our senses we perceive the environment and the vast Universe and by observing within the mind we become aware of [the inner relative reality] of our own thoughts and feelings. Theologians will say God created all things both visible and invisible. Philosophers also believe ABSOLUTE REALITY CAUSED OR CREATED ALL PHENOMENA.

Reason based on the simple principle of cause and effect made many people to believe God was never created (no beginning) and always existed (no ending) and that God created all things. This reasoning is sound because it can be deduced to the self-evident truth "something cannot come from nothing" and "nothing will always be nothing" and "something will always be something." Which means something -- God -- did not come from nothing and something -- God -- will always be -- something -- God -- and -- exist as an Eternal, Absolute Reality with no beginning no ending.

Question: "Even if I believe in God (what's so important about all the abstract reasoning to understand the infinite." With my mind I could grasp most of the day to day finite reality and still manage the ups and downs of day to day life, but I do fear sickness and death and the unknown. I don't think anybody really knows what happens after death although I heard stories about people having a near death experience. People into Religion talk about God, Heaven and Hell and the scriptures as the absolute truth. I feel most of them are too emotionally involved in a belief system taught by self interest groups. For me to speculate beyond the senses and the physical is not sensible and filled with nonsense, sure some of it could be truth but I think half-truths are worse than no truth.

There's not much I can say about your thinking and life style, but I feel the more the minds of people understand the principles of the Absolute Reality or the Universal Principle the better the relationship becomes for a much more secure and happy life.

Since we understand a bit of the physical Relative World, what does it take for this carton box to exist? The box has attributes and without attributes the box cannot exist. The most obvious attribute is matter. Without some kind of matter the box cannot exist. The attribute of space -- it's impossible for the box to exist without space. Motion is a difficult a tribute to follow -- the motion of the cardboard box slowly disintegrates even slower "Diamonds are almost forever." Time is an interesting attribute and seems to go hand in hand with motion. Another attribute is principles that condition the box for existence as a cardboard box and also condition things like paper, diamonds, air and all different forms of creation and existence. Mentally we can analyze each attribute separately but in actual reality all attributes cannot be separated. They coexist and (inherent) in each other. It's impossible for anything to exist if any of the attributes are missing. The cardboard box cannot exist without matter. Relative existence means all the things can be measured, have a limit, are finite and depend on something for their existence.

Does God (or Infinite Reality) have attributes? God has the same attributes as Relative Reality except the attributes are infinite. Matter is not nothing so matter always existed. The other four attributes -- time, space motion, principles, always existed. "The Whole is greater than its parts." Finite attributes cannot cause or create the Infinite Attributes but the Infinite Attributes can cause or create finite attributes. All attributes co-exist with Infinite and finite reality. Even God cannot exist without the attributes. Can you imagine a Monotheistic God not having the attribute of Omnipotence and other Omnis including eternity?

The scientific study of the Universe, Linus Pauling's overview is a good example of formulating the molecular structure of the Universe. It starts by the accumulation of some correct data based on research and synthesized into a whole structure. Further research done would have to fit into the structure, if it does not fit he would recheck the new research data thoroughly and if it was still correct, he would adjust and change some of the existing structure to accommodate the new finding. In this way, the minor and major principles validate each other and eventually all the principles known will be synthesized into a holistic structure and a unifying principle established.

Recently the jargon of scientist and physicist are becoming very metaphysical. It started with Newton's Theories as "sum total of matter is constant." The totality of energy cannot be created or destroyed. "Action equals reaction" and maybe a few corollaries could be added. With the explosion of the Atom Bomb the atomic theory became a reality. Minute particles and electrical charges releasing tremendous energy and power. Particles evaporate into energy and what does energy melt into? The latest is the Super String Theory nothing but waves of energy like the string in the violins and at any instance things could pop up into existence. I think the waves of the Super String are still finite.

Since ancient times some schools taught similar theories. As philosophers they used reason and imagination based on axioms to go beyond the finite waves, energy or motion. Where did the finite motion come from? It came from infinite motion that always existed. Some thinkers thought that matter was made from minute particles existing eternally rather than one Infinite size particle and held together by energy fields in space holding the particles together, two eternal realities, particles and energy, a duality of eternal existence. Particle has size which is measurable and energy that fills the space between particles is measurable space and by the definition of the axioms they are both finite. Do two finites make one infinite? Particles and energy are not nothing so what substance created the duality? Infinite Energy and Infinite Particle as one singular homogenous substance. There cannot be two types of Infinite Energy and two Infinite Particles

Like Infinite Attributes they coexist as one eternal infinite Reality. The Attribute of Infinite Energy is not detectable and not measurable. It exists beyond the rarest and lightest form of energy and by its principle of Contraction and Expansion it concentrates to create the lightest and lighter form of energy. The greater the concentration becomes, the heavier and heavier the energy, eventually becomes modes of energy that we would detect as particles or matter.

This may not be a good analogy but consider water; it exists in many forms. Governed by the principle of temperature it appears as snow, ice, water, steam and moisture all from the one substance – water.

Maybe the finite mind is made in the image of the Infinite Mind. When I close my eyes and concentrate with my mind to form an image of a rocketship travelling at supersonic speed, it never goes beyond the limit of my mind. If I imagine a barrier I can make the rocketship stop before it hits the barrier. The question is "What is on the other side of the barrier?" It seems like Infinite space is within the finite mind. The space is not nothing; my mind fills it and my mind is not nothing, it's still something. I could relate the mind stuff as the most refined energy and when the mind concentrates it creates different shades of density with its own mind stuff and thoughts and imagery is created within my finite mind. The attributes of the finite mind are the same as the attributes of the Infinite mind. When my mind begins to understand the attributes of Universal Principles, it's the first step, I believe, in opening the path to Cosmic Consciousness.

Universal Principles are the same for all of humanity. The simple message is to be in rhythm with the Order of the Universe, or to be in tune with the Infinite.

All this abstract reasoning based on self-evident truth is deduced to the final aspect of Creation and Humanity having a finite and infinite nature. Jesus, the founder of Christianity, was enlightened to his own divinity and knew all people have the same divinity and to those who believed in his teaching would awaken to their own divinity, manifesting the inner spiritual power to create a much more harmonious and secure life. Divine Nature by its own Principles cannot change its own eternal existence.

GOSPEL OF ST. JOHN (VERSE 13)

The underlined words translate as divinity.

He was in the World and the World was made by him and the world knew him not.

He came unto his own and his own received him not. But as many as received him to them gave the power to become the sons of God, even to them that believed on his name.

Which were born not of blood nor of the will of flesh nor of the will of man but of God.

Understanding of the finite and infinite principles helps to redefine the Human Nature, the self-consciousness of mind and body and to find ways to let go of layers and layers of attachment to emotional perception and that causes barriers blocking the path to create an attitude and lifestyle of Cosmic Consciousness.

Synthesize Philosophy, theology, and the advance in Sciences staying in line with self-evident truth causes a clearer overview of finite and Infinite Life.

*****

No wonder Willie H and I seldom agreed on religious views.

Willie loved to play pool. Stubborn, competitive, with mental toughness not to give up is a difficult combination to beat in any sport. Consistency is not an easy act to follow and his game was up and down. Once in a while he'd play a game like a real professional; good position with excellent control enabling him to make one ball after another until the whole table was cleared of all the balls. After any great performance, his face showed euphoric satisfaction. Many times he would say that if he had a choice to make millions in real estate or to become the best pool player in the world, he would choose the latter.

Many people would say hanging around pool halls and playing pool was a wasted life, so I wasted thirty years. I lacked the consistency to be a good shot maker due to a compensating side arm stroke that looked like a chicken with a broken wing trying to stroke the cue in a straight line. The reason Willie couldn't beat me was due to my consistent "Talent of Touch," the man with the golden arm (kept these thoughts to myself). The touch in controlling the cue ball and the object ball never let me down. Even under the pressure of a money game, the touch was always there and the greater the pressure the better the touch. When I had difficulty in making balls, I resorted to strategy and defensive safeties outsmarting the opponent and playing superior safeties by control and touch, hooking the opponent or leaving the cue ball in such an awkward position it becomes a trap. The player takes a penalty or leaves me an easy shot.

Willie would be frustrated with a look of disbelief saying "how could you control the cue ball so well, leaving me no shot, time after time after time? I could see the angle the cue ball is coming back, knowing it's floating into a spot where it's going to trap me." Sometimes I even surprised myself for having the uncanny ability to place the ball where I wanted. Willie would never give up thinking that he could beat me. After beating him game after game until closing time, he would ask the owner of the pool room to let us play after hours Willie would really get upset if I told him I'm getting tired. He didn't want any excuses from me if and when he won. Team sport wasn't for Willie. He preferred individual sports like Boxing and Billiards but never played golf. Being a detail person he had great insight in strategy for pool games and probably in real estate. Willie was like a genius analyzing specific situations but weak on synthesizing, seeing the tree but not the forest. He analyzed the art of boxing to the nth degree and had a love and hate relationship with it. Willie told me his first street fight was through road rage, with a big truck driver. One punch and the driver went down like a ton of bricks and the sound of the trucker's head hitting the sidewalk made him sick in the stomach. Willie never backed out from a potential fight but had a lot of restraint. Through the years, since I've known him, he never threw a punch. Baldy C the famous and toughest bouncer and street fighter in Toronto was watching Willie punch a bag and said, "The way you're punching the heavy bag, if you ever hit me with a punch like that you'll knock me out."

Birds of a feather flock together. Willie told me his father went to see a Doctor for his arthritis and the Doc asked his Dad, "What did you do all your life?" and his old man replied, "Drinking and fighting." His younger brother Jerry and Little Davey went looking for fights especially in beer halls and his Dad would tag along just to watch the entertainment. Willie's father and brothers were not big men, height 5'6" and shorter, all weighing about 150 lbs. or less and to me it's a miracle that none of them got seriously injured. Li'l Davey was one tough son of a gun. Height is about 5'7" and many times he knocked out 5 or 6 guys at a time including twice, a bunch of cops. When he worked for Hydro a fifty-pound metal canister fell from near the top of a telephone pole, hitting his head, crushing the safety helmet. The force was so great it loosened the muscle nerve endings from the bones; the pain was unbearable. He mentioned that the pain was so great that if it weren't for his wife and kids he would have committed suicide. The Doctor told him he was lucky; if the canister had hit his shoulder it would have killed him and also told him to control his temper, it's not good for his hypertension. Dave recovered slowly and even as a senior still works as a self-employed electrician.

Not long ago in a little donut shop, Willie started to argue with the man behind the counter. The man exploded in anger, running around the counter charging at Willie who ended up lying flat on his back on one of those fixed immovable tables. Willie's neck and head were hanging over the edge on the other side of the table and the hot head on top of him trying to reach over to grab Willie by the throat. Willie was already a senior citizen and the guy was a strapping man in his mid-thirties who seemed to know some fighting techniques, so I tapped him very lightly on his back, saying, "Hey take it easy on the old man." He let go and they ended up tussling in the short and narrow aisles. I was close to Willie, standing behind him and while wrestling they managed to switch positions and that's when the donut man bent his leg and kneed me, tearing cartilage on my left knee. After the positional change, Willie had his back to the exit door and the man, wrestling and shoving, pushed him outside, telling Willie to fuck off, and quickly grabbed Willie's hat and coat and threw it outside. Willie wasn't overly angry but did say, "It's a good thing he didn't come outside with a little room to move around. I would have nailed him and laid him out." Willie thought the guy had some training in Martial Arts. The toughest part of the scuffle was when he had to make that positional change so the guy could easily push him out the door. I was impressed with Willie's balance and wrestling with a man who outweighed him by thirty pounds and I thought the guy had some training in the military. Even though Willie is past his senior's age, he's a stickler for exercise. He walks for miles and miles and if he has a bag, he'll shadow box and punch the bag but I doubted he would have knocked the Donut Man out.

Willie told me he met a Korean Tae Kwon Do Master working in a carpet store. The teacher clenched his fist, sticking his thumb straight up, telling Willie to bend or break his thumb and when he gripped the thumb it felt like a steel pipe and when he really put his strength into bending the thumb backward, the teacher would move his forearm slightly backward to relieve the pressure. Knowing Willie, he would ask all sorts of questions on the fighting style and how effective it would be in actual combat. Willie would always say, "I wouldn't bet against Baldy C if he had to fight any Martial Artist, although Baldy might move slower when he throws a punch at an empty space or at a spot, his timing is so good that the guy's head would be there to meet Baldy's fist. I've seen Baldy C when he worked as a bouncer in a Gerrard street tavern, his thighs and legs seemed very big and powerful. He didn't walk, but glided around like a big cat built like a bull and had fists like a sledgehammer. People who had never seen Baldy would talk about his exploits on hearsay. Everybody loves a hero and, like groupies, creates the image of the toughest and best brawler ever. Even though it's a snap shot, it's all about perception. My little friend, Lou St. Lou from the Pool Hall days said, "Baldy C, he's chicken." And told me his experience. One night the cops were chasing him and he was jumping over fences in peoples' back yards in total darkness, running away from the cops and he realized Baldy's house was close by so he managed to get to his place where the back kitchen lights were on.

Running in the dark he couldn't see, so his head would hit a post or a clothesline and his head and face were bleeding and he burst into the kitchen, still holding the gun in his hand and Baldy's face went pale white. Lou thought Baldy was chicken. Anyway, Baldy told Lou to hide in the basement and he would take care of the cops. The cops did come and Baldy said he never saw anybody.

Lou spent some time in the pen and he fought like a maniac against big tougher guys, saying, don't let those big guys get away with anything, otherwise they will step all over you. It's hard to believe a nice pleasant cheerful guy like Little Lou could become a raging wolverine.

Willie was always respectful of the Kendo Master, knowing the blinding speed of forward and backward movement, he realized it would be impossible to punch someone out of range. Apparently he talked with Master after the exhibit and probably quizzed him on how Kendo would stand up against the other Martial Arts in actual combat. Somehow he liked the character and the manner of speech of the teacher. Willie would always refer to the Kata experience of the Master Kendoist as the "Roaring steam engine that almost ran over us."

Certainly, I had fond memories of the sound of pow! pow! pow! Powell Street Kendo Dojo. Powell Street played a great part in framing my state of mind to be rooted in Japanese culture. Kendo training, going to early Japanese grade school and living at the far eastern end of Li'l Tokyo which was like a little community where all my young friends were of Japanese ancestry. Spoke mostly English with each other, felt comfortable, laughed a lot and played hard. When we went out of our area, strangely enough, our personality changed. Spoke softly, acted sheepishly, almost looked forlorn and minded our own business even against racial slurs but when confronted with violence, we didn't back down.

Mother was able to speak, read and write English and Japanese. Born in Vancouver, she felt very strongly, "I am Canadian," spoke mostly English to us and Japanese to Father and we kids spoke in broken English to Dad. If Mother were not cooking she would be reading and during lunch or supper would talk about current events, history, different cultures and anything she thought we should know. She educated us and westernized us. As poor as we were, she always managed to buy things of value for our lives such as the Children's Book of Knowledge, which I read at an early age, the whole set from beginning to end. Like all Mothers, she gave us down to earth advice and taught the horror of drugs and destructiveness of cigarettes. Unfortunately, I didn't listen to all she said. She always stressed the positive side of Japanese culture, saying that we had nothing to be ashamed of. She mentioned that European people were living like Barbarians when the Japanese had a civilization and wore beautiful clothing and had elegant table manners and etc. etc. I equated barbarians with cavemen and, from what I studied in school, painted a picture in my mind about cavemen roaming around Europe. When thinking about it now it's funny. I had no idea of chronological time and pre-civilizations. She felt sorry for the blacks, saying they don't have an ancient culture and civilization to fall back on. Wrong again, this time it isn't funny. The tender young mind will accept emotional imagery and even if the truth becomes known, the spin will keep the feeling lingering on.

Mom used to serve different types of small dried fish saying that to eat the whole fish, "bones and all" was good for the teeth. Quite often for snacks she would say the same thing, giving us baked so-ra beans which were harder to crack than Brazil Nuts. As kids, we enjoyed cracking the hard stuff with our teeth. I don't know how Mom got the information that green tea was good for us. Recent research claims green tea is a good antioxidant. One day the home room teacher talked about how harmful coffee and tea were for health and asked whoever drank coffee or tea to raise their hands and then said, "tomorrow, I don't want to see any hands go up." The next day she asked the same question and my hand was the only one raised. The teacher was upset so I had to tell her my Mother told me that "Green tea is good for me." The teacher was frustrated for a few days saying my Mom was wrong and I kept saying, "I listen to my Mom." She sent me home threatening to expel me.

I finally had to tell Mom about the tea situation. Mother matter of factly said, "Don't worry, I'll go and speak to your teacher." Knowing Mom, she probably went to see the principal first. The next day, the teacher asked, "Anybody drink coffee or black tea to day?" I wouldn't be a bit surprised if my Mom was the first Canadian feminist of Asian background.

Mother never pushed me to study at home or to do any homework, which was great, gave me more time to play and chum around with my pals. If my report card didn't show anything but As and Bs she might have sung a different tune. This habit continued into the senior years in high school where my report card showed Cs and Ds and finally some Es and Fs for failure. Learning how to cram for the final exams helped me to graduate grade 13 in Ontario.

Mom, once in a while would ask me in a nice way to take my brothers out and play with them, saying that they would enjoy my company. At that time, it felt like they would be a nuisance; I figured that they were too young to keep up with the gang's activities. We lived on Powell Street for approximately five years, from when I was 7 years old until I was nearly 13 years of age. Brother Bob, sometimes called Ketchup, was four years younger and Richard was a year younger than Bob. Mom could be so nice and diplomatic, giving me 30 cents to buy fish and chips when we went to the beach. I would take them to Kitsilano beach and whether they enjoyed it or not with me, it's hard to say but they seemed well behaved.

The story goes that if any kid tried to fight Bob, younger Richard would go to his aid and fight for him. Richard is the one with all the scars.

Naomi was two years younger than Richard and Mom couldn't understand why she kept brining home stray cats. Vancouver alley cats were mangy and rangy. Ferocious dogs usually got the worst of it when they attacked one of those alley cats. At night, the cats would yell and meow all night, sounding like a band tuning up for rehearsal and the neighbors would all get upset and yell and throw things at them. One day Naomi came home crying and sobbing that one of the cats was stranded on top of a telephone pole, so Mom called the Fire Department. Tug of War. Mom getting rid of cats and Naomi bringing them home. Named all of Naomi's kittens and cats, Winkle. The one and only dog I ever had was a beautiful German Shepherd with mouth and tongue drenched in purple and every kid seemed to think the more purple the mouth, the more intelligent the dog. My name Rip with a dog name 'Van' and the cats called 'Winkle' – I thought it was cool to come up with Rip Van Winkle.

Dad operated a small wholesale egg business in the basement of the house. Once in a blue moon he would ask me to help him grade the eggs and put them up to a light to spot blood clots which he sold to the bakery. Sometimes Dad would take one of us kids to the country to buy eggs. Most of the farmers were Japanese and Dad enjoyed talking with them and if Dad was ahead in schedule, he would join one of them in having afternoon tea and snacks. Most of the farmers had acres of strawberry and had chickens to sell the eggs. Besides that they would have a little vegetable garden growing some Japanese vegetables like burdock, big white carrots and rhubarb and cabbages. One year, dad thought it would be a good idea for me to have a working holiday on a farm. I believe it was the Sano family's farm. I did chores like cleaning up the chicken coops, collecting eggs, feeding them and later, even picked some strawberries. I sort of felt farm life was not for me.

What made my life on the farm worthwhile was the neighbor who owned a dog kennel business. After finishing the chores I decided to explore the uncleared section of the farm and saw lots of bees and bee hives, wild flowers, pitchy pine and fir trees and tons of ;bushes. I was fascinated to see my first humming bird; amazing how they keep still while the wings are moving so fast it's just a blur, having their beak picking the nectar of flowers. Wild canaries and hawks was a common sight. Ended up on the main road and the position of the sun tipped me off that it was late afternoon and without thinking, I started to head back to the farm house which was set back about 100 yards from the main road. Walking along this big sleek looking dog was running like a greyhound towards me from the neighbors field and a man standing alone beside his house about 200 feet away. No time to have fear but thought of protecting my throat with my right arm in a boxer stance and shove my left fist and arm down the dog's throat or ??? The sound of a whistle, the dog stopped immediately about 20 feet from me, turned around and ran just as fast back to the owner. The man came towards me and said in a friendly voice, "Doberman Pinschers are well trained and you had nothing to be afraid of." Although he was middle aged, we became very good friends. I was welcome to his place any time. I learned more about dogs from him, his wife and a younger hired help. As thoroughbreds, the Doberman had the best scent ability and would be used for tracking. One evening he let a Doberman sniff a coin and told me to go into the woods and hide the big penny. I must have gone a few hundred yards deep into the woods and placed it near some bushes and upon returning, he snapped his finger and the Doberman went off running. Sure enough the Doberman returned shortly afterwards and dropped the coin from his mouth at the foot of the owner.

Dobermans were originally bred in Germany, brought to the U.S. and in California, probably due to some owner's negligence, found themselves running around wild in packs and some of them were shot by hunters or captured and domesticated. Born with big floppy ears, their instinct was to attack and fight and so the ears would be torn. As pups, the men would snip the ears into a small sharp triangle, which made the dog look aristocratic. The kennel raised and trained Doberman Pinschers and had Beta, who won prizes at every dog show. The owner was happy and proud of Beta. She made his kennel well known and famous and through her breeding, the offspring were sold for a lot more money. The Kennel owner loved dogs and he even cared and looked after mongrels when their owners were away on holidays. He said many nice things about mongrels.

Once I watched the hired hand snipping the ears off the Doberman pups and applying bandages. He warned me never to step inside the stall with the pups; the Mother would attack anybody that came close to her pups except the owner. He showed me all the different nutrients fed to the dogs, like iodine, minerals and vitamins and his pet saying was "never overfeed" and all the dogs looked trim and sleek and in good shape. I used to wonder, "how come all the vitamins?"

I guess hanging around feeding, grooming and training dogs every day, he liked talking about the different personalities of the dogs. "Killer", a Doberman, was obnoxious to me; he behaved like a bully with a mean vicious streak. He told me about his "Love-Hate" relationship with Killer. He respected and loved the dog's loyalty but didn't trust it completely because of the reactive killer instinct that would turn on him.

Quite often the owner would take Killer for a walk and let the dog romp around the field. Strangely, Killer was obedient to the owner's command "Here boy", "run run" and he behaved like any other dog. As a kid, it seemed like magic and I wondered if Killer was the same dog who first came charging towards me. Now I think of the owner as the Master with the Magic Touch.

The owner's wife must have liked me. She always invited me into the house to have a drink and something to eat. Grooming and trimming the dogs was interesting to watch. Once she was preparing a poodle for a dog show and said, "Poodles as thoroughbreds are the most intelligent dog" and made the poodle do all sorts of tricks and seemed excited about the coming dog show. The poodle didn't win as many prizes as Beta.

On one occasion I asked the owner about my dog, Van, the German Shepherd. He explained almost everything about German Shepherds in such a great detailed way that I forgot most of it. The Shepherd didn't have the great sense of scent for tracking like the Doberman, but still made excellent police dogs. It was very durable and handled northern climate very well and had the ability to absorb punishment. It would take a bullet or a deadly blow to stop a German Shepherd. Working in a team, they were a great asset to the police and a formidable force against the enemy. Very protective and loyal, they enjoy running over or around rough terrain. When trained, Shepherds are able to climb ladders. They were easy to train as watchdogs for the blind and invalids. The more I heard, the more respect I had for Van. Later when we moved from Powell Street to Prior Street, Dad found a new home for Van. I missed him even though my parents explained that Van would be better off staying on a farm, having freedom to run around in open space. I kind of agreed.

It was a short summer, spending most of the time on the farm and at the neighbor's dog kennel. The farmer paid me $7.00 for the chores and I thought he should have paid me more. Still, I had a few days to enjoy time at the beach with the guys before school started.

As soon as the public school class ended, I would rush home, pick up some books and head on to Japanese School. Everybody had about 1 half hour of fun and games before classes started. The boys, as usual, played the rough and tumble games. King of the Castle was played in the auditorium. Whoever was able to throw everybody off the stage became the King. The "Whip" was another exciting and thrilling game. Somebody stands in the center of the floor as the hub of a wheel and the other kids would join in a fireman's grip, hands holding the wrist. When 15 or more kids grip each other's wrist, the line begins to move like a single spoke of a wheel and the kids near the end of the whip are moving much faster. As the momentum pick us up, the last kid is flying and his feet and body would leave the floor and when his grip lets go, he becomes a flying object, crashing into the wall or anything that's in the way.

Some of the boys really like to show off to the girls. One stunt was to run and dive through an open class room window right on top of bushes outside. The girls would gasp -- oohing and aahing.

One kid loaned me a knife with the blade broken in half with an even edge. Pressed on the back of one hand with a little red ink it looked like a knife stab. I showed it to my desk partner YK. She was shocked and almost in tears. Later I showed her it was a trick and this may have upset and hurt her feelings. She was not her friendly self.

One day I was late for fun and games and walking through the auditorium the kids were already having piggyback fights. Someone jumped me from behind, falling forward, I tried to brace my fall with the right arm and felt a sharp pain in my right elbow. The right arm was paralyzed but still held on to the textbook with the left hand and managed to get up and continue on to the classroom. Left the books on my desk and walked outside where nobody was around. I didn't want anybody bumping into my arm and as long as the arm was motionless, the pain was bearable. When the class started I showed YK my elbow; it was slightly swollen and crooked. Everybody started to write but I couldn't even hold a pencil. The teacher noticed and came over asking if anything was wrong. YK spoke up saying that something was wrong with my arm. Bit of a fuss, sent for another teacher from another class to look at my arm and he decided to take me to a Judo teacher. YK had tears in her eyes. It made me feel good that she cared. The Judo teacher pressed two or three places on my arm and told me the elbow was dislocated. He warned me it would be painful when he snapped it back into position. He cupped his hand underneath the upper arm and held the wrist with the other; a short yank with a sharp pain and it was over. He made a tourniquet and told me to wear it for a while.

*****

Powell Street and the unforgettable Powell ground home of the now famous Asahi baseball team recently inducted into the Canadian Baseball Hall of Fame. Most of us were around nine years old when we started to play baseball with a bunko ball, a hard hollow rubber ball that didn't bounce so well and we swung a regular bat that was sawed off at the end. Two years later we graduated to playing real baseball. We all felt grown up and excited playing for the first time with a hard ball. Ouch! The first time catching a hard ball, the palm of my hand stung. It took a couple of weeks before the stinging went away and then it was pure pleasure playing catch and snagging fly balls. The bats were too heavy to swing so we still sawed off the end. We used to get bats that were cracked from the Ashai players and repair them by using screws and tape. To us a repaired bat was a brand new bat. Akio's older brother Sumio was two years older than us and was the team captain and named the team "Hurricane." In those days, midget baseball was not organized and Sumio went all over the city arranging baseball games for us to play. In the span of two years the Hurricanes played four games and the last game we won. Sumio was elated, jumping up and down, shouting, "We're number one." The Asahi ball club didn't have a perfect record like the "Hurricanes" four wins and no losses. A few years later during the war years, we played two more games in the relocated camp and won both games. Sumio with a big grin kept reminding us about Hurricanes' perfect record.

I can't remember which Halloween night it was but Powell Street was silent and filled with tension. Judo men, Kendo men with the RCMPs were walking and patrolling Powell Street in pairs and some were standing on the street corners. A couple of my friends and myself were nervous and excited waiting with anticipation. One year before, some truckloads of gang members came on Halloween night and wrecked and smashed the storefronts on Powell Street. This year Li'l Tokyo was prepared. The men that were walking the beat kept telling us to go home in case of violence and danger. We kept hiding and watching the streets. Sure enough, a load of guys got off the truck ready to wreck and damage the stores when a whistle blew and a dozen men went running towards the truck. The Mounties were swinging their Billy clubs and the Kendoists were using blackjacks to knock out people and I saw a Judo man almost wrapping some guy around a lamppost with a foot sweep. A few of them escaped by running through the dark Powell Grounds. Other trucks came by but seeing what was happening to their members they didn't stop and kept going. I think the whole scenario was over in a couple of minutes. The half dozen guys laid out on the ground were thrown into a paddy wagon and Powell Street once again became silent.

Powell Street had its history of violent events. Just a month ago I read a book called, "The Phantom Immigrant.", a very interesting story about a Japanese entrepreneur from Miyagi Japan. The mob violence on Powell Street was the result of the American Fisherman's Union who wanted to establish a strong hold in British Columbia.

The Japanese fishermen would not join the Union so the Union members were upset and wanted to "teach the Japs a lesson." The mob, made up of Union members had to go through Chinatown so, for warm up exercise or for some other reason went on a rampage, wrecked Chinatown and by the time they got to Powell Street they did a good job in smashing up the store fronts or any other thing they could damage. . The following year the Union people wanted to do the same thing to Powell Street. The Japanese were prepared for a fight and a half dozen Japanese men who thought they were still Samurai volunteered to sacrifice their life by jumping into the mob scene and with razor sharp swords would slice up everything in sight and whether it was rumor or not, the Union members wanted no part of facing the sword wielding fanatics.

"All is quiet on the Western Front" That's how Powell Street became on Halloween nights with no more gang members coming around, just the usual Martial Artists and police were on guard. It was boring and Shige N, who was two or three years older than us, said, "Let's go to Chinatown" and yesiree, five of us kids got excited and away we went with Shige. When we entered Chinatown it was crowded and I met two of my Chinese classmates and greeted each of them saying "Hi Albert" and "How are you doing John?" As we walked deeper into Main Street Chinatown, it even got more crowded and we began to hear derogatory remarks about us being Japanese. Behind us, a wall of people was beginning to form, blocking us from going back the way we came in. In front, the road was clear and the sidewalk on both sides was crowded with people. As the crowd noise became louder and they started to close in on us, Shige shouted to us to run to the other end of Chinatown which was about three or four blocks away. We all ran as fast as we could and it seemed like running a marathon with the crowd on both sides of the sidewalk booing instead of cheering as they picked up the lingo of the mob chasing us. Some of them joined the chase and the mob scene got bigger and bigger.

Twice I looked back. The first time I saw Shige flip a lone person to the side and the crowd hesitated for a second and in a much louder roar, they charged Shige who ran away from them. We were leading the way about 50 to 60 feet ahead of Shige and the crowd. The second time I looked back, we were close to the end of Chinatown. It was a comical sight and yet it was awesome. Shige standing all by himself facing the crowd with both arms moving like a windmill, trying to hold back a tidal wave of people. When we reached the end of Chinatown the sidewalk was crowded with people walking who were not Chinese. I don't know whether it was some animal instinct of territorial rights, but the crowd stopped dead about fifty feet away. What a guy Shige was. Such an upbeat person, his face and neck covered in sweat, grinning away and he just said, "Come on, let's go" like nothing happened. Even in later years when I met him twice, he was still grinning and smiling like a happy go lucky guy.

*****

Our teacher was the wife of the Principal of the school, very soft spoken but firm. She kept praising me, telling the class that during the painful ordeal with my arm, the Judo teacher said I never cried or uttered a sound. Stoicism was highly regarded by the Warrior Class, a Samurai was expected to bear pain and face death without fear. Some of this attitude probably became part of my consciousness, based on Kendo training, a typical macho trait. Growing older, I still enjoyed some of the Samurai's movies. The actors in the movies spoke very little, had poker faces and looked a little up tight. Subtle facial expression and telltale body language with stylized movement explained the hierarchical class structure together with the discipline to follow and an attitude of loyalty and trust. They didn't have to say too much to understand each other.

Things are changing very rapidly in modern day Japan but I still think Japanese men have difficulty in saying "I love you" to a woman and a woman is expected to understand or read the man's mind for their wants and needs.

Recently CNN News mentioned that Japanese couples find it much easier to say, "I love you" in English. It's an interesting duality of having an island mentality of close-mindedness. Everybody and everything is considered 'outsider' not Japanese and yet their mind is open and accepts everything from the outsiders and either improves on it or makes it the Japanese way.

Through the years, it was easy for me to notice the Japanese did things backward. Their 'yes' means 'no' and 'no' means 'yes'. The hand waving Hi! Means goodbye and goodbye means Hi! Some of my Dad's carpenter tools were made to pull instead of to push. He claimed it was much easier to cut a straight line by pulling the saw towards the center of the gut instead of pushing it towards some vague point in space. Using a plane to smooth out rough lumber was the same principle. Dad, a Judo expert, constantly turned his back against his opponent to throw them on the ground while in Western style wrestling it's a no no to turn your back against the person you are fighting.

Western society is riddled with guilt whereas the Japanese society is sprayed with shame. People still visit the 47 graves and show their respect for the 47 Ronin, a classical historical event in Japanese History. Some cultures may not like treachery and revenge but the Japanese put Honor and Loyalty far beyond a bit of treachery and revenge. The list of Japanese doing things backwards could go on and on but the tourists seem to enjoy Japan and the business people might find it confusing at the beginning but learning the way of the Japanese, it's easy and becomes really easy for non-Japanese people when they begin to understand the Japanese way.

The Japanese written language is based on the Chinese characters called Kan-Ji. Kan-Ji is a pictogram and has a bit of a logical structure. For me, it was a lot of memory work and boring. YK and some of her girlfriends were always at the top of the class when it came to tests and exams. This made me study sometimes just to see if I could keep up with YK, just to prove something - ego, I think. At least the teacher often praised my brushwork when writing classical Chinese characters. We learned two different types of Japanese alphabet. Kata Kana and Hira Gana. Usually Hira-gana was written beside the difficult Kan-Ji so even if we didn't understand the meaning it helped us to pronounce and read the text. I couldn't help but admire and respect YK's academic ability. I was two years older and two years ahead of YK in English public school. During World War II we were relocated 100 miles from the coast in the interior of B.C., a place called Slocan Bay Farm. The Sisters of Assumption started a High School for the Japanese Canadians to be able to continue their education. Myself and another girl were the only Catholic students attending the school and after Sunday Mass, Sister Superior would talk and give me some spiritual guidance. When I first went to Catholic High I started in Grade 10 and the following year, nearing the end of my 11th grade, Sister Superior seemed quite animated, talking about an interview she had with a precocious girl. The girl was trying to decide whether to go to Catholic or Protestant High School, claiming that her two girlfriends, including herself, were geniuses and wanted to make sure they made the right choice. It was a real surprise to hear the girl was YK and I thought "what a bold girl." Over sixty years later at the Toronto Japanese Community Centre we had a Class Reunion with some of the teachers from the "Sisters of Assumption" and I introduced my son Daniel to YK saying she was my first love and her immediate quip was "Yeah, fifty years of could have been." Still sharp and not as shy.

Japan was at war with China. Everyone going to Japanese classes was told to collect tin foil from cigarette packages so Japan could build airplanes. My young mind calculated the amount of cigarettes my parents smoked; they used to hand roll cigarettes in those days and to scrounge around for some empty packs outside on the street didn't make sense. Even if everybody did this, I thought, "They would be lucky to build one plane." I asked my Mom about this and she said, "Japan is a poor country and some people die of starvation." She might have mentioned that people were sending food and clothing besides just tin foil.

In early grade school we were taught about the unbroken lineage of the Emperor and that the first one came down from Heaven to rule Japan and if you died for the Emperor there was some kind of reward. I was too young to reason but I still liked the idea of fighting with honor for the Emperor. For whatever reason, I preferred and loved the stories of "King Arthur and the Round Table." Or "Ivanhoe" and even "Robin hood." The honor and chivalry of fighting for King and Country and a lovely maiden caught my imagination much more. The spin on the Emperor's Divinity was not as effective as the Virgin Birth.

Like most Nation States, Japan followed the same patterns to become a nation.

The usual tribal consciousness which developed a Warlord mentality of protecting only their own people for security and using force to gain more land and material goods from neighboring tribes, use of Hard power, nothing but blood and violence. Eventually threatened by external forces, the tribes united, centralized by a political structure suitable to a Nation State. The oldest form of political power was Theocracy with feudalistic class structure. It takes money to support a military so more often than enough they would plunder and conquer other tribes and Nation States. Nation States always have the potential to become Empires and some have since pre-Biblical times and continue to do so in the Mid-east, North Africa, Europe and the Asian Continent, and, like everything else, empires come and go.

I believe the hard power of Human Behavior is partly the functioning of the Reptilian brain. The Reptilian brain is the first to form in human life and probably the last to end. Understanding the brain itself, the system, Reptilian, limbic, mammalian, outer cortex and other parts of the brain is as complex as the whole Universe. They say the number of particles in the brain is equal to the particles of the Universe. Basic human nature has not changed; emotions are older than the institution of marriage and many of the emotional perceptions of the human being are magnified by the thoughts of the outer cortex to make life either better or worse. It requires a correct and good ideology involving practice and study to create a balanced wholesome lifestyle to raise the consciousness of individuals.

I believe that psychology and spirituality have the means to seek and find ways to tame and domesticate the Reptilian Brain. Most animals are restricted and limited in instinctive behavior to kill for food and to fight for territorial rights. The outer cortex has the ability to reason, imagine and create but at times it is misused and overwhelmed by the crocodile brain which brings out the worst of human behavior. Many people feel helpless and hopeless victimized by the reptilian brain to external forces. To become the master of our mind is to avoid becoming a victim and a slave to that aspect of the reptilian brain.

Fortunately a human being has the outer cortex of the brain that could evolve and give us choices to either live in chaotic disorder or in harmonious order and the brain is always striving and struggling to attain balance between the two. It requires a good ideology accompanied by practice and training to develop a wholesome life style to raise the consciousness of the individual.

Love and War on Powell Street

Love and War on Powell street -- only for me, it was puppy love and the last battle in Li'l Tokyo was between the Japanese. My country was at war with Japan and due to some differences in opinions, the Japanese from out of town and the ones who lived in town had a fight. I didn't see this battle because our family moved to Prior Street, but I heard from the grapevine that the outer towners, especially the fishermen from Stevenson, fought ferociously and beat the hell out of the Vancouver boys, including the judomen.

D.N. was a year younger and small for his age. He followed me around like a faithful dog but was an interesting companion with some new ideas and things to do. Like the time he came up with the devious strategy to get even and punish the strong kid T from Kendo class. D.N. had extraordinary speed and quickness in Kendo for the target area Kote. The first duel he caught me off guard and beat me with the "Kote." After that it made me really concentrate on the space between the tips of our swords to overcome his speed to beat him. It was the first time D.N. talked about a girl and kept bugging me to see her. He was almost like a stalker, knew what time she came out of the United Church on Powell Street, knew her name, knew where she lived and told me she walked home alone. Every Sunday we would wait for her across the street and watch her come out of the church. D.N. kept saying "Rip, she'll make a good girl friend for you." K.Y. was just as attractive as Y.K., my schoolmate.

High school was quite a distance from our house and my parents bought me a bicycle so I wouldn't have to walk to school. I was really nervous and hesitant to go with K.Y. to her house but D.N. kept moaning and groaning, begging me to take K.Y. home. Finally, one Sunday, I summoned up enough courage to at least follow her home on my bicycle staying a distance of 30 to 40 feet behind her. I felt like Tom Sawyer in Mark Twain's novel, showing off to a girl. I could slow the motion or speed of the bicycle or come to a dead stop in perfect balance without my feet touching the ground. All the kids going to High School had bicycles with V shaped handle bars and many times we would ride in formation like the flying geese and when we came to a stoplight, we would turn the front wheel to the right, pull hard on the handle of the V shape handlebar and at the same time push hard on the right pedal of the bike, and, at a dead stop, balance in midair without getting off the bike and never touching the ground with our feet. We learned all sorts of tricks, like a cowboy riding a horse. When dogs chased us we would ride sidesaddle or put out feet on the handlebar. Never tried to ride my bike backward to show off to K.Y. In private practice, it was fifty fifty chance of failing and falling off the bicycle so I didn't want to take a chance and embarrass myself. Once I raised the front wheel too high and was forced to jump off backwards to stay on my feet. It's interesting to note that before K.Y. would open the door to go inside the house, she would not turn her head to look at me but would sort of bow her head forward and tilt her head slightly and glance at me with her eyes almost underneath her arm pit. This walk-a-thon and bike-a-thon didn't last too long. D.N. told me her father was very strict and didn't want her to have any boyfriend. I believe it was the same strictness with Y.K.'s father. At that age, what did I know about the reality of the birds and the bees? It was just another story.

How could I ever forget Prior Street? Experienced a lot of things for the first time. The street was situated near the East End of the Italian community quite close to Atlantic Street where my family lived eight years ago. Had my first orgasm, puffed my first cigarette, attended first year High School and for the first time experienced racial prejudice caused by the War between Japan and my country, Canada. It was also the first time Dad had to leave us, working in a pulp mill over in Port Alice, Vancouver Island.

Britannia High was a little too far away to walk so my parents bought me a brand new balloon tire C.C.M bicycle. It was my first bike and it made it easy for me to keep in touch with the old gang on Powell Street and a few Italian friends nearby. Dimitrio, a red headed Italian, was a very unusual friend, not my type, a nerd, but such a nice person, very sincere, considerate and always happy to see me. We were in the same class throughout public school and here we were in the same class at Britannia High. Miyo I, a Nisei girl, made up our trio, but when the war started, Miyo and I separated from Dimitrio and ended up in the same class in Slocan Bay Farm for grade 10 and 11 and finally we both graduated, still in the same class, from High School in New Denver B.C.

I could never forget Dimitrio's patience and concern, helping and teaching me mathematics. The big problem I had was English and that made it difficult for me to understand the exam questions. Both Dimitrio and Miyo did very well in their studies and exams and Reg was the dunce.

Outside of the trio, everybody else enrolled from other public schools so I can't recall or remember any of the classmates. The only thing that sticks in my mind is the Physical Ed Teacher. I finally realized what my Uncles were talking about playing Rugby with the Great and famous Patrick brothers. The guys in school were not superstars but were awfully big to wrestle and play Rugby with, although in boxing sessions I gave a lot of bleeding noses to the bigger kids. The teacher kept saying I was a good boxer and wanted me to try out for the Golden Glove Tournament. The dilemma was that I hated boxing and felt I didn't know anything about it. I guess play boxing with my Uncles, throwing and trading punches as a toddler, hardwired my brain where the skills developed naturally.

Friendship among youngsters is a precious and amazing thing. Fifty years later when I visited Vancouver, I managed to look up Dimitrio. He did not live in the old Italian neighborhood but an old woman sitting on the verandah knew the red headed Italian boy Dimitrio Santaga. I finally learned his last name, looked it up in the phone book and called him. We met. He still had that boyish attitude; his hair was not red but dark with a little grey. His friendliness and kindness overwhelmed me. He also showed a lot of gratitude towards my Dad who once brought him three crateful's of baby chicks from the egg farms. Most of them died, but Dimitrio managed to raise eight hens out of the whole bunch of chicks. With a twinkle in his eyes, he talked about some hens supplying eggs for the family and the rest ended up in the oven.

I stayed overnight at his home, met his wife and talked about family life. After his wife went to bed, we talked about the pleasant and fun times we had. Every day after school we went to his place and I would sit on a wooden fence right on top of a 2 x 4 ledge, with my back to the vegetable garden and a manure pile just behind me. At the far end of the garden was a shed where the family kept a cow and some chickens. He would dash down into the basement and bring out homemade cheese and French bread. Sometimes it would be natural peanut butter and homemade jam. Mmmmm even with the barnyard smell, the snacks tasted great. The way he talked about his two lovely daughters, both married, and a successful plumbing company, he seemed happy with his life and I thought it couldn't have happened to a nicer friend.

Another new friend I made was a Nisei boy about my age who lived in the neighborhood. T.S. was preoccupied with making knives by filing down old files and when the rough edge became smooth he would keep filing to make a sharp blade. The handle would be wrapped in strands of leather and it really looked like a good hunting knife. He gave me one, as a gift, with a nice leather case and we practiced knife fighting in his backyard. Looks are deceiving. T.S. was about my size, broad shoulders, slightly bowed legs and a wiry body, which to me is a sign of quickness. But no matter how he feinted or faked a stab, I was able to pick and grab his wrist in midair and instead of stabbing him back, I would tap his body with a closed fist that was holding the knife. Even though the knife was encased in a leather sheath, I thought doing it this way was much safer. TS thought the Kendo training helped my speed and quickness but I believe now, in my old age, that a slightly overactive thyroid all my life helped my quickness. TS had over a hundred small leaded figurines of military men. Soldiers, cowboys, Indians, cannon, cavalry, which we would place strategically for battle. We played in his backyard and used natural terrain and built castles and forts to have an imaginary battle. Thinking about TS, my childhood friend, I feel he would have made a great general.

Heading home one evening I met Mother walking. She was a little reluctant but finally sat on the horizontal bar of the bike sidesaddle and kept saying, "Be careful Reg, we don't want to fall." Away we went down a steep long hill, even just gliding the bicycle picked up speed and Mom kept saying, "Be careful, be careful, I'm scared." I finally said, "Mum!" like all kids say when they think their Mom doesn't know anything. "You bought me the strongest bike, a balloon tire C.C.M and I'm the best rider." "Don't worry." It was the first time she got a ride on a bicycle and after her scare, she had a contented, satisfied look when we arrived safely at home. I'm glad she never noticed a slight dent on the slanted front vertical bar. Like a fool one day, I went full speed along an alleyway hoping to make a sharp turn and still stay on the sidewalk. I could have done it except I didn't see a fire hydrant inside the outer edge of the sidewalk, fairly close around the corner of the alleyway. What a collision. I went flying over the handlebar and landed on my body sideways, rolling over a few times. Can't recall any pain, bruises or scratches.

Most of my friends had the Raleigh racing bike, all colored black and white and it looked like it was built for speed but sometimes they wanted to test ride my balloon tire bicycle that handled rough and bumpy roads much better. Riding their racing bike, the handle is much lower and the seat seemed much higher and the body with the head down is leaning forward and no matter how slow it's going an abrupt stop with a hand brake and the body leans forward over the handlebar. Many a time, my body would have gone over the front handle bar but the hips and thighs get caught, trapped by the handlebar and it always made me fall to the ground, bike and all. No broken bones but always pain, bruises and scraped skin.

December 7, 1941, after the bombing of Pearl Harbor, the Government ordered curfew on us, which meant our family and everybody else after 7 o'clock in the evening had to stay at home. One night, during curfew hours, Mom needed something from the drug store. She told me to take my bike and not to worry, the police wouldn't bother me because I was just a kid. Coming home, a police car was parked at the intersection and one of the officers yelled out, "Hey, what are you doing outside -- it's curfew for you." Without missing a beat I kept pedaling the bike and yelled back, "Sabotage! Sabotage!" and ducked into an alleyway moving in and out of pathways to the house. I told my Mom about the police car that didn't bother chasing me. Mom generally showed her feeling by the shape of her lips. Sometimes it was a smile or a grin. This time her lips were sealed stretched out like an elastic band, the corners slightly bent downward, silently saying, and "I told you the police wouldn't do anything. Job well done."

Another event relating to the curfew was some of the kids from Powell Street and myself found a job setting up tenpins in a downtown Bowling Alley. We all had to stay and sleep overnight in the building. After closing, one of the guys found the side of an arcade machine lightly open and we could see a locked cash box inside. One person found a bunch of keys in the cash register and somebody with a screwdriver opened the side of the arcade machine. The kid with the keys started using each key to find the one that would fit and "Bingo!" the lock was opened and the box was half filled with nickels. Everybody decided to take out only one third of the nickels and relocked the box and placed it back inside the arcade machine. We divided the nickels equally among us, which came out to approximately three dollars a person. I learned how to play Jacks or Better, Draw Poker and Blackjack. We gambled until 3 am and then started to bowl ten pins for the rest of the night. When curfew was over in the morning we all went home on our bikes. I didn't know whether I lost or won in gambling, but felt the nickels that filled the two front pockets. It was a strange and yet a wonderful feeling to have all that money. Next day, someone called from the bowling alley and for a moment I panicked, thinking they found out about the missing nickels.

It was a relief to hear that we were all just fired from the job. Bowling tenpins half the night until early dawn made such a thunderous noise it kept the whole downtown neighborhood awake. People were calling the Police, Fire Department and whoever, but nobody was able to do anything. We locked ourselves in the building and it became a prison. We wouldn't go out and nobody could come in.

The Government first started to evacuate the area closest to Japan and my Dad was one of the first to go. Port Alice where he worked was located near the North end of Vancouver Island and if it weren't for the Pacific Ocean, Vancouver Island would be one of the neighboring Islands off Japan. Dad had a choice either to work on the railroad or become a prisoner of war. Dad chose Petawawa, a concentration camp in Ontario. We never saw my Dad until after the war and at times missed him but having no fighting between Mom and Dad made up for his absence. The evacuation was done in an orderly manner and I think they changed the ruling and allowed the men, the ones working on the railroad, to join their families. It was too late for the ruling to apply to Dad. Finally the notice came to our family to move into Hastings Park, a temporary depot, before they shipped us out to some Ghost Town in the interior of B.C.

Never felt the upheaval and hardship the grownups had to go through during the war. Hasting Park was like a new and exciting playground. The men and women lived in separate makeshift dormitories. The children stayed with their Mothers. Hasting Park was the home of the Vancouver Canadian National Exhibition with its large buildings and midway with a big area of well-manicured grass as parkland. Even with a high chain link fence around the park I still felt the freedom of a wide-open space.

I was too old, 13 going on 14, so I had to stay in the Men's Dormitory. It seemed like hundreds of double decker bunk beds were placed in a row in a big CNE building. Small area with tables and chairs was for recreational purpose. Sometimes at night we would lie on the upper half of the bunk beds and watch the men play poker. I never saw so much money, stacks of money on the table, and heard stories, men saying money is useless because of the war.

I was fortunate that D.N. and another friend and I got a job as the Baker's helper. He was a typical redneck type of guy, barking orders and kept us working hard. We did a lot of cleaning of pots, pans, trays and equipment. We kept an eye on the ovens, not to over bake the bread and buns. He showed us how to bake things for the people to eat in the Mess Hall. He sounded tough but was a real softy at heart. He treated us real well. Many times he would take meats from the Mess Hall freezer and cook us fantastic meals, steaks, pork chops, chicken, meat loaves, a real professional cook. His desserts were out of this world. We made whipped cream from natural cream and put it on all kinds of fruit pies and pastries that he made for us. For Christmas he baked a lot of special fruit cake so we could give it to our parents and told us to make sure our parents didn't tell anybody about our special treatment. Mother was happy and quite often mentioned how delicious the fruitcake was.

Once in a while I'd see Mom with the kids going to the Mess Hall to eat. She never said too much except how busy it was looking after the kids and was glad she had one or two women friends to talk with. Mom never told me how but always said to look after myself.

My little friend D.N. was happy working in the bakeshop, always smiling and always talking about girls. He kept saying the girls were better looking from out of town and from

Vancouver Island and couldn't believe there were so many of them. I kept silent and ignored his chatter about the girls but I wasn't blind. Some of my friends found an isolated shady spot near the fence where it became a favorite hangout. We smoked and played penny ante poker. Someone introduced a new game called Low Ball Draw Poker and loved to play it.

D.N. eventually started to bring the out of town girls around. None of us had the nerve to approach girls or knew how to do it, "How sweet it is". Blue sky, warm sunny days, lying on a blanket cushioned by grass and talking to girls we'd never seen before. Catherine had a beautiful face and all the guys said she was a doll. Oval face, straight nose, normal shaped eyes and mouth, a long slim model type of body with a healthy look. Very soft spoken with a pleasant personality. She liked me and I liked her and for me it wasn't the usual infatuated puppy love but having a beautiful girl like Catherine really fanned my Ego. I saw a real attractive girl and it felt like love at first sight and I told N.D about her. A few weeks went by and I was walking along with my friends and when I heard a girl shout out, "Fuck you, Reg."

When I looked at the girl, it was my first love in Hasting Park. I was in shock and couldn't believe what I heard but managed to swear back at her. I could never forget that unbelievable incident; two young teens, without knowing each other, out of the blue start swearing at each other. One adult told me to shut up and stop swearing. In those days, women never swore in public let alone a young girl. Even young guys caught swearing the Mothers would wash their mouth with soap. I was in a state of shock, traumatized, didn't know whether to laugh or cry and walked around in a daze for days. Finally I asked D.N. if he said anything to the F.O. girl and he said, "Her name is Delores and I didn't say anything except you really liked her and you were breaking up with Catherine." I thought maybe she's jealous but that was no reason to start swearing at me. Later whenever I passed by her and her friends they would call out my name, "Reggie! Reggie!" and I was so pissed off I told them to fuck off and again, some grownup told me not to swear. A few days later, Delores moved out of Hasting Park with her parents. I heard the news from my favorite grapevine, N.D. Fortunately or unfortunately we didn't go to the same Ghost Town. Meeting Catherine and Delores in Hasting Park was still an emotional Romantic love for me but a few years' later girls became sexual objects and very frustrating until I had my first sexual experience in my late teens. Now I think Delores was born too soon; she would have fit in nicely with the girls of Generation X.

On the other side of the fence, the midway opened up with all its bright lights showing all sorts of rides including the roller coaster called the Big Dipper and the Barkers shouting to the crowd, enticing them to play their games. We were drawn to the glitter like moths to a flame. We just walked up a wooden fire escape, reached over and grabbed the top of the fence pole shaped like the handle of a cane facing outward and gingerly stepped on and over the barbed wire and climbed down the chain link fence. None of the outsiders seemed to care or even knew we were breaking curfew. In fact, I met some schoolmates that just said, "How's it like inside the Park -- glad you're able to enjoy the Midway." The fire escape was really handy to go AWOL. A few times during the day we went over the fence and visited downtown Vancouver. The last time going home we were close to the park and the cops chased us and we just ran past the Mounties guarding the gate. They were laughing and just yelled, "Watch out for the cops."

I loved the game of baseball. In the darkness of the night we would climb to the top rail of the roller coaster called the Big Dipper. High above the ground we could see the baseball field all lit up by the spotlights. The green outfield, the uniformed players playing their positions, the crack of the bat, the roar of the crowd. It was like observing a crystal ball all lit up. We didn't even know who the teams were and argued so loudly which team was going to win our voices attracted some adults and for our own safety they barred us from climbing up high structures of the Big Dipper.

I never heard of Karate until this little bow legged man with a shaved head bragged about the power of Karate -- empty hand. His arm was slightly long for his size but he became believable when he showed me his hands. All his fingers seemed to be the same length and the tip, flat and square. He claimed to punch a pillar with his fingers and said that his finger was like a steel rod. With one swipe of his finger he could take a chunk of flesh from my forehead. His knuckle was all callused, the result of punching a tree every day and the side of his palm was like a real blunt axe where he later demonstrated breaking a two by four. He kept saying he would challenge MR T 2nd degree black belt judo man and wipe him out in no time. Mr. T was a friend of my Dad and rumor says that he tossed a half dozen Mounties around when they tried to grab him and then voluntarily walked to their headquarters without any cuffs. The fight between the Judoman and the Karateman never happened. I asked him if he would have a chance against a swordsman with a real sword and I didn't believe him when he said that he would win. I even told him that I would beat him with a samurai sword and he just said with a grin, "Go and find a sword." I didn't challenge him but I did have thoughts about whether I would have a chance with my knife. Now I realize there was no chance to beat him even with a sword unless I trained in Karate and could anticipate the moves. We became kind of friends and he would invite me for a drink and began to tell me about his life. He told me he made some money boxing in a ring but had a very difficult time winning the big gloves, bigger opponents and he couldn't use his feet, was too much of a handicap although he claimed to have won the odd fight. I realized then why he was a little punchy. In those days nobody had heard of Karate or Kung Fu. Now the whole world knows. Gradually we were all moved out of Hasting Park to the interior of BC. Most of us called the new and different locations 'Ghost Towns.'

Train ride in the Rockies, three or maybe four coaches powered by two steam engines, the one in the front pulling and the one back of the passenger cars pushing. Sitting beside an open window, I could hear the heavy breathing of the steam and the huffing and puffing of the engines moving on the track that winds through the mountains and steadily climbing upwards. Avalanche territory, a sheer wall up one side and a deep gorge down the other side. Hundreds of feet below, water is running towards the Pacific Ocean. The shrill whistle of the train and the mournful echoes playing with the mountains presses my heart. It feels heavy knowing that I would miss the Ocean. The vastness of the salt water that gives life stretched my imagination. The sound of the waves, the smell of ocean air, the fun times, and the life of the ocean was part of my life. The feeling of letting go of the past and reaching for the future is difficult to explain. The trip to Slocan was like taking off and discarding old comfortable clothing for something new. My state of mind was naked, stripped from everything.

The tempo of the train quickened, travelling faster on the flat land of a valley. Once again the laborious climb begins; nothing but peaks and valleys going to "No Man's Land."

We arrived in Slocan City, a small deserted mining town with a few dilapidated wooden buildings and shacks. What a contrast to the pristine untouched mountain peaks, the clean pure water of the lakes and streams with abundance of fresh air from the sky so near. The new surroundings motivated me to seek and explore and to find new clothes to wear for my (naked) mind.

Not too far from downtown Slocan City was a big barn converted into a mess hall where people could eat. Besides the building were a few acres of cleared land with tents making it look like an army base. Inside the tents were wood burning stoves and double decked bunk beds and the ground was covered with wood flooring

The men were very friendly and helpful. They allotted tents for the families and helped unload and carry the luggage from the truck to inside the tents. One person gave us instruction on meal times and told us where a long trough was with dozens of water taps where we could brush our teeth and wash our faces. There was no hot water. Later a person told us how to get to the Public Bathhouse. All we had to do was walk along a dirt road about 200 yards to a silver mine. I believe that the use of the bathhouse was scheduled at different times for men and women or they could have had two separate bathhouses.

Most of the men were busy building cottage type houses so families living in tents could move into them. Eventually our family moved to Bay Farm, the closest location from the tents. Two miles further, Popoff was another cottage community being built. Seven miles away, Lemon Creek was another community in the making. All the houses were like wooden matchboxes with a triangular roof. Inside the house, it was divided into three sections. Walking in from the outside was the middle room with a wood burning stove, sink and cupboards and a kitchen table. The other two sections were used as bedrooms. One end of the house outside was an open shed where we kept and piled the wood for cooking and keeping warm in the winter. I think a few households used a common well for water and shared the outhouses.

The streets were named after numbers like 1st Avenue, 2nd Avenue, 3rd Avenue, etc. It was simple to say, 'I live in number 7 on 7th Avenue.

Most of the time for breakfast they served hot or cold cereal, boiled eggs and toast, sandwiches for lunch and I believe we ate a lot of stew.

One evening before dark, I was walking towards the Silver Mine to take a bath. Suddenly out of nowhere a huge cat appeared in the middle of the road, about 40 feet ahead, paused, and looked at me. I didn't know the difference between a Mountain Lion, a Cougar or a Lynx. Hearsay reminded me not to move and just stare into the eyes of the animal. In the stillness and silence of the twilight, the cat's eyes were luminous only for a fleeting moment and then it vanished. The brief encounter with a real wild cat was stunning and awesome. I felt the cat was a friendly acquaintance, perhaps an aloof neighbor, but still, a friend. With this thought in mind, unafraid, I continued on to the bathhouse.

It was a typical Japanese Bath built by the old-timers. In the middle of the room was a square wooden tub filled with hot water and against the wall was a large wooden bath filled with hot, hot water. Nobody washed in the big bath; it was used to soak, relax and heat up the body. Everybody used a basin to scoop the water from the smaller tub and soaped, washed, scrubbed the body. After that I would keep scooping the water, rinsing and splashing water over my body until the soap was cleaned off. The Japanese way of doing things backwards, washing the body first and then soaking in clean hot water didn't bother me. The Western way of soaping and washing and soaking in the dirty water was neutralized by finishing it with a shower.

B r r r r ! The morning air was cold, overnight the top of the mountains were capped in snow and the beauty of the sunlight glancing off the white peaks warmed my senses. Naked from the waist up, I had to run to the water taps to keep warm and brushed my teeth in a hurry and washed my face and neck with soap and bending over the trough, cupping icy cold water from the running tap, rinsed and washed the soap off my face and neck. Using a dry towel, I wiped off the chilly cold wetness and kept scrubbing the body to keep warm. Back at the tent I put on a thick shirt and jacket and went to the Mess Hall to have breakfast.

Returning to the tent, I never saw my Mother so furious. She picked up a broom handle trying to hit my head. I could have easily grabbed it from her but let her hit my forearm a few times and all the while she cursed me saying, "I'm stupid that I don't care about my brothers and sisters, that I should make a fire first thing in the morning when everybody is freezing." All the while, I'm stepping backwards and forwards out of the tent and I told her I'll have the fire burning every morning for sure. Mom had the habit of complaining and nagging for days and sometimes weeks and some things she never forgets. But this time, (in the days after), she never breathed a word about the firewood not burning in the morning.

Shortly afterwards, before winter really settled in, we moved into our new cottage home, a place called Bay Farm. No insulation, no basement, no running water and no electricity. I don't know whether it was any warmer than living in a tent. I kept the stove burning by chopping an awful lot of firewood. I enjoyed using a double blade axe; to me it was the next best thing to a samurai sword. At least that's how I felt. The Government wouldn't allow any of us to train in Martial Arts.

The underside of the mattress would frost and at times get wet and then freeze, keeping a supply of firewood was a necessity to keep the stove burning because it heated the whole house. I kind of think we had some coal to burn during sleeping hours. Splitting and chopping a log with a big knot was awkward and difficult. One log was almost chopped except for a small portion of a knot that was holding the two pieces together. I gripped the left piece of wood and axe blade between the split wood and tried to pry it apart by pressing the axe handle with the right hand. The bottom blade of the axe slipped and shot upwards. I wasn't fast enough to release my grip and the blade cut my hand between the thumb and slightly closer to the forefinger. The cut was an inch long on the back of my hand and continued around the edge of the hand and the cut continued on another inch above the palm of my hand. My Dad wasn't around to stitch the cut so I had to walk to Slocan City for a doctor to stitch the wound. The Doctor was amazed that the one blade only cut the flesh around the front edge and the back of the hand. When I show the scar by flipping the open hand over back and forth, people swear that the bone was cut. I reckon it was my quick reflex that saved me from any bone damage. Richard, my little nine-year-old brother, playing some stupid game called "Executioner" with a friend got cut on the forehead by accident. Double blade axe is a little more dangerous than a regular axe. Sometime later, working in a logging camp, I always made sure nobody was standing behind me and never stand behind somebody who's on the verge of swinging the axe backward.

Dry cold or not, when the temperature makes a big drop everything freezes. Families living in Slocan City had no water. Some of us volunteered to make water holes in the thick frozen ice of the lake for people to fill up buckets of water to take home. It's amazing to see steam rising from the holes in the ice and in seconds a thin layer of ice forms over the water. The men kept breaking the thin ice by dipping their buckets and filling them with water. Steam was rising not only from buckets filled with water but stirring the water hole with a stick, breaking the thin ice kept the steam constantly rising. Stop stirring with the stick and a thin film of ice covers the water instantly and the steam disappears. It finally dawned on me that the water was icy cold but the thick cold air was much colder, causing the water to steam. It didn't take too long with so many people helping for the all the households to have plenty of water.

When it was cold we had to watch out for frost bite because the nose and ears would freeze. We never touched metal, otherwise the skin would stick to the metal. Like my friends, I wore long john underwear, a thick flannel shirt, work pants -- usually denim -- boots, and thick socks, a big scarf to cover the neck and used the end of the scarf or glove to protect the mouth and nose, and a cap or bandana to cover the head and ears. This was enough protection for the normal subzero weather and when it got real cold we just put on an extra jacket.

Female fashion always puzzles me; like the temperature, the skirts go up and down. That year, when school started, the girls were wearing the shortest of miniskirts. One morning, it was freezing and I asked a girl if the cold bothered her legs and her reply was like a slap in the face, "No, it doesn't bother me!" and she looked at me as if I was stupid for asking such a silly question. I learned never to question a girl's clothing, and much later in life, to praise whatever they had on. I recall the Principal, Sister Marie Crucifix, asking me what I thought about miniskirts. I just shrugged my shoulders. She seemed perplexed and was mulling things over in her mind and finally said, "The miniskirts were just too short, but it was not a sin for girls to wear short skirts." The grown up women like my mother only wore dresses and skirts just below the knee.

These days anything goes. The women are wearing suits (usually black), pants, shorts, short skirts, long skirts and the top and tank tops are getting shorter and shorter, showing more of the midriff and having tattoos and mutilator jewelry all over their bodies. At least we can say young girls are economical, saving on material by wearing skimpy clothes compared to the young guys wearing huge saggy, baggy pants that cover a lot of air.

I enjoyed going to school. The reason was that I never did any homework. I liked to listen to the Nuns teaching and unfortunately I forgot most of the things they talked about. The nuns introduced us to 500 West, a card game similar to Bridge, to play at school parties. Sister Superior thought it was a good way for the students to socialize, playing with mixed partners. Dancing was taboo -- no dancing at school parties.

One of the great events was preparing for Christmas celebration. The nuns were quite excited; after all it was their first attempt to celebrate with non-Catholic Asian students. The sisters taught the traditional songs of the Church for Xmas. Ave Maria, Glory Glory Hallelujah, and some Xmas Carols.

Singing was not my bag and I just went through the motions of singing, moving my mouth. It surprised me that the girls were enjoying the rehearsals and really into singing. On the night of the performance, Father Ernest was present, including the family members of the students. Sister Superior conducted the choir and had tears in her eyes, waving the baton. I kind of understood her feeling. The songs seemed to constantly hit the high notes that sounded like voices from heaven above. It touched me. Sister Superior always praised the students during rehearsals for how good they were, and how everybody put great effort into the choir practice. I think the final performance surpassed Sister Superior's expectations. She was so happy. Later she told me that Father Ernest thought it was the best Xmas celebration he had ever had.

What little singing I did, I began to enjoy listening to music on the radio. Bing Crosby's "White Christmas", Christmas Carols, pop songs and jazz. I think later the kids from Protestant High School held dances for the public, but my Mom wouldn't let me go, saying, "You are too young."

Spring came early and with the warm weather it was baseball time. Most of us as kids played for the Old Hurricane Team of Vancouver added a few outsiders and we still had the "hurricanes."

On a hot sunny day after practice, we all decided to go swimming. The lake was just behind the ballpark and we all knew the water would be icy cold. It was the first swim of the year and by the time some of us got to the sandy beach; a few of the guys were already in the water swimming. I took my clothes off slowly and like everybody else just left the underwear shorts on. The two guys I was with ran and jumped into the water swimming towards the rest of the swimmers, just floating around forty yards from the shore. Being the last person, I ran and dived into the cold water and swam as fast as possible, hoping to catch up with the guys in front of me. The cold water didn't bother me and when I came close to the rest of the guys, I tried to roll over on my back to relax and to catch my breath. Somebody was splashing and swimming beside me. I couldn't even say, "Help me!" My voice and body were paralyzed. I thought "Oh no, I could die by drowning with everybody so close and all around me." I was in an upright position and my body and head sank underneath the water. I was waiting to pass out and see my whole life flash by me. Everybody had heard this story many times.

I could see the sunlight on the surface of the water. My head bopped up and I tried to gasp for air but couldn't' breathe and my body again sank below the water. The motion of going up and down was happening. I don't know if this is a natural movement when the body is upright in the water. I experienced it many times as a kid. Jumping off a high diving board feet first, the force of the jump would take me down deep into the water and when my body reached a certain depth, it stopped and then almost naturally started to rise to the surface. After going up and down a few times I still couldn't breathe, but the natural rhythm of up and down in the water must have helped to get a little air into my lungs. The position of my arms was spread-eagled and I felt a slight movement in my fingers. The finger movement wouldn't have had any more power than a butterfly flapping its wings. It gave me hope. Ever so gently and slowly, fluttering the fingers seemed to help the natural motion of bobbing up and down, up and down.

The shoreline of the rocks was to the left and the sandy beach was in front. The big rocks and boulders were much closer. It took a long time bobbing up and down up and down until my hand touched and held on to the edge of a rock. I stayed in that position for a long time, the body sapped of energy, floating in the water anchored on the rock by my hand. Finally I had enough strength to pull my chest and part of my stomach onto the flat part of a rock which was a foot above the water.

Then little by little, I crawled like a snake until the last of the legs and toes rested on dry rock. When I rolled over on my back to welcome the sun and the fresh air it was the happiest moment of my life. Another person came by and asked "if everything was okay." I said, "I'm okay, just catching my breath."

In bed that night I rehashed the moment of truth. I was relaxed and aware of what was happening but even as a kid I knew not to go all out for a swim on the first day, but to swim a little every day until the body worked itself into shape. I also suspected that smoking caused a lot of the shortness of breath.

The old timers were playing baseball so I decided to climb a cliff near the ballpark. Lots of guys enjoyed mountain climbing. The cliff was no higher than 50 or 60 feet and did not look threatening. I had a relatively easy time to climb three quarters of the way up, then I was stuck. To go up I had to hang onto something that was a foot or so away from the wall and I didn't like the idea of my feet and body dangling in midair although it would be only about 30 feet fall to the ground. Standing on the ground, the cliff didn't look high but where I was stranded and trapped it looked dangerously high. The down slope was almost vertical for the first twenty feet and the last ten feet or so, it sloped out slightly and would be easy to slide the rest of the way down the slope. I saw a few little bumps and some small rocks jutting out from below me and I hoped to grab some of them to slow down my fall. With my teeth and hand I managed to wrap a kerchief around my free hand and then when I let go of the other hand to drop, I used it to grab my cap and with both hands tried to grasp, grab and claw the things that were sticking out of the wall. The plan did work to slow the speed of the fall but it was still the fastest slide I'd ever had. The cap and the kerchief protected my hands but the forearm bled because of the rubbing and scraping of the cliff and my backside was in pain from sliding down the last few feet on my ass. I don't know which would be worse: death by drowning or death by breaking a neck.

During winter we entertained ourselves gambling in poker and even gambled playing 500 West, the card game the Nuns taught us.

Slocan City had a truck depot with a shed used as an office. The truckers would report daily when they took a truck out or brought it in. When I entered the shed, they were playing Poker. I watched them play Poker, curious to see how these older guys played. They didn't seem to mind a young teen watching and when somebody dropped out, the man looking after the office asked me if I "wanted to join in." I loved the game they were playing -- "Low Ball Draw" -- and was happy to be playing with grown-ups for the first time. I learned all the moves gambling with my young friends -- when to drop out, how many cards to draw, when to bluff and how to make the pot bigger when you think you have the winning hand. Card players all know the saying "Beginner's Luck." I had it. You cannot imagine the feeling when you pull in or draw the card you need. Especially to make a bicycle 1,2,3,4,5 the best low ball hand. Many times, if I had 1, 2 and 4 and drew two cards, it would be a 3 and 5 making a bicycle. Some would go broke and leave other drivers standing around to replace them. We played until the last truck checked in about 5:30. The adults didn't seem to mind a young kid like me winning the money. Some of them would be moaning and others would laugh saying I had beginner's luck. The lucky streak lasted all afternoon and my winning was close to $50.00. That was big money in those days and I was lucky to win all that money playing for nickels and dimes. Rumors travel fast and about a week later my Mom asked me if I won any money playing Poker. I gave her over $40.00 and she seemed pleased but didn't know whether to scold me or praise me.

It wasn't too long afterwards my friend quit playing cards and we started to play "Shogi", a Japanese Chess game. Some of the guys still wanted to play for a quarter but eventually the game was so absorbing and fascinating, that we didn't have to gamble to make the game interesting. The older "Shogi Club" members mention that students in Japan were not allowed to play because Shogi was too addictive and the kids wouldn't study or do anything else.

The game of "Shogi" was so consuming and absorbing we would play all night and then go to school to sleep during classes. Watching the real top players, some from other communities was fascinating. Most of the games were over quickly, sounding like a fencing duel. Instead of snapping Kendo sticks, the players would slap the flat pieces made of wood onto a thick (6 inches) Shogi board. The movement of the arm and hands taking pieces from the opponent and then at times using them by slapping them back on the board was done with lightning speed. They didn't waste time thinking and looked like fighters trading punches over the Shogi board. Sometimes a player would concede in the middle of a game, which speeded up the playing time. I'm under the impression that people who know what they are doing, do it quickly and well.

Japanese chess is similar and yet different from the English or European version. The game could never end in a draw. All pieces taken from your opponent could be used by placing them back on the board to your advantage. All the pieces are flat and shaped like the front of a cottage house with a triangular "A" roof. Every piece is inscribed with Chinese the character defining the hierarchy of feudalistic power. Naturally the pawn pieces were the smallest in size, having the least power. However if a pawn moves into enemy territory, it could be turned over and written on the back face of the pawn is the new increased power of the pawn. The player has the choice of flipping pieces over to increase their power in enemy territory if it is to his advantage. Many of the Japanese men with homemade tools were good finish carpenters like my dad. They made beautiful chess pieces from a Yew tree but I'm only guessing since I've never seen a yew tree. I believe the outer core of small yew trees are small and when the bark is stripped off the outer core and the trunk is reddish brown which surrounds the inner whitish core. Thin sheets of wood are cut out of the tree where one side of the sheet is reddish and the other side, whitish. From the sheets, they would handcraft the pieces, cutting shaping, planning, polishing and then carving and engraving Chinese characters on every piece. Each piece is a beautiful piece of art. The board was made from a thick hardwood block made square with only lines patterned after a checkerboard to fit in all the pieces. Playing with one of these sets brought out the feeling of playing a prestigious game. Primitive, playing with pieces of wood in the wilderness. Mother Earth watches the game of War and Peace.

We enjoyed holding the flat piece with the three middle fingers and like the Ki-eye in Kendo, shout "O tei" (checkmate) at the same time slamming the piece on the board. It was so spirited and fun we practiced slamming even if it wasn't a checkmate. If we missed the target, the other piece could go flying off the board. It was bad etiquette and not becoming a Shogi player to disturb the board.

At times a man would show us a book with diagrams of pieces on the board and certain pieces in our hand to checkmate the Emperor. Very simple once you know how but many times my buddies and I would put our heads together and still couldn't figure a way to checkmate the emperor.

I started to play pretty well so the club asked me to play in a C tournament. Win some lose some, it was good fun. One game after a couple of opening moves, I didn't know what to do so I just moved a pawn ahead one square. The man took such a long time staring at the board I had to bend down to see if he wasn't sleeping. Finally he muttered out loud to himself, trying to figure out why I moved the pawn. It made me chuckle thinking that he thought moving the pawn was some kind of a Master Plan. One young player, Bob, could have been a child prodigy. He defeated a lot of men in the tournament. Playing him was like our bush League "hurricane" against the "New York Yankees." I had no chance.

Warm spring, hot summer. Warm weather is the best time to play baseball. The muscles are relaxed and react to the ball easily, swinging the bat was effortless. Hurricane wins again so what else is new. Can't remember whether my base hit contributed to the winning run or kept the rally going. I didn't wear my glasses and the sun sets behind the big mountains quickly and it gets dark sooner than you expect. At bat could not see the ball leaving the pitchers hand and could only pick up the ball when it was in front. I could remember thinking "Hope the pitcher would not throw a bean ball." Must have guessed right when the pitcher released the ball. Imagined the ball coming in on a certain location, stepped forward with the left foot, saw the ball ten feet in front of where it was supposed to be made good contact to the right of the second baseman for a hit. To this day, I sometimes wonder if my reflex was that fast or not.

Another pastime was related to sexual frustration. Curiosity kills the cat. Not knowing what the female genitalia looked like was far more tortuous than not having sex. In those days there were no books or porno magazines showing everything. The odd night we would go to the Ladies Bathhouse to get a peek. I couldn't relax or enjoy it from the fear of getting caught. One fellow, M.M., pushed us to go every night until he saw his sister bathing and realized the other guys were watching the same peep show. He was embarrassed and after that he wasn't too keen to push us to be peeping Toms at the bathhouse. The intense short lived curiosity was kind of satisfied which made life much easier to live, by just using imagination and the hand.

School over, summer holidays. My friends signed up to work in the logging camp. I was too young to work as a lumberjack so I went as a cook's helper. The bus ride along the Selkirk Range to Revelstoke, from there a short train ride west through the mountains to Golden. The City of Golden had a sawmill, gas station, and a post office, part of a Dry Goods Store. Then we had a truck ride for 17 miles to the Camp where we stayed and worked for the summer. The place had a Mess Hall for chow and a Bunkhouse where 12 beds fit in comfortably. The first thing the men did was to build a Bathhouse over a little creek that ran behind the Mess House. The Cook and I shared a little room that was part of the Mess Hall. When I went into the Bunkhouse most of the beds were made and a hardened old bachelor was trying to bounce a quarter on top of the bed, testing if the sheets and blankets were stretched tight.

Nobody could make their bed sloppily. It had to be neat and perfect just like in the army. It's a good thing, sharing a room away from this Bunkhouse with Fred the cook who was a Nisei and just as sloppy as I was. Fred was a perfectionist in the Kitchen and I wasn't a good kitchen helper. It was easy for me to get Fred upset and at times he would be livid and raise a ladle or a big heavy spoon in a threatening manner. I give Fred a lot of credit in having restraint. Things never came to blows. He did apologize saying that I was too young and didn't know anything about responsibility. Unlike the old bachelors who behaved like low rung Samurais, they never argued, the fists would fly first -- then if you fought back it became a duel "fight to the death." My friend M.M found that out. He was lying on his bed with his shoes on and one of the gentler looking Japanese men told him to take his shoes off while lying on the bed. M.M talked back and in the morning while he was brushing his teeth beside the creek, the old man had in his hand a rock the size of a bread loaf to smash M.M.'s head while he was bent over the water. Someone just came out of the Bunkhouse and yelled to warm MM who quickly stepped away. The rock was too heavy for the old man to run after MM. MM could hardly speak Japanese but kept apologizing in broken English. The other Samurai boys talked to their comrade, not to do anything, and they all warned M.T. if he didn't behave or do what he was told, they would bust his head. M.T. was two years older than I was and quite strong. Maybe a bit of a bully but the hard-nosed old timers sure tamed him. My attitude to work in the kitchen was really negative, however I enjoyed cutting logs with a buck saw and chopping it up as firewood for the kitchen stove. Back at Bay Farm, one of my friends was able to chin himself with one hand. To me it was an amazing feat. I used a two by four to make a bar, nailing one end to a tree and the other end to the corner of the building. The height of the bar was seven feet above the ground. I would jump up, grab the bar with two hands, and pull myself up until the chin was slightly above the bar and let go of my left hand, the right arm not strong enough, could not hold my body and the arm would straighten out leaving me dangling with one arm holding the bar. I kept repeating this routine until finally I was able to hold myself with one hand, my chin at bar level. After this, I began to lower my body slowly, which worked all the muscles of the arm slowly. It didn't take too long to lower the body two or three inches and pull it back to chin level. Eventually, it got to a point where I could lower myself six to eight inches and pull myself back up to chin level. At this stage of development I would only jump up, grab the bar with one arm, elbow bent, and pull myself up. It always started with the elbow slightly bent to chin myself with one hand. I only knew one person GY who would have his elbow straight, shoulder loose and dangling, and then jerk himself into position, the elbow slightly bent and then chin himself.

Fred knew I wasn't afraid of hard work but realized kitchen help wasn't for me. Even though I was underage, he let me go so I could work in the bush. This younger Japanese man about 45 years old seemed happy to take me as a partner to teach me the ropes. I assumed he was like the old Japanese bachelors, emotional perfectionist control freaks. All the saws and axes were razor sharp. He would be upset if I didn't hit the same spot with an axe. The notches made in a tree with an axe were so smooth it felt like it was sandpapered. One time we were sawing off a fallen tree in sections and he kept saying to hold the saw lightly. He was still yelling at me so I let go of the handle and he was still yelling until he realized that I wasn't even touching the handle of the saw. He sensed right away that the saw's teeth were not sharp and started filing the teeth. When we resumed sawing the log he was smiling and said this was much better. He never apologized for yelling at me but was happy he found the solution to the heaviness of the saw. I didn't mind his close minded attitude, at least he wasn't as crazy as his other older cronies.

He taught me a lot, like how to fall a tree between a big boulder and another tree, watching for the wind and twisting of the tree. To make sure no dry limbs come falling down, he would hit the tree with an axe to test it, or, if it got too windy, we couldn't work. A couple of his countrymen not only looked like gorillas but were as strong, carrying heavy cable wires, tying and strapping them around the logs to be dragged out and by the big caterpillar. The men seemed to be running all the time. Long before this my Dad told me he was a whistle punky. Instead of the big cat machine, it was a train called Donkey, a strong steam engine, and it pulled logs four, five feet in diameter and hundreds of feet long, and it was dangerous because the logs would whip around. He had to make sure nobody was in danger before he blew the whistle and if anybody showed a bit of carelessness he would get upset. Our trees weren't as big as the ones on the coast or Vancouver Island but still, they were two to three feet in diameter.

None of the workers died or had any serious injury working in the bush but they still worried about me being under age and all that, so they decided working me in a saw mill was a much safer place. It wasn't like working in the shady forest but in the opening called a landing where all the logs were cut to a certain length to make lumber. These shorter logs were piled on to a huge tractor trailer trucks to be delivered to a saw mill in Golden City where they were sawed into 2x12, 2x10, 2x6 2x4 or any other size.

The noonday sun felt like it was going through a magnifying glass and the guys wore flannel shirts and a cap or pit helmet to keep the skin from burning. Sawing logs in the heat was tough enough but the constant sawdust in the air would stick to our sweaty necks and body, which became very uncomfortable. After work, washing the dirt and sawdust off the body and soaking in a hot bath was paradise. It's interesting to note a real hot bath would help the body keep cooler in the summer and warmer in the winter.

During the war everybody was under food rationing. It did not apply to lumberjacks. We had plenty of steaks, chops, roast beef, sugar, coffee, never a shortage of good food. Occasionally a local worker would bag wild life for extra fancy meat. On Sundays we fished for mountain trout and it tasted great as sashimi. Once, along the creek, a flock of birds were walking along and none of them would fly away. Excited, I grabbed a stick to kill one of them for food. The pheasant or grouse just stood there with its beautiful brown eyes. "Dumb Bird" I thought and didn't have the heart to hit or kill it.

On a Sunday, the younger Japanese man that taught me how to cut trees down took me fishing. We hitched a ride early in the morning on a truck that dropped us off on a bridge seven miles down the road. The width of the river was anywhere from 100 to 150 feet and the water was very fast moving. The man had fancy fishing equipment and he made me a simple fishing rod from a tree branch with a light sinker and hook. We always put our line in where the water was (turbulent?) and swirling, usually behind a big boulder or logjam. After trying for nearly two hours or so, I caught the first fish. It pulled so hard that I thought my rod would snap or the line would break. He yelled to me not to bend my fishing rod and to straighten it out. He kept telling me to pull and let go, pull and let go and this must have gone on for about five minutes, then finally he helped me to pull in the fish. I was surprised that the rainbow trout was only about 12 inches long and had so much power and strength. I don't know if it had muscles or not but fighting the rapids must have added strength to the fish. He put the fish in a container filled with water and we continued to walk along the river for another two hours, putting our lines into ideal spots here and there, hoping to catch another fish. Finally the expert caught a fish and the way he played with the line, I realized the fish could tire too and by the time he reeled it in the fish probably was tiring. One hour later he caught another rainbow, which made me happy. I could tell he was filled with anxiety, trying to save face by catching more fish than me. We had to be back at the bridge where the truck drivers said he would pick us up at 5 o'clock.

We hiked a long way, at least ten miles down the river so we had to hurry back to the bridge. He kept telling me to stay close to him in case a bear attacked us, saying he would protect me by fighting the bear. I didn't believe he could handle a bear in a fight but at least it would give a little time and a chance to escape. I was getting used to the Japanese men talking with the Warlord mentality of "fight to the death" creating the air of invincibility. Neither liked nor disliked that attitude, just had enough sense to avoid them in a confrontational situation. Anyway, the fishing trip tested my endurance. It might have been harder than chopping and sawing trees down all day. Another test of stamina was a hike with a 50-year old Swedish man. He was 6'3" and carried a knap sack weighing 60 to 70 lbs. It's a good thing I only had to carry a bit of water and some lunch. Five hours of steady climbing, him and his long legs and me with my shorter legs, taking two steps to his one. His favorite spot, a small cave, a secluded, beautiful haven and a few steps up, the highest peak overlooking the southern range of the Rockies I was relaxed and calm contemplating the magnitude where heaven meets earth. He kept smiling, happy to share his ownership "where no man set a foot."

Black bears started to come around the back of the kitchen. They would rummage around the garbage looking for food. I threw some food over the 10-feet wide creek for them to eat. The bears seemed harmless enough and I thought that maybe they would eat food out of my hand. Everybody said the bears are dangerous "and stay away from them." Somebody's yappy dog kept chasing the bears. I was surprised to see the bear run up a bushy hill as fast as any animal I've seen. The bears smashed the meat-shed cooler and ate all the meat. The shed was built over the creek where the cold water kept the meat storage shed cool. Anyway, a couple of rangers came and hung around. When a bear showed up they placed the rifles on the windowsill and bang! The poor bear dropped dead. It was a strange feeling to see a bear eating something to stay alive and then raising the head to look at us and bang it was dead. The hunter carried a long knife, telling me a wounded bear is a very dangerous animal and by law they would have to track it down to kill it, sometimes with a knife. I asked them what chance a man would have fighting a bear and, like me, they heard stories on rare occasions a man had survived.

One of the things the old timers feared most was fire. One hour before dawn the kitchen bell was clanging away and the cook shouted, "Reg, it's a fire, get up." I reacted like a Jack in a Box. Smoke was smoldering from underneath the floor and through the open door I saw sparks flying through cracks of the Mess Hall floor. My first thought was to crawl through a small window above my bed. It had no glass, only a screen. Hitting and pushing with the palm of my hand. I realized the screen was made from heavy wire mesh and was just too strong to push and pry open. Quickly grabbed my pants and while rushing out the door, noticed Fred the cook was still putting on his pants. Not only the sparks but now flames were shooting through the cracks of the floor so I hopped on and ran on top of the long dining table and jumped off at the other end, ran through the kitchen and out the back door. Fred was a few seconds behind me, saw what I did and followed my footsteps, jumping and running on top of the table. The men, half-naked, formed a human chain passing buckets of water from the creek, pouring it all over the floor. I assume the sawdust underneath the floor was put there for insulation. Anyway it didn't take too long to get the fire under control.

It wasn't too many days afterwards, before it got dark the bell was clanging again. This time it was a bush fire beside the road 60 or 70 yards from camp. Never saw the hardliners so upset and up tight, cursing in Japanese, blaming the truck driver who must have started the fire by carelessly tossing a lighted cigarette butt out the window while driving. I never dreamt about how tortuous it was to carry buckets of water the distance of about 60 yards. The first 20 or 30 yards was fine but the longer I carried the water, the more my arms began to ache and get cramps and numb. Continuously carrying buckets of water, my arm felt like a raw piece of meat in pain. Couldn't believe the old timers were actually running with buckets of water in each hand. They moved like robots, never tiring. They all had the look of fear and yet seemed ferocious. I gave them plenty of room when they passed by me, whether they carried water or empty buckets back to the creek. Didn't want to bump into them or interfere in their movements under these stressful conditions. Most of my Nisei friends were further away, digging and cutting pathways around the area of the fire to stop it from spreading. The creek became a natural barrier, stopping the fire from spreading. The 73 year old Englishman was amazing. He ran 17 miles to Golden and returned with a truck in about three hours, bringing back an eight-man crew to help fight the fire. The whole area was a tinderbox and fortunately the men caught the fire in time to contain it. Some of them stayed up all night and others came back in the morning to watch the smoldering wet ash burn itself out, making sure there was no more signs of smoke or hot ashes. The Samurai-like men were relaxed and almost looked human. They told me how fearful and deadly a fire could be when it's out of control Raging fire could create its own gale like wind and our camp could easily turn into ashes. The side of big mountain with pitchy evergreen trees would be like a flamethrower burning the whole side of the mountain in minutes. They were a tough, stubborn close-minded bunch of guys but I respected their knowledge based on their experience. Throughout the history of Japan, I know the people lived in constant danger of earthquakes and typhoons.

The last two weeks they sent me to Golden to work on the green chain next to the sawmill. It looked like I worked the gamut of the Logging and Lumber Industry. From working in the kitchen, to cutting trees in the forest, to sawing logs at the landing, to stacking the final product in different lengths and size lumber and being shipped out from the sawmill. Another young Canadian and I worked the Green Chain. The 2x4s, 2x6s, 2x8s, 2x12s were coming out of the sawmill like a never-ending assembly line. We had to be quick and work fast to pick out 2x4s and stack them in a pile. All the sizes had to be separated and stacked properly. The green chain never stopped and we had to keep taking off the lumber and pile it in its proper place, otherwise the lumber would fall off the end of the chain and create a jam, causing unnecessary extra work. When a stack was completed, a forklift or a truck would come and take it away. Did I learn anything doing all the different jobs? I realized how hard the men worked in the good ole days and for me it was better than working in the kitchen washing pots and pans. It's a wonder nobody died or had a serious injury considering the volatile temperament of the hard-liners and the hazardous environmental and working conditions.

Back to school routine and the only consistent activity was smoking and puffing hand rolled cigarettes. Played Shogi when we had time and seldom played cards. It happened that on a sunny day in early October we were playing Black Jack out in an open field. The deck of cards was so old and worn out we had difficulty to shuffle and deal them. This person came over and introduced himself as 'A', a half-breed, asked us if he could play with us. We all thought, "why not?" and said, "Sure, join in." when it came his turn to deal, he surprised us. He dealt with one hand, dealing out one card face down to each of us and then with one hand, dealt each of us a card face up and then dropped the Ace of Spades for himself. We'd just finished complaining about how difficult it was to play and deal with such worn out old sticky cards. Naturally he had a Black Jack but wouldn't take our money even though we were gambling for nickels. He showed us how he cheated. It was unbelievable. With one hand he dealt out the second card from the top to each of us making it look like he was giving us the top card and dealt himself the Jack of Spades. He showed us the top card in the deck: Ace of Spades and dealt us each a card that looked like it was coming from the top and then dropped the Ace of Spades to match his Jack for another Black Jack. Not one of us could believe what he did and I told him we had trouble dealing the top card using both hands and how could he, with one hand, deal the second card from the top? He showed us the tip of his finger saying it was smooth as a baby's bum and used sandpaper to keep his fingertip smooth. Some of his stories were interesting; how he went to different places where men worked on the railroad to play cards. Sometimes in a game, another card cheat would be playing and sooner or later by sign language they would know each other. When he dealt he would shuffle the cards to make his new found partner win and when his partner dealt the cards he returned the favor so they both won all the money and nobody suspected anything. When Mr. A had no partner, he would win most of the money and would leave some money on the table under the pretext of going to the washroom and just leave the place, not returning to the card table. Later we found out he was always winning playing cards and players knew he was cheating. Everybody watched him like a hawk but could not catch him cheating. It's only afterwards, when they wouldn't let him deal or touch the deck of cards, that he began to lose money. One of my buddies' friends had a father who was a good poker player and he told me that Mr. A was not a good player and would not be able to win in an honest straight game.

A week later at the same place where we played cards, a group of men were milling around. A short time later, a smaller group joined them. We went over to see what was happening and some money was exchanging. They were betting on this strong man that he could lift a log lying on the ground onto his shoulder and walk at least 20 feet. The man lifted one end of the log, raising it high enough so the log rested on his shoulder. Then he would raise the log slightly with his hands and move his shoulders forward. Bit by bit he raised the log, adjusting his shoulder until the front end of the log on the ground gently lifted and the centered weight of the heavy log in balance rested on the man's shoulder. He walked forward, his legs wobbling and shaking, but managed to walk past the 20-foot mark. Big uproar and cheering so I assumed most of the men bet that the strong man could do it. It was a man thing and a fun thing to do. The next day, walking by the log it struck me, "I wonder how heavy the log could be." It blew my mind. I could hardly lift one end of the log a few inches off the ground. The log was about 12 inches in diameter and close to 20 feet in length. I thought I was strong. It sure brought me back to reality that some guys are that strong.

One of the guys had a skeleton key and wanted to test it at the commissary store. Every community had a store run by the Government. We waited until dark and the guy went to the side door and the key actually opened the door. So the five of us went inside. Once our eyes got accustomed to the dark we could make out the counter and the soft drinks (?) and the other goodies on the shelves. We made ham sandwiches, drank pop and enjoyed eating the cookies and other things. We went every night and ate just enough so none of the daytime staff would suspect anything was wrong. We decided to hoard some canned stuff like soups, corned beef, peas, corn, etc. to a little Mountain Hideaway across the street. We must have had five to six boxes of canned stuff stashed away in a small cave thinking that if something ever happened to the food supply because of the War we would have enough food for us and our families to survive for some time. We decided to let a clumsy outsider into our group and sure enough he knocked over a big bottle of Ginger Ale on the counter and it smashed and splashed the glass bottle and the drink all over the floor. We made him clean up as well as possible and a few nights later the key wouldn't open the door. Everybody missed the rendezvous with the soft drinks and the sandwiches. One of the guys was so desperate he talked us into going to Slocan city store. Unfortunately we couldn't open the door so we had to break a window to enter. We had our usual goodies plus a bonus chocolate bars. Wartime rations made it impossible for most people to get their hands on chocolate. It was the last criminal act. We did realize it was too risky and dangerous to be breaking into a store. I don't know how true the stories were but we heard that other kids did the same stealing act in other communities.

Unlike Vancouver, living in the Rockies was Winter Wonderland. Glacier Peaks, the mountains stocked with evergreen trees dressed in white, the snow was always white. We enjoyed skating and playing hockey at the Harrison's Ranch. Clumps of bushes stuck out from the ice so we practiced stick handling the puck, weaving and faking, skating around the bushes. In a larger ice surface area we would play a scrub game of hockey. I saw a photo of myself wearing a dark jacket and a bandanna around my forehead, carrying a hockey stick with a pair of skates on my shoulder. I can't remember how I was able to have a hockey stick and a pair of ice skates.

For skiing, we made our own skis. Some man showed us how to curl up the front part of the lumber by steaming it to make it look like a ski. With the right size lumber and a rope to strap our feet on the makeshift ski it looked great. We went to the ski slope where men were skiing. It was a long walk going up the slope and the guys were flying past and some of them would zig zag, slowing down the speed. We went half way up the slope and started to ski downhill. Nobody taught me how to ski and even having a stick in each hand I couldn't control the direction of the skis and hoped to stay within the narrow boundary of the ski slope. On the side of the slope were stumps, sticking up about a foot or so above the snow. Didn't want to smash into one of those. My brother Bob, riding a Bobsled with his two chums sitting behind him, hit a stump and snapped his leg between the knee and ankle. Speeding down the slope the skis overlapped and crossed over forming an X. I tried to change back and make them parallel but the rope strap was too loose and I was at the mercy of the crossed skis speeding down the slope. I lost my balance and fell. Skis, sticks, arms, legs and body flying in all directions. It's a wonder I didn't break an ankle. My ankle twisted with one end of the ski stuck in the snow, the other ski went flying somewhere else, and sticks were gone. It took a little while to untangle myself and find my gear.

Little mountains are deceiving. Across the street from our house, further in, was a small mountain. There were two slopes, one for the kids sleigh rides and the other was so steep the kids played at the bottom of the slope.

On the weekend, a beautiful sunny day, a number of girls from school were watching the kid and guys having fun riding down the slope with all kinds of homemade sleighs. W.T., a school acquaintance of mine, was chatting with the girls. Whatever was said, he must have talked himself into bob sledding down the steep slope just to show off to the girls. "Hey Reg, let's borrow a sleigh and come down this hill." W.T. was a nice person, wore glasses and looked like a nerd. Type of person that wouldn't harm anybody and it surprised me that he would attempt something so physical and adventurous. W.T. scurried around and found a younger boy with a Bob Sled who wanted to see us come down the steep slope and was happy pulling the sleigh half way up, looking back, it already looked like the Big Dipper roller coaster ride in Vancouver. I yelled to Willie, "This is high enough!" We had to concentrate on the footing to make sure we didn't slide back. Willie never did look back and I kept yelling to him this was high enough and he kept answering back -- "to the top" "to the top." He was about 30 feet ahead of me. Dragging the sleigh slowed my climbing and looking down it seemed the crowd was getting larger and the people smaller. I kept shouting to W.T., "This is far enough" and he kept saying "To the top, to the top." He sat down to take a rest and when I caught up to him his face was white. He realized the frightful dangerous predicament we were in. As I said, little mountains are deceiving. At the bottom it looks like a molehill but from the top it feels like Mount Everest. I was so upset and pissed off with W.T.'s blind stubbornness, I started to say "to the top! To the top!" He was really scared and wouldn't budge. I guess my ego was bigger than his, the typical chauvinist attitude of showing off our physical prowess and being the hero to the girls. W.T. was scared and it took a little coaxing for him to sit behind and hang onto me. "Holy shit" I was scared. Swoosh went the sleigh so fast, hit a little bump and we went flying five or ten feet in the air. Landed on my back and my body became a human bob sled, hit another small bump, went flying through the air and landed still on my back, spinning like a top, and by the time I stopped spinning and rolled over a few times I was at the bottom of the little mountain. Still conscious, no bones broken, maybe a few muscle bruises, I felt Okay. Everybody was clapping their hands and W.T. was okay outside of a little bruise on the side of his face and losing his eyeglasses. Some of my friends came by and happened to see the show. They were grinning, knowing that I was able and willing to put on a circus stunt to show off in front of a big crowd but were surprised that W.T. would do such a thing.

Uncle Michi and his wife lived in a house behind ours. Even in winter on sunny days he would practice fly-fishing in the backyard. He would flick the rod and throw the line 30 to 40 feet away, landing the fly softly on the snow. It took skill not to lose the fly while throwing out the line. Bob was the lucky one.

Uncle Michi took him quite often to the second and third tier of the mountains and found pure pristine lakes to fish in. According to Bob, Michi always caught fish and later when he moved to Kaslo, B.C. he met his Vancouver buddy, David Suzuki's father, and apparently they were the two best Sports Fishermen in the world, competing with each other.

Michi, like my Mom, was an atheist and very outspoken. He worked with a doctor (name?) as a mortician. Whenever somebody tried to convert him to Christianity he would get upset, telling them that the Christians who ended up in the morgue had twisted faces that made them look like they were in Hell. His job was to make them look nice.

He also subscribed to some sort of naval magazine and would tell me Japan cannot win the war. He would show me the pictures of warships the U.S. had and how many Japan had Mom really got upset and called him stupid and told him to keep his mouth shut, otherwise he'd get killed by some immigrant Japanese. Michi always said his father and mother spoiled me. I think he spoiled me the most. For Xmas he would buy the most presents for me and my brothers and sisters. He invited us over for Xmas and Holiday dinners and treated us like his own children. Both my Uncles were big-hearted men. Although they were atheists, they lived like God fearing men, never got in trouble with the law, worked hard and all their kids graduated University.

Sometimes we would go to the Public School Gym. The only thing I remember was doing a bit of boxing. Again, word got around that I was pretty good. Only one person, M.M., who was bigger and a very athletic southpaw, gave me trouble. It was the first time I boxed with a southpaw and couldn't anticipate his moves. The old Kendo trick -- hit first M.M. was like me and didn't like to get hit and we quit after a round. I don't know, with his southpaw style and longer reach, if I could have out-boxed him.

Just around the corner on the other side of the street, SS lived with his family. He was a good friend of my Uncle Hank. In fact, when they lived in Vancouver they belonged to a gang called "The Purple Seven." I believed they were more like the Rat Pack of Hollywood. They never avoided gang fights and occasionally fought some toughie stranger one on one and always abided by the Queensbury rules. Never heard of any of them ever losing a fight and like me, avoided having any trouble with the immigrant hard liners. S.S. was a weight lifter, body builder and boxer. For a Nisei he had a big chest, big arms and puffed on cigarettes all day. I don't know the reason why he was training YH, the childhood bully from Vancouver, to box and saying that YH would beat Reg in a fight. He kept bugging me to come to the other side of the railroad track and do some boxing. Word was getting around that nobody could knock his cigarette out of his mouth while sparring with him. The area across the track was porcupine territory. Whenever we had the chance we would try to hunt them down with a long stick to see their quills stick out. As usual SS was showing some kids how to box. "Reg, put on the gloves and see if you can knock the cigarette from my mouth," SS was always puffing a cigarette. Without thinking I said, "Okay."

While someone was putting on those big 16 ounce boxing gloves, I kept thinking that whenever I feinted a duck at the same time threw a left jab, I never failed to hit a guy's face. These guys were around my age or a little older and S.S. was an older mature man who trained in boxing and might have enough experience to block my left jab. Soon as I felt within range (Kendo space training) I ducked and at the same time threw the left jab. All I can recall was sparks did fly from his cigarette tip and a sharp pain between my elbow and wrist. S.S. kept his forearms parallel spaced about 10 inches apart, the gloves at chin level. With those big gloves, his mouth sucking a cigarette, it was a small target. When I feinted a duck, he must have flinched and that's all the time I needed to shoot my left glove between his two forearms, hitting the tip of his cigarette. After my arm went between his forearms, they shut tight like a vice grip catching my arm, not my glove, so painful it felt like my forearm was broken. Later I thought the distance was misjudged by three inches. Otherwise I might have stuffed the cigarette into his mouth and yet, if my arm went deeper he might have snapped my elbow. My reasoning told me that S.S. used his forearms to block punches and his gloves to protect and block punches to the head, and yet his gloves were in a good position to counterpunch. What I know about boxing, I was always grateful not to learn or train in boxing, which helped me to avoid fights.

Apples

Seasons come and go quickly and for the summer holiday we heard that many of us were able to go to work in the Okanagan Valley picking apples. Many girls were going and unfortunately none of them stayed at our orchard. Ten of us mostly my friends worked together thinning the apple trees.

We had to learn how to use and handle a 16-foot ladder. The base of the ladder was approximately four or five feet wide and tapered towards the top. On top of the ladder was a small platform 14 inches long and eight inches wide. When the ladder stood straight up, a single pole on the other side rested against the ladder. The pole was a little shorter than the ladder and bolted with hinges at the top. Holding the ladder with one hand and allowing the ladder to lean forward at the same time pushed the pole outward so we could control the height of the ladder. Pushing the pole further lowers the height of the ladder. The more upright the ladder, the closer the distance of the pole to the ladder and the higher the top of the ladder.

The two wooden rails on each side of the ladder… not only hold and anchors all the steps but with the pole becomes a tripod. The tripod will stand up on its own and the sixteen footer has great balance and stability. Once we got used to the ladder we could walk up and down or even run up and down as if it were a stairway in a house. All the trees in the orchard were trimmed for the 16 footer. Standing on top of the ladder we could reach the highest branches. All the trees were trimmed into major and minor forks where the ladder could be placed between the two branches of the fork. We could usually strip the whole area of the fork without getting off the ladder. Standing in the middle of the ladder we could lean back, pulling the ladder with us as the pole lifted off the ground and swing back to us. We leaned forward and pushed the pole closer or further depending on where the branches were. Sometimes we balanced ourselves on one leg of the ladder, twisted it to change direction and then pushed the pole. This saves a lot of time, not having to go down to the ground to keep adjusting the position of the ladder. Everything was done in midair.

The apples were small and green but on many branches they were bunched like grapes. It seemed wasteful thinning the apples, dropping most of them on the ground, leaving only one green apple every eight to ten inches apart. With the ten of us, mostly my friends, it didn't take too long thinning all the trees in the orchard. Bigger orchards in the surrounding area needed help that kept us working. Thinning was finished in all the orchards and we had to wait around for weeks for the apples to mature and ripen.

I phoned my Dad's brother who was staying and working on a farm in Kelowna, B.C. We talked about things in general and he said, "He was excited and would be happy to see me." Of course he meant come and do some work on the farm.

I may not have reported to the RCMP which we all had to do when we traveled, but told my working friends that I'd be visiting my uncle in Kelowna and would be back in about three weeks, just in time for the apple picking season.

Our orchard was quite close to Vernon, B.C. where I hopped a bus to Kelowna. Beautiful valley with abundance of water, the famous Okanagan Lake where everybody talked about some kind of monster lurking and living in its deep water. The bus route was beside this lake and then along the river. The thousands of apple trees on rolling hills made it a scenic route.

Uncle was waiting for me at the bus station with a pick-up truck and then we drove back to the farm. He mentioned being partners with two other men leasing the farm and under contract to grow tomatoes and onion. As I thought, since I wasn't doing anything he told me to do some work and make some money. It was getting dark and supper was ready. The three men took turns in preparing the meals and sharing kitchen work. Typical Japanese meal, tasty and salty. "God, did I ever get tired of eating rice three times a day."

It was nice to see Uncle looking much healthier and stronger. When he first came from Japan he was not as physical as Dad and had a weak constitution.

At first Uncle lived with us for a while in Vancouver. One evening during supper, Dad, without warning, gave Uncle a backhand slap on the side of his face. All Uncle said was he "found it tiring to be working hard." I could tell by Mom's face she didn't like what Dad did but never said a word. She knew the chauvinistic macho temperament of Japanese men. Mom got slapped around for another reason and she fought back verbally and physically. Mom bruised easily but never had any permanent marks. Dad, on the other hand, had marks and scars all over his body. When Mom flipped she threw the steam iron, frying pan, plate, everything but the kitchen sink. For some strange reason, father never hit me or slapped me at any time yet, according to my brothers, if they did anything wrong dad punished them physically. Thank heaven most of the Japanese men mellow down after they marry; not like the old, hardened bachelors who seemed to lack tenderness. Maybe a woman does relieve the uptight stress level.

Morning breakfast was at six o'clock sharp. Rice gruel made from hot water or green tea, miso soup, scrambled eggs, sometimes replaced with small dried fish and pickles. Western men will lose weight and even die of malnutrition eating skimpy Japanese meals.

At seven o'clock in the morning we were working in the field. Rows and rows of tomato plants at least 50 to 100 yards in length. Each plant covers an area of a 4 feet diameter circle and the height of the plant weighed down by tomatoes is about three feet. Place a tomato crate that barely fits between the row of tomato plants and pick only the ripe ones for the cannery and other times, the semi ripe ones for the markets. A back breaking job, uncle told me not to put the knees or even one knee on the ground while picking tomatoes because his partners would not like it and by standing and bending over it would be much faster picking tomatoes and when the two plants were stripped of tomatoes it's much quicker and faster to move the crates forward for the next two plants. Sometimes a few hired help came to work and were allowed to be on their knees picking tomatoes. They were all on piecework. We had a half-hour break in the morning (teatime), one-hour lunch at noon and another half-hour break for tea and dessert in midafternoon. The rest of the time we all worked like hell. I worked overtime after supper for the first time because of a rush order for cucumbers. It could become dark pretty quickly so my Uncle and his comrades were working as fast as possible to fill the quota. Before it got really dark, I was tired so I put one knee on the ground still picking the cucumbers. Walking back to the house, my uncle was beside me and very softly told me not to put my knee on the ground. I thought this work was just as bad as washing pots and pans at the logging camp last year. After a Japanese hot bath it always put me in a good mood to sleep and yet when I woke up in the morning it felt like I'd only slept for three seconds. Three weeks also went by like three seconds. It was time to go back to the orchards in Vernon.

Uncle was not as handsome as Dad but he was a kind gentle person, not a stereotype Japanese bachelor. He didn't give me too much money but promised to visit us when the season is over and give Mom the rest of the money. I was very happy with that. Every time he visited us he always gave Mom money.

The guys were happy to see me and they all kept asking me "what happened to my hands?" It looked like a dark dirty green stain, something that cannot be avoided with a tomato plant. "Hey Reg, the RCMP were looking for you, better give them a call." They just warned me to report any time I was going to travel. We all heard the saying "RCMP always get their man" and stories of the heroic exploits of the men in Red, but to me they seemed like Okay guys.

What a difference a few weeks make, the trees now were loaded with red apples; some branches looking like a bunch of red grapes. I saw a limb broken because of the weight of the apples. No wonder the bosses kept checking us to make sure the apples were thinned properly in springtime.

The owner finally said we would start picking apples in two days. Everybody was on piecework getting paid seven cents a box. We each carried a bucket like a shoulder bag; the front made of metal and the back a sheet of canvas that rested on our stomach and top. The bottom of the bucket was made of canvas; when opened it acted like a chute and the apples dropped out. The canvas extended about a foot below the metal bucket with metal rings at the bottom edge of the canvas. A rope wove through these metal rings and when we pulled the rope, the bottom closed and stayed closed if we hooked the loose end of the rope onto a clip attached to the outside of the bucket. A knot prevented the rope from loosening and opening the bag.

Now the fun begins. When the bucket is filed with apples we bend over a wooden apple box -- unhook the rope, keeping both hands underneath the opening of the canvass and gently allowing the apples to drop into the box. Owners are paranoiac about apples being bruised. You gently lift the apples with the palm of your hand and the stem parts from the branch and careful not to hold the apples too tightly with the fingers. It took less than a week to master the 16 footer. Run up the ladder, fill the bucket with apples, turn around, back to the ladder and run down. All the guys were running up and down the ladder like monkeys. The best is when you are standing on the top platform of the ladder, your bucket fills up and you turn and run down the ladder. After two pickings there were hardly any apples left on the trees and owner said, don't bother, he'd finish picking all the apples.

Apple Haven.

They sent us to one of the biggest orchards in Vernon and the apples were getting too ripe so they told us to strip the tree. Other crews and even some girls came over from other orchards. The owner wanted us to pick as many apples as possible before they were over ripe. I was surprised to hear some girls picked 220 boxes in a day. My average was 250 boxes. One day, everybody decided who would be number One apple picker. With my quick hands, I figured to have a good chance to win. I worked fast and furious and steady for the day and picked 305 boxes. I couldn't believe K.K. picked 316 boxes. Next day I was so tired, my quota dropped to 200 boxes.

Hardly anybody fell from the ladder except one person. He would be shouting help! Help! At least once or twice a day. Once I slipped on a top step trying to run down the ladder and the heel of my boot caught the edge of every step of the ladder sliding down, sounding like a woodpecker pecking a tree and such a smooth ride, never missing a beat. In piecework, time was of the essence and mastering the 16-foot ladder saved a lot of time.

Vernon was a beautiful town. The streets and stores were clean and neat and looked civilized compared to the Ghost Town of Slocan. Even though there was not that much to do, we liked eating in a restaurant and going to a movie. There were lots of soldiers in town from a military base just outside of Vernon.

Occasional the men in uniform made racial remarks. It never bothered me and those things never bothered my Mom, and Dad was trapped in the Code of Honor. During the training of the military, there were some close calls, bullets whizzing through the trees. I don't know if they were firing at us or missing their own targets. Anyway, we were happy going back home.

The mountains were becoming part of my life and found the bus ride relaxing and comfortable. Carefree, half awake, half asleep, not a worry in the world. Thought about how well we did picking apples and the money we made. Macintosh was the biggest crop, next came Delicious, and lastly Golden. These were eating apples. Crab apples made delicious jam and jelly and the rest -- I've forgotten the names -- were cooking apples

Back in Bay Form the routine was pretty much the same as last year except I was in Grade 11 and my marks got worse, Es and Fs. We did more hiking and met a hermit, a shell shock victim of World War I. He could only live in the wilderness to have peace and quiet. He managed a couple of goats and some chickens and with a small vegetable garden. He had a fishing rod but no firearms, a very pleasant old man who took a liking to us and showed us where to go to pick wild berries.

On another occasion we encountered some Doukabours. We heard stories they had problems with the government because of nudity. What did I know about culture, religion, politics and different institutions? They seemed like friendly and harmless people. Another story was circulating that the Japanese had a choice: either to stay in Canada or go back to Japan. Mother was Canadian and she would never go to Japan.

In early spring while snow was still on the ground, we hiked up the little mountain that was in front of our house and camped there over the weekend. It took a little while to build a good fire on the wet and drenched ground caused by melting snow. We brought potatoes to bake and with the canned goods -- corn beef, peas, beans and peaches -- the meals weren't that bad. Late at night, having a rap session, the hot Campbell soups tasted the best. Most of the time during the day we went looking for animal tracks on the snow and to us it was a guessing game. None of us had a clue what a bear, deer, wolf or mountain lion track looked like. Even when the snow was gone we spent a lot of time exploring. We found an Indian graveyard. Japanese may not like Ghosts, but they love telling ghost stories. We told YH, the bully from Vancouver, about the ghost hanging around the graveyard and sometimes they would come out to our community. People used to take short cuts through the haunted ground but when they heard it was a graveyard, they started to take the long route home. It was a cold winter night and the full moon lit up the snow white landscape. I could clearly see the road, the houses and some trees. Walking along the road with my hands in my pockets I felt two chilly hands grip my shoulders. I stopped cold. Could it be some one? What could it be? The graveyard was close by. I didn't believe in ghosts; why let my imagination get carried away? I raised an elbow and swung around, expecting to hit someone's arm. No one was there, just cold air and I had to laugh, the motion of moving my arm around must have loosened the shoulder muscle and some of the chilly grip lost its hold. Moving the shoulders up and down and around, the feeling of the chilly grip disappeared. I told my friends about the chilly grip experience and some of them believed it was still a ghost. The chilly grip story added more fuel to the rumors of the burial ground and the last I heard most of my friends and other people felt the chilly grip on their shoulders, still thinking about a ghost.

Chilly early spring, we loved the sunshine and the blue sky. M.T. talked us into going to Slocan City and maybe even go for a swim or at least see the Ferry Boat. I felt the water and it was cold; any colder and ice would form. M.T. and S.T. were still arguing whether any guy could swim in this icy cold water and S.T. got so upset he threw a quarter into the water saying "go into the water and get the quarter for me and I'll give you five bucks." The quarter was lying at the bottom, about 15 feet below the surface. M.T. had such a stubborn nature, he said, "You have the money and I'll do it." I think he stripped naked and he'd lost most of the tan from last year so his skin was fair. The embankment was steep and he didn't dive into the water but sank into it as if he were going to take a

Japanese bath, and as soon as the water level reached his lower chest, he dove down to the bottom.

M.T.'s skin turned light blue immediately and I thought, "Holy shit, I hope we don't have to pull him out, if his body becomes lifeless. From my experience the previous year, I knew all about not being able to breathe in cold lake water. In seconds he was at the bottom, grabbed the coin and came out of the water just as fast. His mouth was chattering, mumbling a few words he quickly put on his shirt and pants. If something happened, none of us would know what to do and had never heard the word 'hypothermia.' Later M.T. told me he wouldn't have minded if his body froze a bit but not his balls. If he'd known that could happen he would have never taken the chance of going into the icy cold water, about ten times colder than normal cold early spring water. Five dollars was a lot of money in those days, but S.N. said, "It was worth it to see a goof ball like M.T. diving into that cold water.

I don't know who the kid was who drowned swimming close to the big paddle wheel at the back of the ferry. The big wheel, churning in the water, created an undercurrent that sucked the boy deep into the water and he was probably not strong enough to swim out of that situation. Fresh water is much tougher to swim in than salt water. My father and his brother both said they used to swim 14 to 15 miles a day in the Sea of Japan. They both claimed that the hot sun evaporated a lot of water and the warm water had more salt than the cold water of the B.C. coast. I don't know if people swim in the Dead Sea. Maybe in that area people walk on water.

Whenever we talked about swimming, the school term was coming to an end.

Some my friends at school, including my sister Doreen and some girls signed up to work in a potato and tomato ranch in Ashcroft BC.

The previous summer, picking tomatoes at my uncle's farm was not that exciting. At least Ashcroft was a new and different place. Boy! Was it different! I never would have thought a place like Ashcroft BC existed in the heart of the Canadian Rockies. We went by bus to Kamloops northwest of the Okanagan Valley and then a train ride further west to Ashcroft. We arrived at the train station around 3 o'clock in the morning, no welcoming committee, not a soul in sight. Only one light bulb invited us inside the station where there were a few benches and a ticket office. Outside, it was pitch black. Hot and humid for a mountain town. Instead of waiting around some of us decided to check out the town. The street was lit up with lamps. Ashcroft was much smaller than Vernon, with a few well-kept stores and a huge cannery building near the train station. I noticed the trees on the boulevard were irrigated with pipes laid on the ground, sprinkling water. Returning to the train station and standing outside on the platform staring into the darkness, I thought about the strange and weird feeling I had. It was predawn, still dark. I began to see the dim outline of the mountains against the sky. As the darkness began to evaporate, I saw that the mountains had no trees. They were bare. Ever since I could remember, mountains were always covered with evergreen trees. The sunlight bouncing off the reddish brick mountains made the place feel even hotter. "I wish I had a camera" to take a picture of it. Only one tree was growing on top of a mountain. The scene looked like Death Valley that we see in Western movies. Plenty of sagebrush, some rolling around like tumbleweed, and small cactus plants growing here and there

Finally the truck and vehicles arrived and with a bit of apology for being late, they took us to our new home, two houses on each side of the road. The guys stayed in one house and the girls in the other. Canada's Death Valley was extremely hot, between 120 and 130 Fahrenheit in the shade. On the third day, one person had to be sent home.   It was strange to see someone foaming at the mouth being taken to a hospital for treatment. We all sort of felt he had a weak constitution. I'm glad my sister was able to handle the heat. The only people working the field were older Chinese men and Native Indians, and a few Caucasians working inside the Cannery downtown.

The Chinese wore straw hats with a big brim, long underwear, denim shirts, work pans and covered their clothing with overalls. At first I thought they were crazy. We never wore that much clothing in subzero weather. Not until I wore a light shirt and got a sunburn on my back did I realize that clothes protect the body. It's a good thing we all brought our pith helmets like hunters wear in Africa.

At the beginning we did a lot of hoeing, getting rid of weeds that could choke the tomato and potato plants. The owner of the ranch was a Chinese man called Benny who had 500 acres of crops. It wasn't like my Uncle's little farm in Kelowna. The hoeing never seemed to end. Rows and rows of growing plants as far as the eye could see. A few weeks later they sent us to another location where we had to sleep in a barn. Attached to the barn was a shed big enough to be a kitchen with a dining room to feed eight of us. The cook didn't know how to cook and we found flies in our soup and food. At the beginning we all got sick, then the body must have developed immunity to the flies

The Chinese families lived in houses not too far from our barn. When working, they only drank warm tea from big pots, sharing the tea with us they told us "not to drink water, it will make us sick" It didn't take too long for the tomatoes to grow and to become ripe for picking. They seemed much larger than the ones my Uncle grew in Kelowna and of course I picked the tomatoes with one or both knees on the ground, the Canadian way. What a relief from heat -- sometimes in mid-August, the evenings became cooler and the harvesting of potatoes started. The soil is dry and powdery and the crops are constantly irrigated. All the potatoes are shipped overseas. Ashcroft potatoes are famous in England. If we peeled the potatoes, boiled them and then strained the hot water from the pot, the surface of the potatoes became fluffy and dry. Cut a potato in half and there would be no wetness or sogginess inside and all the boiled potatoes were light and dry.

Between the rows of potato plants, a bit of earth is removed to both sides making a small ditch. The plant appears to be growing on the top of an earthen ridge and when the dam is opened, the water flows along the ditch, supplying water to the crops. On top of a single seat wagon, a Chinese man steers two horses which pull circular looking steel claws that dig up the potatoes. It's wide enough to turn over two rows of plants and dirt, rolling and scooping everything, drop on a steel mesh slanted slightly to the back. The dirt is sifted and falls through the mesh and the potatoes drop off the end to the ground. Now, I worked the Japanese way throwing the potatoes into a burlap bag until our section of the row was finished. Each man is stationed fifty feet apart and when we finished the section, we moved over a few rows and waited for the horse digger to return. It wasn't back breaking because we spent half the time standing around waiting for the horses to come back. When we filled the burlap sacks, each weighted approximately 80 pounds.

Sunday was a day nobody worked and with slightly cooler days we had some fun times. Two Native kids, age ten and twelve, came by our barn, each riding a beautiful sorrel. I believe a sorrel is a male horse, with a reddish chestnut color, that cannot breed. The boys were friendly and before I could ask, they offered their horses for us to ride. The kids seemed to be expert riders whether cantering, galloping or jumping over fences or prancing around in a circle or having the horse stand on its hind legs. He showed me how to get on a horse without a saddle, using the stirrup and grabbing the mane to pull myself on. They both told me to squeeze my legs if my foot slipped out of the stirrup so I wouldn't fall off and I'd have a chance to regain my balance. I asked how to steer the horse and he said, "Pull the rein to the left or right." The horse began to canter, a real bumpy ride, so I stood up on the stirrup, otherwise I could have bounced off the horse. I pulled the left rein with my left and the horse did not turn. I tried with my right hand and the horse would not turn to the right. I thought, "What the hell's going on." The other kid came galloping from behind and whacked my horse in the rear end and what a rush. I felt the power of the horse surging forward. What a great sensation! Without the saddle, I felt the aliveness and warmth of a living being underneath me, the stride so smooth and powerful it made me feel like half man half horse. I always liked and felt good being born a Sagittarius. I could see why men throughout history valued horses and stealing as horse was punishable by death. I found out later to hold both reins with one hand and move it to the right or to the left and the horse will turn whichever way.

One Sunday the kids invited us to their family home, a community called Dead Man's Creek. We thought it was a funny coincidence that Dead Man's Creek had a funeral service that day. What a wonderful surprise, a fantastic feast. Moose meat, bottled deer meat, some kind of roasted pheasant, roast and mash potatoes and all kinds of vegetables. Plenty of yummy desserts with a variety of fruit pies. The boys' Mother was an excellent cook and I didn't realize that sort of food existed. The Father told us a story about a Silver Moose, relating to the tasty moose meat we had just eaten. I can't remember the story whether it was true or just another Legend.

The next door neighbor had a small orchard. The most delicious peaches, pears and apples I ever tasted. WE all enjoyed the fresh fruits for a while until our boss Benny came over and told us not to raid the fruit trees at night.

Another enjoyable day was when the Natives invited us to their Stampede Day it was fun watching the men riding the bronco horses. Girls were having fun, laughing and screaming, riding a mechanical horse. It was a seesaw with a saddle attached to one end and some guys on the other end making it go up and down and a little sideways. When a girl began to fall off the men would stop the movement to prevent injury. My friends were gawking at the beautiful Indian girls. I found some of them very attractive, especially the mixed blood, but they were all bowlegged worse than some Japanese girls. The young men and teenagers love to wrestle. They were not afraid and kept challenging us for a match. We had talked and argued among ourselves before about whether Judo can handle a wrestler. The argument came around to boxing and one guy, B.S., wanted to fight me over an argument. He was two or three inches taller than me and weighed maybe 20 pounds more. Since there were no boxing gloves, I made him feel good by saying, "I don't want to fight you." One of the guys trained in Judo as a kid in Vancouver and showed me some technique. My argument was, Judo men are used to grabbing a uniform or a jacket to throw a person to the ground. What is he going to grab when the wrestler is naked from the waist up I stood in a relaxed position and when he stepped into position, "bip" my feet were six inches off the ground, my stomach resting on his hip and part of his back, completely at his mercy. He could have thrown me over his shoulder, goodness knows how far, or slammed me down on the floor as hard as he could. Without using a grip he positioned himself much closer to my body, holding my right forearm and his other arm around, just above the waist, and swiveled his hip all happening at the same time. My body was much higher off the ground and again at his mercy. Considering all things are equal, the person with the best athletic ability will win.

One day the sky looked strangely mystical. The sun's rays were beaming through the clouds. All the five or six rays were symmetrical and looked like the Japanese flag used in war, except the sun and its rays were not red but astral white. I don't know whether it was an omen or not but someone came around telling us, "The Americans dropped the Atomic bomb in Japan." I stood watching the sky, my mind in silence as if paying tribute to the dead and knowing the war would end.

The season was also coming to an end and everybody was going back home. For whatever I needed extra money so I volunteered to stay and work another ten days. They needed help to store the potatoes in a cave dug inside of the mountains. Trucks after trucks loaded with sacks full of potatoes came to the storage caves. I could just barely lift two sacks of potatoes by gripping the sacks in each hand.

Pulling them off the end of the truck while lifting both sacks, one in each hand, the sacks hanging but most of the weight resting on my forearm and chest and hurry into the cave to pile them in an orderly fashion. It requires much more strength when the stacks become higher. I would lift the 80-pound sack, making sure it was well balanced on my forearm and then push and shove it on top of the other potato sacks. Regaining my balance, I would do the same with my other arm. I felt all my body parts were getting a real good workout. The hardest part of the job was not being able to breathe. Inside the cave was like a desert storm and we all wore a kerchief to cover the mouth, nose and most of the eyes. Grab the sack, take a deep breath, hurry into the cave and stack the sack, run out of the cave and start breathing deeply. The work became a routine deep breathing exercise. Without air, any job is tough but for me, it was still better than washing pots and pans. Macho Man Rip. It never rained when we were in Ashcroft. Sometimes in the late afternoon heat of summer, we would feel a hot breeze and, as if we were in a sauna bath, our faces would be dripping with water and the clothes became really wet. This would last for about a minute and then, the dry heat moved back in and it didn't take too long for everything to be dry again. Winter is supposed to be cold and windy. I can't remember if anything was said, whether it snowed or not. Sitting by myself riding the train from Ashcroft to Kamloops, it was nice to have a chance to contemplate and enjoy the scenery. Canada's Death Valley had its own beauty. I thought about Mom and the kids. They had moved to New Denver, B.C. Bay Farm was gone forever. The family first stayed in Roseberry, a community four miles from New Denver, until a house became available for them to move again to new Denver.

All this was happening while I was in Ashcroft. Mom always managed, but moving twice in such a short time must have been hard on her. Approaching Kamloops, there was no drastic change in the landscape. At least I saw some Evergreen Trees but still plenty of arid land and treeless hilly mountains. I had to wait three hours in Kamloops for a bus to New Denver, B.C.; plenty of time to do some shopping and have something to eat.

Kamloops looked like a bigger town than Vernon and the weather seemed much warmer. Walking along Main Street, a dozen soldiers were milling around on the sidewalk. As I walked towards them, I began to hear racist remarks and realizing it could become a dangerous situation, I stopped. They were about 25 feet in front of me. I wasn't afraid, figuring none of them would catch me if I ran. When I noticed all of them were wearing big shiny army boots compared to my light running shoes I became more confident. They all looked sharp wearing their khaki uniforms with a cap shaped like an envelope. Two soldiers came forward and I was ready to make my run when a voice boomed out, so loud that maybe people heard it at the other end of town. "Re—eh – gie!!!" He was behind the group of soldiers, towering over them, pushing his way through, his arm stretched out for a handshake, still saying in a loud voice.

"Reggie! How the hell are you! What are you doing here? I can't believe it's you." I couldn't believe it either. It was Frank Agostino Demitrios' friend and neighbor and my friend from Vancouver's Little Italy. Frank was a tall kid and grew even taller and filled out to look like a Giant of a man. He didn't even know his buddies were going to give me a rough time. Frank showed me where to buy my brogue dress shoes and then we sat in a Restaurant and talked and talked and talked about the guys in Little Italy and my time in the Ghost Town. We stayed together talking until it was time for me to leave. To this day I think of Frank as my General Macarthur, the Supreme Commander of the Pacific War who saved and restructured the Nation of Japan.

Physical Enlightenment: my body felt invincible. Working out with those sacks of potatoes strengthened my whole body. No wonder I wasn't afraid of the soldiers. Thoughts about my Dad, who moved, wrestled and stacked 400-pound pulp bales all day at a Pulp Mill in Port Alice. It amazed me how he did it. In those days, the Hindus and Japanese did a lot of heavy backbreaking work. Never worried about father during his time in an Ontario concentration camp. While in Camp Petawawa, dad trained and earned his black belt in Kendo with the same teacher who taught me as a kid in Vancouver. He also told me a High-ranking officer said, "Ted, with a little training you'll be the best Sergeant Major in the Canadian Army. As loyal as Dad was to Japan, he always said, "If a Nisei was going to join the Canadian Army he should not disgrace his heritage and should fight to the best of his ability with courage and honor. I think some Japanese Canadians and a lot more Japanese Americans joined the military, like my friend T.S., because they were bored with community camp life. Is it a residual from the Japanese Culture or is it in the genes?

The ride back to the green Selkirk Mountains was comfortable and exhilarating. The Rockies were now part of my life. I never dreamt that New Denver would be such a beautiful place. It was paradise. The lake was approximately 100 feet from our house. Every morning, weather permitting, I would run out of the house and dive off a floating platform into the lake. The water was not only refreshing to swim or bathe in; we were able to drink it. Outside the house was a high bar, my favorite exercising equipment; two posts spaced six feet apart and a steel pipe two inches in diameter across the top and about seven feet high, joined the posts. It looked like small football goal posts. I would jump up, get hold of the bar and do chin-ups. Sometimes I'd pull myself up to my waist a number of times and then do the half giant or try to do the full giant. The full Giant starts off by doing a handstand on top of the bar and letting the body swing down clockwise for one and a half rotations and ends up in a handstand on top of the bar again. I never bothered practicing this stunt because once, while trying to do this, my hands slipped off the bar and the body went flying through the air and I landed on my flat tummy and luckily I didn't kill myself

Mother was happy to see me and was even happier when I gave her the money. Labor of love. I don't know if my sister Doreen enjoyed her experience in Ashcroft. All she could say was, "It was so hot. It was so hot."

I could never forget the first morning I went to school. The sky was blue and the cool morning air was energizing. I wore a grey flannel shirt, black denim pants, boots and a red bandanna with white spots wrapped around my forehead and covering most of my head.

The school had two buildings, a large two story white house and a rectangular flat roofed building. Walking through the front door of the big house, immediately to the left was an open door that looked like the back of a classroom. On the other side, directly across from the door was a wood-burning stove. This beautiful girl was on her knees stoking the fire and adding firewood. When she looked up and saw me standing in the doorway, her jaw dropped. She stared at me as if I were some – who knows what. I know I was still feeling physically invincible. "Don't tell me this girl is really impressed with me. No it can't be, or maybe I'm dreaming." I managed to ask her "where is the office." She stood up, came close to me, still taking a good look at my face and without taking her eyes off me pointed with her finger saying – end of the hallway. I must have been staring too and, beginning to feel a little embarrassed, said, "Thanks" and walked away, my heart singing. She really fanned my ego. I passed by M.M. many a time during the year but we never talked or said "Hi" or "Hello." She seemed to have lost interest or so I thought.

Too many attractive girls to be hung up on the idea of one and only. My grade 12 home class was on the upper floor of the big house. We had three male students and twice as many female students. There were some cuties, but none of them seemed interested or paid attention to me. We were in the same age group and I thought they were too old for me. The desk and seat benches were made for two people. The two desks at the back of the class were just enough for us three guys. All the girls sat in front of us. The position of sitting at the back was great because at times I still had the habit of taking a nap during classes. The nuns left me alone. The single drawer below the desk came in handy. I would leave the textbooks there to sleep for weeks. Then it got interesting

I found a grade 10 textbook in my desk drawer that didn't belong to me. Between the pages was a big piece of paper with short love note. "Reg, I know a girl that likes you." Please write to us and leave it in your desk." It was initialed V.O. and R.K. This woke me up. During the day, depending on which subjects we were studying, we would go to different classrooms. I kept looking, trying to find out who these girls were. One clue: they were in Grade 10 and I hoped they would be baby dolls. When I did find out they were really attractive and beautiful unfortunately, the early bird gets the worm and unfortunately I was two weeks late in starting the new school and most of the nice looking girls were taken. I don't know where this attachment to an emotional perception originated. I would never try to take a girl away from my buddies. Friends were much more important than a passing fancy. Emotionally caught in a love triangle, sometimes it really hurts. Love notes started to come regularly from different girls and I thought V.O. and R.K. were instigating the whole groupie thing, which I didn't mind. At that age, it was pure emotional naiveté of romantic love. Temperamental, sentimental, swing music and the marvelous beat of jazz no other generation of youth could ever experience the era of romantic music. I never heard of an abortion or a single girl having a baby.

Fall brings out the beauty of the Selkirk Range. Standing in front of our house, we saw green mountains across the lake soon to be capped in snow. The base of the mountain was like a dress hem, a ribbon of autumn colors from the leaves of maple, poplar, birch and oak trees. Among them were wild plants and bushes with their own fire, all displaying seasonal colors to the eternal evergreen.

The morning power of the sun mirrors the whole panorama of the sky, clouds, green mountains, with the rugged snowcapped peaks and the band of blazing autumn colors stretched out onto the lake. Nature's awesome splendor.

Cold weather comes easily and early, the fury of winter storms blanket the area. The drudgery of walking to school through deep snow becomes routine. Dancing sparks the boredom. The school allowed dancing on weekends and at seasonal celebrations. The Sisters came from Victoria, B.C. and when questioned about the morality of dancing, Sister Superior said, "I went to many school dances and I turned out okay. Nothing wrong with dancing." Mom never said anything. Of course I was two years older now, since Bay Farm. I went to school dances just to watch. Most of my friends including myself didn't know how to dance. Oddly enough most of the girls knew how to dance. Near the end of January, T.S., a handsome girl, offered to show me how to dance. Not too long afterwards I was able to dance the fox trot, waltz and a bit of jitterbug. One evening I finally drummed up enough nerve to ask T.S. if I could take her home. She said, "I will let you know later" because she had already promised someone else she came up to me for the last waltz, which meant I would take her home. At the door, her friend was standing and waiting with a despairing look. She went over to him and then she started to cry. The guy never looked at me and I believe the only thing that existed in his life was T.S. I could tell he was such a nice guy and I felt his pain. My fickle mind felt the same pain over V.O., R.K., M.M. and even others I forgot. Even as a teenager I was aware of my self-consciousness of Ego. I sheepishly told T.S. to talk to her friend and she understood. I went home alone, wondering if it was a noble thing I'd done. It didn't keep me from feeling sorry for myself.

Life wasn't all about relating to the opposite sex. The old gang from Bay Farm and Slocan broke up, some going to Alberta, others scattering around the interior of B.C. and some were going to Japan. Out of the old bunch I chummed around with G.Y. and a newcomer, M.A., most of the time. Some of the other guys I knew were going to the High School run by a Protestant Church. M.A. was a handsome looking guy and girls like him. He was much more mature in his attitude towards girls than G.Y. and I. G.Y. really had difficulty socializing with females. He kept telling me how much he liked S.T. but was too shy to approach her. From all my buddies, G.T. was the only person that confided in me about girls and at times I reciprocated. He must have been desperate, asking me to set up a date with S.T., saying she looks like a twin sister to V.O. He was right. S.T. looked like my secret love. I might have tried to set things up for him with any other girl, but with S.T. I didn't have the courage, somehow feeling that if she rejected G.Y. she'd be rejecting me.

However G.Y messed things up royally. He was timid with girls but after a few drinks he became very bold and no girl would accept an invitation from a guy who was drinking. G.Y. moaned for months about her and finally said, "If I can't get her why don't you get her. She's no different than V.O." I said, "Yeh." But my thoughts were, "I have enough problems with girls and no way am I going to add more.

In my age group, G.Y. was the strongest teenager I knew. Once he showed me, placing a spike or big nail underneath his forefinger and placing it across the two fingers beside it and clenching his finger, eh bent the spike. I couldn't bend one of those big nails with two hands. He said, "It takes practice." He was also the only person who could chin himself with one hand without cheating. He'd dangle from a high bar with one hand, arm straight and his shoulder loose. Then he'd jerk his arm, putting his shoulder in place, elbow slightly bent and then pulled himself up so that the side of his chin almost touched the bar. Then he'd straighten his arm, shoulder loose, and chin himself again. G.Y. was able to chin himself with one hand three or four times. I was able to chin myself three or four times, starting off with the shoulder tight and elbow slightly bent. It took me a month of training before I was able to do clean one handed chin ups. Sometimes we would go to the other school and hang out in the Gym. B.S. would brag about doing ten one handed chin-ups and I believed him because I saw him do seven chin-ups. Of course it was the easy way, but I still respected his strength and power to be able to do ten, even if he cheated a bit. Walking into the gym one day, I said, "oh no" some of the guys were boxing. I remembered from Ashcroft, B.S. had said he "could beat the shit out of (me)." He got his chance. I was surprised that he never laid a glove on me and I tagged him a few times. He seemed slow and clumsy; it was very deceiving, especially since he had a well-proportioned muscular body that appeared to have speed. I think that after that he had some respect for me. Years later, I was even more again, when I heard that B.S. became a 5th Dan Karate Master and was teaching somewhere in Ontario.

It's a good thing G.Y. was a good friend of mine and I only boxed with him once. I hate to think if I had to box with him a few more times. He was pretty quick and his punch felt like being hit with a sledgehammer. When he threw a punch at my head, I caught it with my glove. The force was so great it just pushed my glove back, jarring my head. I didn't want to be knocked out by my own glove especially if I was wearing it. G.Y. didn't know too much about boxing and he was swinging wildly. I kept busy dodging his fist, waiting for an opening to nail him and slow down his aggressiveness. Boom! I hit him with a good right hand, felt the hit in my hand, and knew I stunned him. It stopped his wildness in slugging and we kind of boxed away the round. Later I told him, "G., I'm not going to box with you anymore. You hit too hard and I don't want to get into a slugfest. Otherwise I'll end up punchy." G.Y. was good natured and said, "You hit pretty hard yourself, Reg."

G.Y. was fearless. He stepped between two guys and stopped a fight. One man was a tall Canadian and the other guy was short like us. I asked G.Y how he could fight a tall guy like that. He just said, "put him on the ground and we're all the same." I heard from a good source that G.Y. was like greased lightning wrestling on the ground. The Canadian was lifting oil drums onto a truck. When the oil drum is standing it has a three inch rim about three eights of an inch thick around the top of the drum. He would grip the rim with his fingers and lift the oil drum onto the truck just with his fingers. Even if the oil drum had a handle, I doubt if I could lift it a foot off the ground, and strong as the guy was, I agreed with my friend G.Y., lightning speed will win the fight. Boxing with K.I. helped me to make a very important decision in regards to fighting. I was just toying with him and gave him two or three left jabs to his head. KI was so upset and angry, he wanted to take the gloves off and go outside and fight to the death, talking like the old Japanese hardliner. I thought he was crazy so I apologized to calm him down.

That night I thought very seriously about matters of violence, imagine -- a couple of love taps and KI wanted to make it into a do or die issue. Many guys were stronger than me but did not have the speed. Poking an eye out or stabbing someone's throat with a pencil or small object would maim him for live, all over nothing. It just didn't make sense to act or react violently to somebody who disturbed me emotionally. Angry, yes, but not to the point of injuring him for life. Mom often said, "Sticks and stones will break your bones but words will never harm you." They say a cornered rat will fight and I would probably do the same. Fortunately, up to now, I've never had to resort to physical violence over emotional differences. I'm grateful to KI for helping me make the decision towards non-violence.

Winter went quickly, attending classes, going to school dances and hanging out with the guys over at the other school gymnasium. G.Y. and I spent a lot of time confiding and talking about "She loves me, she loves me not." Secret love from afar, dreaming and pretending of love never to be, melody of aching heart. It hurt.

Life goes on and spring is around the corner. M.A. was able to borrow a rowboat from his relative. We oared across the lake for camping and hiking. Easter holiday was an opportune time.

The lake was still too cold to swim but the sun was warm enough to melt some of the snow off the mountain. We pitched our tents in an excellent location beside a small hill, the other side cut like a wall forming a perfect barrier and lessening the roar of the waterfall and protecting us from the misty spray when the water hit the bottom. We would make the campfire in front of the waterfall for cooking and the misty spray together with the smoke made it impossible for the Forest Rangers to spot our camp smoke. In the Gang of Five – myself, G.Y., W.T came from Slocan Bay Farm, and M.A., B.T. – can't remember if they were the original New Denver Group or if they came from somewhere else. We found what appeared to be an old mine trail that lead upwards so we followed it going higher and higher. At times the trail would be five feet wide with a drop of 3 or 400 feet down. Other times the trail was a walk uphill through a forest. We came across a small level clearing with plenty of wet snow on the ground. Looking up, the snow peaked mountain seemed much foreboding and formidable, supreme in its existence, arrogant and untouchable. No wonder that, since ancient times, people believed in the Mountain God. W.T. was really excited about this trip. After the bumpy sleigh ride down a small mountain in Bay Farm the last year I thought maybe he wouldn't be too keen in climbing mountains, but he was enjoying it and really liked being one of the boys. I noticed he was careful and stayed as far as possible from the edge of the cliff. We were grateful that W.T. volunteered to make a campfire and cook lunch. I asked him, "How are you going to make a fire when this snow is wet and the dead branches are all soaked with water?" He said, "Reg, I was a boy scout when I was a kid and I learned how to make fire in the rain." We told W.T. we would all be back in two hours for lunch. None of us liked cooking and I doubted W.T. could start a fire.

M.A. led the way. The backpacks with food and cooking utensils were left behind with W.T. and the only thing we carried was some rope, flashlights and I had my usual hunting knife. None of us really liked to cook and we were happy to have W.T. to do the cooking. M.A. was grinning and chuckling at our jokes about W.T. and said, "I'd rather drop dead than to be caught cooking." He almost dropped to his death. He was leading us towards another cliff hanger when his body disappeared, only his head and part of the shoulder and arms spread eagle were on top of the snow G.Y. reacted quickly and yelled to me to "stay back." He pulled a rope from his knapsack and threw it about six feet to M.A.'s hand and told him to secure his hold by wrapping the rope around his wrist and then to grip the rope with both hands. We were at the other end holding the rope on solid ground, and G.Y., helping us, told everybody to pull the rope slowly to pull M.A. out. In order to pull M.A. out we had to step to the right a bit. Then I clearly saw M.A.'s leg and feet dangling in midair hundreds of feet above ground.

When we first approached this man made walkway we couldn't see it from the left side. The suspended walkway was five feet wide with logs six to eight inches in diameter spiked into the side of the cliff. When we pulled M.A. on to safe ground he gave a sigh of relief, sweating around the neck and face. M.A. was well built, handsome and the girls liked him. He trained with weights, did a bit of High Bar workout but was not into boxing, martial arts and sports. He was quite macho and just chalked up the incident as a close call. Heading back down I said, "It's a good thing W.T. wasn't around. He might have passed out. Everybody laughed and forgot about the deep drop that might have been.

W.T. had lunch ready. Steamed rice mixed with a can of peas, and every time he threw a water soaked cedar branch onto the fire it would sputter and spit out ashes and some of it would end up in the food. I must have been hungry. It was the best pitchy-tasting mixed rice I ever ate. Although we teased W.T. a lot we liked his good nature and easygoing ways.

Back at the base camp again, W.T. made a campfire in front of the waterfall. We had meats, wieners, potatoes, rice, fresh vegetables, fruits, and everybody's favorite marshmallows. There was so much food some of us helped W.T. to cook supper. After the meal, two guys took turns in playing the harmonica. It was a sing along mostly the simple "Country and Western" songs like "You are my sunshine", "Oh Suzanna", "The Yellow Rose of Texas", etc. and a few sentimental pop songs. Then we talked and laughed and joked about everything until the wee hours in the morning. My thoughts went back to the time when I was a boy going camping in North Vancouver looking at the stars. The stars appeared much bigger and brighter in the Rockies. I was secure and happy thinking I'd solved the mystery of the Holy Trinity. Three of us decided to watch the sunrise so we went to a section with a pebbly beach, lay down naked with feet pointing towards the east and fell asleep. "Reg wake up!" the guy beside us yelled. I heard some guy laughing and shouting and girls giggling. The sun was bright and my body felt like it had a sunburn. I sat up squinting my eyes and saw a rowboat 50 or 60 feet from us. As my eyes became adjusted to the bright sunlight, I realized they were the Roseberry crowd. Oh no, I thought, "One of the girls could be my secret heart throb." At least my knees were close together. One of the guys on the boat wanted to come ashore and we threatened him with obscenities. After this embarrassing incident, I received a few more love notes in my desk; most of them were out of context.

He never drove one of those big tractors. We were heading east, four miles to Roseberry. The highlight beams were on and nearing a bridge a man tried to hail us down. M.A. gunned the pedal to speed up the truck while we shielded our faces with our arms. Away we went hoping the man didn't recognize us. M.A. was doing well switching the high beams and low beams to see the road. We only saw the low wall of the cliff to our right and it was pitch black on the other side. We knew that some parts of the pitch black highway were a sheer drop hundreds of feet to the bottom and other parts were just steep slopes. M.A. turned left to Roseberry and in a short distance there was a clearing to park "the big sucker" as M.A. called it. Well the "Big Sucker" made a lot of noise and a lot of kids from our school came out to see what the big commotion was about. I didn't feel good, realizing now everybody would know we took the truck for a ride. I sort of thought what R.K., V.O. and some of the girls would think about this escapade.

The three of us had a disagreement about how to get back to New Denver. M.A. wanted to walk back along the railway track. I wanted a ride back with the truck and G.Y. was neutral but wanted to learn how to drive. G.Y. and I decided to take the truck. M.A. wanted to stay for a short time holding hands with his girl. When G.Y. let go of the brakes, the tractor-trailer started to roll backwards. I was at the back of the trailer and had to yell, "Stop the truck." G.Y. came out and realized the back wheels were only ten feet from the water. We were on a beach like elevation and began to fear that the truck would start to sink immediately. I figure we had 15 to 20 feet before the back wheels would be under water. "George, you can't let the truck go backwards. Do whatever you have to do to make it go forward. I'll be in the back pushing or holding the truck from going backwards. I felt like a mouse trying to push an elephant. The motor roared and G.Y. did it. The tractor-trailer jackknifed bouncing three or four times before the motor went dead. G.Y. and I were laughing that at least we were on solid level ground. I had my doubts whether he would be able to drive but the big tractor was moving fairly smoothly. He made a right turn and was driving the biggy buggy nicely. Just when I thought I could relax a bit, the truck started to veer left and when he turned the wheel it went sharply to the left and smashed against the wall of the cliff. Now the tractor-trailer was blocking the whole road. My idea was to leave it and walk home but G.Y. said it was too dangerous to leave it that way, so using the flashlight to see he started the motor and parked it parallel to the wall so other vehicles could pass by. Before we could make up our mind what to do, we saw the beam of headlights bouncing around the mountains coming towards us. We thought they could be people looking for us so we went down the slope using a flashlight to make sure there was no cliff like drop. It's a good thing we weren't too far from Roseberry where the section of the Highway was not too high and the slope wasn't steep. When we got to the bottom and came across the railroad tracks and before we started towards New Denver we saw a light coming along the track and knew it was M.A. with his flashlight. Together again we all felt better like the three musketeers. I asked G.Y. "How in the hell did you manage to drive the truck into the cliff?" He laughed saying, "I was so used to driving boats; when you want to make a right turn you turn the wheel to the left. It's the opposite of driving a car.

I thought it was lucky that the truck veered towards the cliff. If it had turned the other way the truck would have gone off the highway crashing down the slope and goodness knows what would have happened to me and G.Y. M.A., with his flashlight was leading the way. Never was I aware of so many deer in the darkness. All we could see were the eyes, so many of them shining and moving in the darkness. I didn't think they traveled in the dark. The howling of the wolves alerted my senses, heard the monotonous shuffling of our shoes while walking on the railroad track, saw lights in the distance, knowing we were not too far from New Denver.

As we came close, we saw people standing on the bridge and M.A. thought maybe they were waiting for us and he spotted one of them with glasses who looked like the guy who tried to wave us down. We decided to wade across the mouth of the river rather than let them see who we were. We were in the dark and far enough away that they couldn't see us so we walked towards the mouth of the river. The river was maybe 60 feet wide and the mouth was at least 100 yards from the bridge and it was too dark for any of them to see us. We joined hands in a fireman's grip and started to walk across. Halfway there the water was so deep we all sank, letting go of the grip and started swimming to the other side. It was such a short swim I hardly felt the icy cold water and on dry land started to squeeze the water from my shirt and pants. I was surprised the water was so deep near the mouth. During the day the water under the bridge looked shallow, only about two feet deep. When I went home Mother had a visitor and looked at me funny. I was shirtless, carrying the shirt waist high and trying to hide my wet pants.

Next morning sitting in my classroom on the second floor I heard knocking on the front door downstairs and a voice asking to see G.Y. and me. Some girl came through the open door, whispered to the teacher and then left. Sister came over to me and said, "Someone wants to talk to you." I expected to see a red uniform, but the RCMP officer was wearing brown. G.Y. was already outside standing around. The first thing the Mountie asked me was, "why did you steal the truck/" all I could say was, "we went for a joy ride." He mentioned that M.A. was already picked up and waiting for us at the headquarters. We sat in the back seat of the car and he drove to his headquarters, which looked more like a small office, and sure enough, M.A. was sitting on a chair. The officer was an okay guy. He said, "Listen, you kids are lucky I picked you up. If it were the Provincial Police you would all be put in jail, maybe prison. I'll have to ship you kids out of town in a hurry." I told him we only had a month or so to finish school and to graduate. He agreed, "Okay, as soon as school is over, report to me and we will send you wherever you want to go." We were brought up to respect the RCMP and I thought the officer treated us well and felt the prestige and class of the Federal Police Force.

The war was over and people were moving to other parts of Canada. Every time someone from school was leaving we'd have a farewell dance party. After school was over, the parties continued for a few months. I waited around for two months before going to Toronto. It was a continuous party and I never ate so many sandwiches and cakes. The M.C. announced, "Ladies' choice." This dream girl came up to me for a dance.

She introduced herself as the older sister of V.O., talking about how good V.O. was in helping Mom to cook and to help her wash dishes, clean house, learn to knit and whatever good women did in those days. I was struck with mixed emotions. "Is she trying to say I have a chance to go steady with V.O.? I believed her sister was sending a message on behalf of V.O. that she at least liked me. I was hoping it was the truth or maybe she even loved me. I acted as cool as possible on the outside but my heart was singing inside. Love eternal. That feeling lasted a long time.

Finally we got a notice from the RCMP to leave in ten days. We couldn't go with our families but it was better than going to jail which was a fair exchange.

The dance was our farewell party. It was a pleasant surprise when M.M. asked me for a dance since we ignored each other all year, partly due to the fact that she was going steady with one of my buddies. It was the same situation with V.O. M.M. asked where I was going and what my plans were. The conversation was nothing out of the ordinary until I told her, "I'll be staying with my Uncle." She dropped a bombshell: "If your Uncle looks like you, I'm going to chase after him." I choked. All I could say was," He's already married." Tongue-tied, my mind was racing. "I was right that first morning at school; I made a big impression on her." I could have said a million things like, "I'm not married" or "I love to chase you." I just couldn't say how I felt. It took me a long time before I could express my feelings in words to girls.

Train ride through the prairies was not as exciting as going through the Rockies. Quite a contrast with the high mountain peaks and valleys of BC to the flatlands of the Prairie Provinces. Thought "what a country for baseball, it would never run out of land for building ballparks.

M.A.G.Y and I might as well have been going to a foreign country; we didn't know what to expect in Toronto, Ontario. Moving into Ontario was a welcoming change of scenery with its trees and rolling hills but I still preferred the mountains of BC

Toronto Union Station – I felt like a hick town boy, the world did not have TV, websites, fax and computers. Most people in the rural provinces didn't have a clue what a big city was like. Royal York Hotel in front of Union Station – wow! It looked like a manmade mountain dwarfing all the other downtown buildings. Now, in the 21st century, the glass and steel skyscrapers dwarf the hotel.

I stayed with my Uncle Hank and his wife in the east end of

Toronto and worked in a downtown factory until my Dad was released from the Concentration Camp in Petawawa. Dad decided we should go up north and work in a logging camp. Mom and the kids later came to Toronto and stayed at a place called Somerville and waited until the government found a suitable place for our family.

Father and I went with a group of guys from the Toronto Employment Agency to cut pulpwood way up in Kapuskasing. The weather was dry cold, 30 to 40 degrees below zero. Every morning while it was still dark we would walk for an hour to the work site. Build a large fire to keep guys warm if they became cold during the day. The foreman was disgusted with a lot of the men from Toronto who couldn't chop enough firewood just to keep themselves warm.

Dad and I, between us, cut five cords a day and I believe the company paid us 2 dollars a cord. Some experienced Quebecker cut five cords on their own in a day.

It was much tougher working in the bush in Northern Ontario than in BC everybody used a little Swede Saw shaped like a bow approximately four feet long to cut the small trees down. The diameters of the trees were approximately eight to ten inches and the height of the spruce trees were less than 30 feet. We could only get two eight-foot sections from a tree and pile the eight footers into a neat 8x4x4 cord. The metal handle of the saw is shaped like a bow with a thin blade saw two inches wide attached to each end of the bow. Sawing the trees on the ground was easy. The left hand holds the top of the handle with knuckles up and the right hand knuckles out grips near the end of the handle. We used our arms and body weight to push downward and the other arm to pull. When the Swede Saw is used properly it cuts the soft Spruce tree like a knife through butter. The hardest part of the job is to cut the tree down. First the snow is removed from the base of the tree and then, bending the body over a difficult position to breathe, cut the tree three inches above the ground with only arm strength. It took my lungs and body over a week to learn to cut a tree down with only one deep breath. Making a bigger notch into the tree for less sawing helped. One thing about Dad, he had the knack of filing any saw or axe razor sharp. In BC we used the double blade axe to make big notches in a tree and to chop off the large branches. Some of the limbs of those big evergreen trees were as big as the trees we were cutting down here in northern Ontario.

I used the blunt end of the hatchet to knock off the small dried branches of the Spruce trees. Dad had in his toolbox the head of a double blade axe, sharp as a Samurai sword. When he showed it to the guys they raved and marveled over it. Some men from Toronto had never seen or used a Swede saw or a regular axe. It wasn't surprising that they couldn't cut and chop enough firewood to keep warm or work hard enough to work up a sweat. Most of the time they stood around the fire trying to stay warm. On real cold days we couldn't work too long and I would stay in front of the fire, arms and hands stretched out and when my back began to feel cold I would turn and warm the back. In this manner we all rotated trying to keep the body warm and the foreman told us that if we ever got lost or without a fire, to bury ourselves in the snow to keep warm.

Northern Ontario was cold and the thing Dad and I enjoyed was the old-fashioned sauna bath. Inside the wooden hut was hot stone on top of burning embers and the rest of the room had a wooden floor with a couple of benches to sit on. Just had to be careful not to put too much snow on the stoves, otherwise the steam would scald our skin. Our body became so hot, walking back to the bunkhouse in subzero temperature we never felt the cold.

Father was a light eater. All the big men ate two to three plates of stew. Dad would only eat half a plate but he sure loved his pies. Many times he would have a second helping, claiming it gave him stamina and strength.

Once the bunk house door was frozen and Dad, with the other guys, couldn't budge it. The foreman came by, a huge man with a barrel chest weighing 270 lbs., gripped the door handle and rammed the door with his shoulder and the whole thing flew open, hinges and all. Even Dad was surprised with his strength. Later I asked Dad, "Can Judo handle a strong giant like the foreman?" Dad bent his head slightly, as if looking at the floor, and between breaths made a soft humming sound as if in deep thought. Father always took combat seriously. He looked at me and said quietly, "You could hit a vulnerable spot, paralyzing or even killing a man before you slam him to the ground." That's all he said. Its common knowledge, no matter how powerful the opponent in Judo, that you use the opponent's power to defeat him. Even a horse could be slammed to the ground. By whacking the nose and, as the horse rears up on its hind legs, step in quickly pushing the side of the underbelly and foot sweep or trip one of its legs and the horse would flip to the ground on its side.

Mrs. Ban and Mother were good friends from the Vancouver days. While living in Toronto they often visited each other. Mrs. Ban moved to Farnham Quebec and still managed to visit Mom once or twice a year. Her eldest son Tad was a little drunk and went to see Dad at Lichee Gardens and wanted to borrow money. There was an argument and I believe Dad told me he slapped him. A slight tussle followed, each having a Judo hold on the other, and the sparring of legs double, triple foot sweep a standoff and Ban was pushed outside the door. It wasn't long after this when Tad came looking for Dad. I could still smell alcohol on his breath and he told me he was going to beat up my Dad. I ran home and told Mother. Mom went outside and confronted Tad, yelling and screaming, "The fury of Mother's Wisdom." She just shamed Tad into the ground and Tad timidly and sheepishly walked away never to bother Dad again.

Tad was a natural explosive fighter, plus the skill of Judo almost made him unbeatable. Dad mentioned even when he is drunk he's a dangerous Judo man. I remember as an eight year old boy Tad would be sitting on the ground outside reading and studying Japanese Judo books. He talked about the theoretical aspect of Judo, which I didn't understand. But the photos of different throwing techniques were interesting to see. The story goes that Tad was working in a logging camp up in Timmins Ontario and in a town bar fought two men trained in the French style kickboxing. In the bar they were the type of guys that liked to show off kicking the ceiling with their boots. Tad went to the hospital for treatment for about an hour or so, one of the other guys stayed in the hospital for three weeks and his buddy had a rest for a half year. My educated guess is Tad not only threw them on the floor but gave them a controlled boot to the head as they were trying to do to him. Ban was that type of person, after disarming and paralyzing them with Judo; he would use his fists, boots, or broken bone technique depending on what his opponent fought with. Tad's reputation spread and they all called him "little Tiger." Many of the guys wanted to learn Judo and Tad felt he was pressured into teaching Judo classes. I heard later that he opened a Judo school in Quebec. Similar thing happened to Father when we lived in a logging camp in BC He was helping the foreman to fix a roof and was carrying a pail of nails up the ladder to the roof. The foreman kicked Dad in the face. It was a low roof and Dad fell onto a pile of sawdust. Dad was so upset he climbed up the ladder, grabbed the foreman, and they both came tumbling off the roof into the pile of sawdust. They scrambled on to level ground and Dad, using the foot sweep, threw the foreman to the ground, put an arm lock behind his back, and with the other hand ground the screaming foreman's face into the sawdust covered ground. One of Dad's friends came running over with a pee vee and stood in back of Dad telling everybody not to interfere and shouted to Dad that he was watching that nobody attacks him from behind. After this incident, Dad and the foreman became the best of friends and some of the guys at the camp wanted to learn judo. So Dad, after a hard day's work, would still have enough energy to teach them "the gentle art of Judo." I was too young to understand or know why all that happened. For five years dad and – or rather his friend – rehashed this story to their friends. I heard this story many times but once Dad made me laugh saying in perfect English, "I had to teach the son of a bitch a lesson." With Dad's temperament I consider it a miracle that he never hit me once.

Dad received a notice from the government saying that Mom and the kids were moving to Mount Forest and for him to join them. We sat on our luggage inside a metal caboose, which was like a freezer. I remember wearing a gabardine rain coat, dress shoes, and light clothing, continuously rubbing the hands, nose, ears and moving the shoulders and limbs and wriggling my toes to keep them from freezing. It's a good thing the caboose ride to the train station in Kapuskasing didn't take too long.

In Mount Forest our family lived in a second floor flat in a big house. Two small families lived in the apartment downstairs on the first floor. We all got along fine with the Satos and Kanos. Some other Japanese families lived in a big triplex not too far from us. We all worked for Mr. Truganno who had a basket factor in Mount Forest and a peach farm near St. Catharines. Mount Forest was not as cold as Kapuskasing but had more snow, a real snow belt. When the main country roads are cleared with snowplows the snow banks would be high as the Hydro poles. Walking on top of the snowbanks one could just step over the Hydro wires.

Cutting cordwood for the basket factory was a lot more dangerous and tougher than working for the Pulp Company up in Northern Ontario. The swamp and bush land of the farms had trees like Maple, Elm (all died in Ontario), Poplar, Diamond, Gillard, Oak were all suitable for making bushel and quart baskets. Up north, the trees grew in density so the trees were cut three inches above the ground for the team of horses to pull the sleigh loaded with cordwood over the stumps. In the bush land of the farms those big trees were further apart and the horse team had plenty of room to move around the bigger higher stumps. The trees were much bigger, having trunks about one to three feet in diameter with so many big branches a wind or breeze dictated which way the tree falls.

It complicated things when we fell a tree that ends up leaning against another tree. Sometimes we waited for the breeze or wind to die down to avoid the snags. Our familiar tool was the double blade axe to make big notches, a crosscut saw to bring down the tree and a buck saw to cut the log into cord wood length. Many of the branches were bigger than the trunk of the trees up North and to use a Swede Saw or an axe, time wise made no difference. So we preferred the axe. The hardest part of the job was to carry the cordwood forty or fifty feet and pile them into cord wood stacks 54 inches wide, 48 inches high and 96 inches long. The logs were cut every 54 inches in length, which suited the machines in the factory that made the baskets. I carried the lightest cordwood with my arms and at times I carried it on my shoulders. Anything heavier than 150 lbs., I let my Dad carry on his shoulders. If the log was really heavy I had to help Dad put it on his shoulder. I would lift one end of the log into an upright position and Dad would lean down low, his shoulder into the mid-section of the log and as I slowly lifted the one end off the ground, Dad would gradually become upright and the cordwood would slowly balance itself on Dad's shoulders. Dad guessed the heavier logs weighed 350 to 400 lbs. Sometimes the path to the cord pile wasn't firm enough and with the extra weight on the shoulders, the right leg would drop into the snow. But Dad had the knack of letting the log fall to the right side of his body. It happed to me, and the log bounced on my shoulder. I believe it weighed less than a hundred lbs. So no broken collarbone. My boots touched water so the path was over swampland and we tied a rope to drag the cordwood one at a time to the pile.

Dad, my uncles and their friends claim the toughest job was to carry cedar bolts over a rough terrain for a long distance. Even a burlap sack on the shoulder did not protect the skin from bleeding. It took quite a while for the shoulder skin to develop calluses. Uncle Hank called it Donkeywork. He also said, "Only the Japanese, Hindus and Donkeys were dumb enough to do that kind of work."

When the snow began to melt, the bush land became too swampy to work so we all started to work at the Factory. In the yard of the factory was an enormous pile of cordwood we had cut during the winter. A dozen men in pairs would pull the cordwood using cant hooks and slide them onto a belt chain and like a low sloped sidewalk escalator, the cordwood would go up to the second floor. I worked with two Caucasians and as fast as the logs came up we started piling them at the far end of the factory. When the first row of cordwood got too high to lift the logs on top, we would start a second row and use it as a step to pile the logs higher on the first row. We would start the 3rd, 4th and 5th row so the back rows could all be piled up to the ceiling. As more rows were added it came closer to the chain belt which made our job easier. The real big ones we rolled on the wooden floor and left them for the first step. Two hours after lunch the two Canadians would be tiring. I felt freshened, still full of energy and I thought with all this stamina I was becoming like my Father. I was okay but the other two slowed down and the cordwood kept coming. They yelled to the guys outside not to work so hard and to slow down. After all, we only had three guys up here and they had an army outside to keep us busy. Our foreman, a Nisei, was a typical anxiety ridden bureaucrat who watched us and never said anything when the Caucasians told everybody to slow down. If it had been a Japanese work force he would have become a whipping boy and make us work harder until the 5 o'clock whistle.

Now, in my old age, I become aware that he was just another anxiety-ridden perfectionist. No matter how stupid his thinking and actions were, it had to be done his way. Emotional perfectionism causes emotional tunnel vision. That robs him of alternative and flexible views for a greater vision. A perfectionist attitude creates anxiety ridden control freaks. Generally speaking, I believe terrorist, fundamentalist, addicts and any other unbalanced human behavior is the result of emotional control freaks going out of control. Pursuit of excellence is wonderful but to be perfect is an illusion of thought that leads to unhappiness, chaos and suffering. To observe the inner state of mind is a difficult act to follow. Even more difficult is understanding the functions of the physical brain especially the reptilian part of the brain that dictates the thoughts and actions of human behavior. I think animal trainers could help psychotherapists to dominate the beastly aspect of the human brain. Anyway, the scientific understanding, the physical brain will validate the Universal Principle of other disciplines. I feel it won't be too long before somebody will integrate my mouthful of words so everybody can take advantage of the angelic nature rather than the devilish nature of the brain.

That last winter, like a perfectionist, the foreman would arrive at the work site at 4 o'clock sharp to take us home. He would drive the truck over the cropland to the edge of the bush where piles and piles of cordwood were gathered. Now the stupidity begins. We would load the cordwood on the truck, secure it with chains, and all of us would lie on top of the load. I would wrap my arms around the chain to avoid falling off. Then the fun began. The truck would go for about 40 to 50 feet and both wheels began to spin and sink. We would get off the truck and the eight of us would try to push the truck but the load was just too heavy and the wheels kept sinking until the axle was on the ground.

We would unload most of the wood, put some stuff in front of the back wheels to prevent them from spinning and push as hard as possible to get the truck on solid ground. Load up the truck, strap the load, jump up on top and go for another 30 or 40 feet and the truck got bogged down again. We did the same thing and the truck would get bogged down after 20 feet, or if we were lucky, it could go 60 feet. By the time we reached the main road and got home it was always after midnight. On a bad night it would be 2 o'clock in the morning before I went to bed. This went on night after night. Tak, who lived below us, told the foreman (take) half a load to the main road and drop it all off and come back for another half a load and pile up the other load and the truck will not get bogged down and we could all be home before 6 o'clock. This nonsense went on every day and we all came home after midnight. Once I walked behind the truck, figuring it's going to get bogged down anyway. The foreman yelled to me to get on the truck. I told him I didn't want to waste time climbing up and climbing down when the truck got stuck. He yelled back like a yapping dog, saying that if the truck doesn't get stuck he'd drive back without me. I mumbled, "yeah, sure." And never missed a ride home. Tak Sato, who lived below us with his parents, told the foreman to "fuck himself" and quit the job. The foreman went berserk, screaming and hollering, "You are under contract with Truganno Farms." And "You will never get a job anywhere else." A few days later, Tak found a job working in a Foundry in Mount Forest. Dad almost had a run in with the foreman. Thank heavens Dad had restraint. Tak was different. He just came out of the Army and didn't want to take crap from anybody and just kept saying, "I'm just a guy trying to make a living."

Warm Spring weekend was a great time to fool around at the ballpark. My Nisei friends enjoyed hitting fly balls to snag and a few young kids were having a great time playing catch and chasing balls that went out of the ballpark. Even after a long layoff, I still had the feel for judging fly balls and made a good running catch in foul territory beside the sidewalk. The catch might have impressed the elderly gentleman standing nearby on the sidewalk. In a friendly voice he said, "Why don't you try out for the Baseball Team? Mount Forest Ball Team needs help." Three of us made the team. Tak as catcher, Kano as pitcher and I played second base and at times, outfield.

The town players were mediocre except Doucette whose average was over 330 and he hit line drives like a major leaguer, and John Englesby who played hockey for the Toronto Maple Leafs, hit those long towering drives. John was a skillful fast skater but he was a slow, clumsy base runner. John was a big, good defenseman in hockey and kept telling me he'd rather get hit by a puck than a baseball. I wore rimless glasses and one of the lenses was broken completely in half. I feared the puck more than a baseball. When I crouched down in my batting stance, my head would be over the plate. Englesby would close his eyes when the pitcher threw the ball over the plate. He was deathly afraid of the ball hitting my glasses or head. Pitchers were intimidated by the broken glass barely hanging on to the top rim and they didn't want to hit my glasses, so I walked an awful lot of the time. One pitcher from the town of Ayton threw right at my head. Dusted me quite often. I know he tried out for the Inter County League, a Triple A team, so an experienced pro that didn't fall for my tricks trying to gain a psychological advantage.

I felt good robbing Buster of a home run. Playing left field, I made one of those Willie Mays type catches and the fans gave me a standing ovation. Whether we played baseball or not, all the townspeople were very friendly and I didn't sense any prejudice. I expected one or two racist remarks, but that never occurred. It wasn't like Vancouver. Mount Forest made it to the finals and we lost out to the town of Listowel.

I said goodbye to the factory and went back to school to finish grade 13. Nobody seemed interested in basketball but they sure liked playing hockey not much to do during the cold winter nights but to go skating at the rink. Surprised myself by becoming a fast skater, so fast that I kept up with the guys who were born on skates.

Played only two games of hockey, the last game I was flying down the ice, trying to go through the two defense men, but they managed to sandwich my back leg, making me fall forward. Sitting on the ice with the puck between my legs, they kept swiping the puck and a hockey stick conked my nose. The nose did not break but swelled up and I couldn't wear my glasses for weeks. I never wore glasses when playing hockey and with my poor eyesight I was always a step behind, just couldn't anticipate the movement of the puck bouncing off the boards and sliding around the ice. I valued my eyes more than playing half-blind hockey, so I quit. I still enjoyed skating and, better still, joined the Curling Club. A game of broomstick and stone. What a fun game, sliding a round flat stone on ice, 100 feet or so into a center bull's eye of targets made of outer circles. My brain must have a paneled end hardwired to any game of touch.

The two most attractive girls were in my class. They were untouchable to all the guys. They were going steady with the star hockey players on the school team who were, of course, also good looking. The brunette, I think her surname was Trua, was friendly and talked to me often like I was a regular classmate. Emotionally there was a barrier against the girls of Mount Forest. I don't think it was racism but the culture of marrying your own kind and shame society could have been the factor. However, Sadie was different; a pretty girl, red hair, some facial freckles, always a smile, a few inches shorter than me and a well-proportioned body. She must have liked me.

Every time we met by chance she would tag along and we would end up in a restaurant having coffee and talking. I felt she was like a stray dog, popping up out of nowhere and following me around. Maybe her clothes gave me that impression; she always wore pants with a T-shirt and sweater that looked like hand me downs.

One evening Kano and I went to the schoolyard to practice shooting a basketball. Darkness was approaching when Sadie and a friend appeared from nowhere. We all liked to smoke and the other side of the school was a perfect secluded place to light up cigarettes where nobody could see us. We sat on the school steps talking and laughing, smoking and puffing until we ran out of cigarettes. Sadie and Kano volunteered to go and buy cigarettes. Sadie's friend was a big girl with big boobs. It's pitch black, silent and scary. She grabbed my hand and put it around her waist. Instinctively I tried to touch her breast. There I am, my hand going all over and I couldn't feel her breast. Meanwhile, Sadie came back with cigarettes and we all left the schoolyard. Walking home, my mind was mystified, the biggest tits in Mount Forest and I couldn't find it. Years later with another girl, the same Karma haunted me. Felt like a dumb duck.

Halloween had to be a special night and we were going nuts just walking around doing nothing. Somebody finally suggested we should sneak into the lumberyard and let the cops chase us out of there. Sure enough, someone yelled, "Cops." We all scattered and I must have been holding hands with Saidie, pulling her towards the lumber piles. One end of the lumber pile looked like a flat uneven checkerboard while at the other end, some pieces jutted out and because of the varying lengths created small tunnel-like openings. Sadie and I squeezed into a small opening, the space so tight we could only lie sideways belly to belly. Sadie's body was soft, sensual with warm moisture coming through her clothes. My mind was completely consumed by her closeness but still aware of the flashing red light and the radio voice of the police and the noise of the slow moving tires circulating around the yard. To me, time felt like a short (element), with only a feeling of exquisite touch. I don't know why, deep down, I felt sorry for Sadie and could only treat her with respect and kindness. Sex was out of the question.

Going to St. Catharines to pick peaches for Truganno Farm was a great experience. It was exciting to see the fruit trees, the flower branches almost touching the ground, weighed down by the clusters of ripe peaches. The number 200 bushels a day comes to mind. Miscalculation, I only averaged a little more than 100 bushels a day. We were paid 15 cents a bushel, which was still a lot of money. It was fast and easy picking, standing on the ground, stripping the peaches right into the bushel basket. Above the ground, the twelve-foot ladder was a nightmare, very unstable; you just couldn't run up and down the 12 footer nor stand on the top platform of the ladder to stretch out to pick peaches. It was a flimsy, shaking ladder that tilted easily and fell to the ground with the picker. Another thing that slowed the picking was that the trees were not pruned and the thick growth of branches was not suitable to place the ladders deeper into the tree without breaking branches. The peach trees were not as big and high as the apple trees of the Okanagan Valley. The Valley trees were pruned so that it ( ) four or five major forks with some smaller forks branching above them. The sixteen-foot ladder was so stable we didn't have to come down to the ground and move it to pick all the apples from the spreading forked branches. I could stand halfway up the ladder, lean back so the ladder became upright, the tripod pole would swing back automatically to catch it with my right hand, lean forward, pushing the pole to any location in front. The further away the pole, the lower the top of the ladder, the closer the pole lands the higher the top platform of the ladder. Sometimes I would lean back, balance the ladder on one leg, turn the ladder slightly and throw the pole where I wanted it to be. In this way the ladder was moved only four or five times to pick all the apples from the tree. The sixteen-footer was a remarkable piece of equipment.

Good old fashioned faces from the Okanagan days; it was almost a pleasant surprise to see some of my old buddies and to be working together again. With our experience in picking fruit, we finished way ahead of schedule.

Dad had already gone to Toronto when I returned to Mount Forest. He joined the carpenters' Union and was working on a building in Chinatown to be the place for the future Lichee Garden. Dad was such a capable trustworthy person, the Boss of Lichee wanted him to continue working for him. Dad looked after the repair and maintenance of the restaurant and building -- looked after the shipping of incoming goods for Lichee and associated trading. He managed the labor force of people of Japanese origin for dishwashing, cleanup, making bean sprouts and moving around the heavy stuff for the Trading Company. Besides all that, he baked all the almond cookies for Lichee Gardens.

We left the quiet town of Mount Forest for the noisy big town of Toronto. The Boss was good enough to let us move into his apartment building near Yonge Street. It was only three blocks to Lichee Gardens and two blocks to Yonge and Dundas, the center of downtown Toronto at that time. Elm Street began at Yonge Street and went to University Avenue, four short blocks. Our apartment was half a block from Yonge and behind us, to the north, was the block long notorious and famous Walton Street that no longer exists, demolished and buried by the huge Chelsea Inn Hotel.

So what else is new? Lived in an Italian community in Vancouver and now, in Toronto, lived in a small Italian neighborhood called the Ward. Mob territory, bootleggers, bookmakers, enforcers, 6 for 5ers and violence. Never heard of drugs or prostitution from any of the guys on Walton Street. I got to know a lot of fun guys who played craps on Sundays on an empty lot on Walton Street. They all liked to gamble, betting on horses, sports games and cards. Even in Vancouver, Italians liked the accordion and on Walton Street, Anthony was a famous accordion player in Toronto being busy working and going to school helped me to avoid law-breaking activities.

One Irish family on Walton Street had a reputation for touchiness and violence and another Italian family had the same reputation. They didn't like each other and kept their distance to prevent a feud. One thing about the Walton Street boys, they would fight everybody else in the world but wouldn't fight among themselves. One fellow from Walton Street had a beef with guys in Wasaga Beach and he arranged a gang fight for the following weekend. I heard that over 200 cars went to Wasaga Beach for a big battle that never took place.

I remember one evening Josh and I walked along the Danforth expecting to see a gang fight. Two guys jumped out from a dark entrance way asking "where you guys from?" Josh replied, "From the Ward." The spotter said, "Anybody from the Ward is okay with us" and he let us through, signaling the other spotters that we were from the Ward. One of the guys told Josh that they were waiting for the Parkdale gang to have a rumble. Josh said to me, "See what I mean, Reg, if anybody gives you a hard time just tell them you're from the Ward and they'll leave you alone."

Roncetti just came out of the army and lived in his father's house. His second floor little front room looked like an arsenal, nothing but all kinds of guns, knives and hand grenades. Sometime later he told me his father pissed him off so he threw a live hand grenade into the kitchen and laughed, saying, "never seen my old man move so fast; he just flew out the back door. 'Put-Tum' – you should see all the shrapnel all over the kitchen!"

Years later I met Roncetti while I was living on Spadina Rd. I told him about the tenants living in the Triplex next door. They wrecked the absentee landlord's building and they thought it was a big joke tearing the wooden railing of the front porch and throwing it onto the street and waiting for the oncoming traffic to see what happened. I passed off their behavior to the beginning of the drug culture. After all those years Roncetti still said, "If any of those wackos give you a hard time, let me know. I'll throw some hand grenades through the windows and fire a few rounds at the front doors and the windows and plaster the whole front of the house with bullets. That would teach those bastards a lesson." It's hard to believe that a slightly built, quiet well-mannered person didn't talk like a mob hit man but sounded like the recent movie character 'Rambo.' There wasn't too much difference between the old Japanese hard liners and some of the young guys living on Walton Street, all part of the Reptilian tribal consciousness.

Relating to the Reptilian brain, I finally lost my virginity living on Elm Street. I didn't brag or say anything to anyone about my first conquest like most of the guys did and it saved me a lot of embarrassment. She was oversexed and everybody in the area had sex with her. One other experience was a woman I met near the Bus Station. She needed a place to sleep for the night so I invited her to my room. The room was a good pad on the top third floor of the building and my parents and the rest of the kids lived in the back of the apartment on the main floor. She was a nice woman, about 30 years old who lived and worked in Windsor, Ontario and was just passing through Toronto to visit a relative in Bowmanville. She was very tired and promised to have sex in the morning. I can't recall if I had a good sleep or not but she kept her promise. She seemed like a decent person and open minded about sex so I asked her if my younger brother Bob could have sex with her. She was happy to oblige and Bob jumped at the chance to learn about the birds and the bees. I remember when I was around Bob's age, the greatest stress and anxieties I had was not knowing what a woman's vagina looked like. It was funny when I asked Bob, "Maybe we should give Richard a chance to have sex" and Bob quickly said, "oh, no, he's much too young, much too young.' Anyway, Richard was the handsome one and all my brother's friends would say, "Richard is so handsome he should become a movie star." Of course Richard was too young and I never felt sorry for him for missing this chance of having sex. According to these older women, sooner or later he'd have more than his share of girls.

Won Gee was an old Chinese man who was a tenant in the building. He had a pudgy face, a little on the heavy side, looked tough but had a good heart and an easy to smile personality. I guess he got lonely just cooking and eating by himself so he volunteered to cook for our family. Mom was happy; it was one less meal she had to make and we all loved Won Gee's cooking. Mom learned to cook Chinese meals by just watching Won Gee prepare the meals. Won Gee even educated us in nutrition. Every different soup he made he would say, It's good for the stomach, or heart, or kidney, or liver and some of the dishes were always food for some parts of the body after Won Gee left to work out of town in a restaurant, Mom kept making steamed fish the way Won Gee made it. I think Mom became a better cook than Dad in Chinese dishes.

A Japanese man who just came out of prison dropped in to see my Dad. They'd both spent time in the same concentration camp during the war. After the war he worked in a logging camp up in Thunder Bay. I don't know Japanese that well but got the general drift of their conversation. Apparently the foreman was abusive and wanted to fight Dad's friend, so he picked up an axe and raised it for a fight to the finish. The foreman dropped to his knees and begged for mercy. The man said, "Kimura-san, it was like drawing a Samurai's sword; once drawn, I had to draw blood." Dad was listening very intently, nodding his head and agreed with what his friend did. Later I told Dad his friend was crazy. Dad did agree I was born in a different country with different values but his friend abided by the "Japanese Code of Honor." So he just nicked the foreman's leg to draw blood.

Father gave me a job as a dishwasher in Lichee Gardens. They had one person washing pots and pans all day. I would have hated the job if I were that person. Lichee Gardens was a big restaurant seating hundreds of people and on top of that, a line of customers stood outside. Night after night, the lineup was one to two blocks long. I never saw lines of people waiting to eat in a restaurant, except for Giovanni's in Montreal. Mountains of dirty dishes brought in from the dining room by male waiters (the only female was the hostess) who threw the dirty dishes on a long counter made of stainless steel. Front, back and one side were a steel ledge six inches high to prevent the dishes from sliding and falling to the floor.

The other side was a wall where the stainless steel counter made an L shape turn towards the dishwashing machine and behind the machine, the counter continued to the wall where it made a 90 degree turn at the corner and continued to the other wall. The room was the perfect size for the U shaped counter and dishwasher, with a small table in the center for stacking extra clean dishes, to handle thousands of dirty dishes. Believe it or not, I enjoyed working with mountains of dirty dishes in front of me. It was a challenge for my hands to move fast. Near me was a round twelve inch diameter hole with a rubber rim around it, and as the pile of dirty dishes came pouring in, I would grab in each hand, different dishes and snap it on the rubber rim where the leftover food and sauce would shoot into the hole and throw the dishes into the corner. The man standing near the corner would stack the dirty dishes in a rack and push the rack of dishes into the machine. It was fun trying to create the sound and rhythm of a drummer hitting the rubber rim with the dirty dishes. The drummer act worked so well that the washing machine could not keep up with our speed. At the other end where the clean dishes came out, a man would slide the rack of dishes around the corner and stack all the dishes in separate piles and another person would take them to different parts of the kitchen. The only thing that slowed down the operation was the machine. They didn't make it fast enough. Working until 2 o'clock in the morning and attending classes at school during the day, people thought I was burning the candle at both ends and that was the reason my health broke down. One could add on the heavy smoking and breathing polluted city air didn't help either.

One day in Gym Class the guys were trying to work out on the parallel bars. They all looked big and strong but had trouble doing the dip. The starting point is the upright body between the two bars near the end; the hands grip each of the bars, bare arms straight, holding the body up in.... air. Swing back the feet and body almost parallel to the bars and then dip forward and the feet and the body swing down, elbows bent, the shoulders just above the bars, then swing back, straighten the arms, the body returns to the original position.

I had never worked out on a parallel bar and couldn't figure out why the guys were having trouble even doing the dip once. When my turn came to try out the bars I thought, "Geez, to do the dip 10 or 12 times should be easy." Unexpected shock; the first dip felt like somebody punched both the front socket of my shoulders and felt excruciating pain and the second dip felt like my arms were being ripped off the sockets and the third dip was done in an unconscious state. The pain in my shoulders was short lived but the tiredness and exhaustion of the body was long lived. I felt the tiredness even while resting and my body felt exhausted and trying to rest my tired body lying in bed was worse. Sleepless, feverish nights sweating, coughing and spitting out phlegm mixed with blood. I experienced a constant hellish condition of tiredness. I ended up in Mountain Sanitarium, which overlooked the city of Hamilton, Ontario.

During my ride to the Sanitarium, thoughts were wrapped up in "time." How short it is! It seemed like yesterday that my friend Roy Ozawa, two years younger, died with the same disease I had now. He talked to me about his love for music (piano) and the art of painting. As a kid, time seemed to pass so slowly and I could hardly wait to become a grown man. I realized that the first twenty years of my life was just a blip. I thought 100 years, 1000 years, were just a few blips in the eyes of the Corpus. In fact, the life of our solar system is only a bleep compared to the existence of some galaxies. Does it really matter if I died yesterday, today or 10000 years from now? Stars twinkling in the night sky died millions of years ago. Trying to understand finite and infinite time opened up a whole new can of worms.

I might have died like my friend Roy but a new antibiotic, Streptomycin, arrested my TB. It was a new drug and still had impurities that caused all sorts of side effects. Some patients went blind, others went deaf, and a few broke out in a rash and boils, but for me it made my stomach extra sensitive. I vomited every meal I ate for six months. The ninety shot treatment was cut down to 60 due to the side effect of upset stomach and what really helped was the X-ray showed the spreading shadow on my lungs cleared up and just a spot was seen on my left lung. The surgeon performed a simple operation collapsing my left lung to stop it from pumping and moving too much in order to give the thing a chance to heal. Two months after treatment, I was able to eat supper without throwing up and a short time later, I was able to keep lunch down and finally, after six months, everything I ate stayed down in my stomach.

All through this miserable ordeal my body weight dropped from 130 lbs. to 90 lbs. fortunate enough to regain some weight before leaving the Sanatorium and for most of my life I weighed between 105 and 110 lbs.

What a pleasant surprise when a young Japanese girl started working the ward making beds, dusting and cleaning the rooms and serving meals. She spoke very little English and I spoke less Japanese and yet we had fun trying to communicate. Occasionally she brought "Bento? A Japanese lunch box and seemed pleased when I enjoyed eating the rice, an item that was lacking in the Hospital meals. Shortly afterwards they moved me from the bedridden Ward to the Freedom Building. For the first time, I was allowed to walk about. I felt free walking to the dining room and sitting on a chair to have my meals and to take a stroll outside, breathing in fresh air, absorbing the natural heat of the sun. The softness of treading on grass and the scene of Nature's greenery lifted my spirit. After being cooped up in a bed for a year, the change in the style was a rebirth of life. On her day off, the little Japanese girl would visit me and sometimes after work she would drop by to say "hello." She wasn't little, almost my height, shapely figure and nice facial features. She always brought lunch and we enjoyed the picnic-like setting. Outside of the Freedom Building it looked like a large parkland with many shady trees, shrubs, and well looked after grass and park benches. It was the most perfect romantic place without a script. One evening we decided to sit on a park bench overlooking the city of Hamilton. Silently and stealthily, the shadowy darkness crept in and the city lights went on. I never thought Hamilton could be so beautiful with all its lights twinkling. The city disappeared, only a large egg shaped bubble shining and existing in the vast darkness. I put my arms around her waist and she moved closer, "With her head on my shoulders? Feeling the warmth of her body, my hand instinctively wandered up to feel her breast. Again a surprise. I just couldn't find and feel her breast. She liked the cheek to cheek contact but didn't like kissing. In my old age I think the mystery of the disappearing breast was the result of the girl turning slightly towards me, creating a bigger gap between my hand and her breast. What else could it be for a naive young man at that time?

The mind is a fickle thing. Six months before it was disturbed, filled with anxieties and the thoughts racing out of control and now meeting a wonderful, beautiful girl, my thoughts were dancing in the clouds. After spending two years in the Sanitarium, I left for good, never to return. My diseased lung was permanently healed without any further relapse. She visited me once in Toronto and after that her younger sister phoned me a few times, trying to be a matchmaker. How could I ever forget her loving spirit and kindness? My love and fondness for her lingered on for a long time in my memory. The partial collapsing of the left lung and the side effects of the drug treatment made me feel less than a whole person. The doctors told me not to do any strenuous work or activities. Losing my love for playing sports was just as bad as losing my girlfriend. Even worse, I felt handicapped and would not make a good husband so I told her, "Marriage is not for me." I thought to myself, "Maybe another life, another place, things might have been different." After a year or so she married some lucky guy. I was happy for her but still felt sorry for myself.

What gave me hope during the miserable times I had when I entered the Sanatorium and even after, was my interest in Eastern Philosophy, especially trying to understand the nature and reality of time. Within the limited and unlimited time of past, present, future and within the limited and unlimited space of gas, liquid and solid, all vaporized by visual reasoning into a

Universal Principle of motionless motion. Without motion, there is no time, space or substance. Consider a colored wheel of a chart, different rainbow colors painted on each spoke and as the wheel begins to turn and move faster and faster the colors begin to blur and then the wheel becomes a colorless vibe and as the wheel approaches infinite speed it disappears. At that speed "Time Warp and Speed Warp occur and when things slow down, the first could be last and the last could be first.

Visual reasoning is unlimited and has infinite potential to create (thoughts in action) reason and imagination help to network and integrate the interconnectedness of all minor and major principles manifesting as phenomena. This method is like trying to fit the pieces of a gigantic jigsaw puzzle and as more pieces are fitted into place, we get a glimpse of what the greater picture of reality would look like. Another good example is everybody only sees snapshots of the great flow of "Life of truth." It's like trying to understand a movie by seeing bits of the preview. Snapshots are momentary awareness of consciousness implanted into the brain and they occasionally arise to the surface, most of the time by reacting to feeling and memory. Between the snapshots are unknown realities, blind spots of unawareness, the origin of "Illusion of thoughts" constantly assuming partial and half-truths as the only whole truth. Blind faith is the result of too many blind spots. Most everybody has their own opinion based on partial truth, creating a value system of likes and dislikes. Recently, pop psychology and self-help books are explaining close-mindedness by using words like "Box, Tunnel Vision, Hardwired, Fossilized, Color Lens, Attachment, Self-Limit, and Self Indulgence." The brain goes through a super-complicated system to create a closed mindset and once it's hardwired it becomes a very difficult reality to let go. Ask anybody hooked on tobacco, drugs, sex, gambling, sweets, junk food and negative life styles. The power of thought, the power of perception, could change an existing reality to a new reality. To let go of the old mind set and to open the mind to a new mindset, words like "paradigm shift, alternative views, choices, emotional quotient, think outside the box help to break down the emotional barriers. Almost everybody self-indulges and when indulgence goes off balance and overboard, victims are born. Victims are forever at the mercy of the changing environment and the inner habitual mindset reacting to the environment like a puppet on a string. Emotional imagery of limited self creates a box of close-mindedness filled with self-service and self-indulgence which always create emotional disorders.

Emotional choices guided by common sense and common ground seem to get the best result for a balanced and orderly life style. Who or what makes the decision and choices.

Most say, "I make the choice." Others say, "God or the Devil", "I think therefore I am." Many thinkers call it the I am, Ego, Soul, Being, the list goes on. The Principle "Oneness of physical and spiritual helps to view the physical brain as a Spiritual Machine" and I believe in the advancement of "the Science of the brain" will validate that the material, spiritual, emotional, intellectual, instinctual and other aspects of the mind, whether active or inactive, exist in some section or compartment of the brain. The part or section of the brain that is most active structures the mindset and that's where the mind's eye, the choice maker, resides. If only the materialistic section of the brain is active and functioning, the mind's eye perceives reality as a physical existence. If the spiritual section of the brain is active, the mind's eye will lean towards a spiritual reality. In most cases, different sections of the brain are active and if the building blocks of the mindset, with "thoughts, voice and deed" are congruent, the mind's eye will find a balance and work in unison with the different parts of the brain. If the building blocks of the mindset are not in unity and harmony, the different sections of the brain will compete in a conflicting way and a dis-ordered mindset is structured. In extreme cases, the most weird and outrageous acts are committed by an unbalanced mindset.

Another way to not only activate and open new compartments of the brain and still avoid pitfalls of structuring and wiring a disordered mindset, is to practice and train the congru-ency of thought, words and deeds. The Brain Trusts Loyalty. Show loyalty to the brain and brain will show loyalty in return. Con men and cheaters think they are smart but they cannot fool or outsmart their own brain. Thinking things one way, saying it another way and then doing things whatever. Mindset filled with ambiguity, deception, secrecy and distrust leads to all sorts of emotional complication -- talking the talk and not walking the walk or making promises that are not kept. Self-syndrome limits the brains expanding awareness although within its own horizon it has limitless ability to create and unlimited ability to create illusion of thoughts. Unfortunately the Reality of Life exists and functions beyond the emotional barrier of Self-Syndrome. Wrapped up in the syndrome of self-limit, self-service, self-selection, self-deception, self-indulgence and other selfishness, the mind is blind to anything outside and beyond the self. This close minded self-syndrome is found in all strata of society. In extreme cases, individuals completely absorbed in emo-tional self-syndrome structures a disturbed mindset that would rather die than to receive help to change the perception of the mindset and some would kill rather than change. The most troubling situation is when leaders of powerful nations are emotionally self-blinded by the aphrodisiac of power and wealth to conquer and expand the Empire, caus-ing millions of people to suffer and die. Hopefully the day will come when humanity will avoid treating the brain as a piece of baggage and awaken to the fact that everybody's brain-body is the priceless jewel of the Universe.

For years I heard we only use three per cent of the brain. It seems a little high but the question is "How do we activate and awaken the rest of the brain", the inner dialogue of "Question and Answer" helps to build new pathways and activate the uncharted territo-ries of the brain. In some cases, the active section of the brain is hardwired in a comfort zone and whether it's good or bad becomes a difficult habit to let go. Congruency of thoughts, words and deeds may help the mindset to have greater freedom. This practice of congruency will help to rise above and transcend the fixation of emotional attachment to restriction and limitation.

Closed mindset	"I can't do it"
Open mindset	"How do you know you can't"
Closed mindset	"I just know I can't."
Open mindset	"Maybe you can or maybe not."
Open mindset	"If you don't try you'll never know."
Closed mindset	"I feel hopeless because I know it's hopeless."
Open mindset	"Maybe a little workable plan could help."
Closed mindset	"Plans don't work; it's a waste of time."

Open mindset   "What was that Chinese proverb" Something to do with a man who removed the mountain by starting to carry away small pebbles.

Closed mindset   "Chinese are dreamers; they like to pretend and fantasize."

Open mindset   "Maybe you like to fantasize making molehills into a mountain."

Endless dialogue, pros and cons, advantage, disadvantage, question and answer, cause and effect, until the mind identifies the old belief system. Reason to be together with new meaning and feeling will alter the old perception to a greater awakening

The wonder of the brain is never ending. Which would be easier -- to follow every snow flake that falls from the sky in a blizzard and track it to where it falls on the ground or to keep account of every nano vibe the brain receives from the environment and outer space and then to monitor, maintain and regulate the brain-body function 24 hours a day? Snow flakes, what a magical moment experience. A few days before Xmas just before it started to get dark, I turned a corner from a busy street and on the other side of the road was a dark brick wall of an old church was the background for the fresh falling snow. I stopped dead in my tracks, my mind stunned with silent stillness. Not one snowflake flickered or wavered out of place. All the snowflakes, evenly spaced, fell softly to the ground. It seemed like they were all tied to an invisible thread, sliding straight down. Time stood still till the rumbling noise of heavy trucks broke the silence. Seeing is believing, the closest thing to perfection.

Everything in motion appears to move in waves and cycles. It's amazing that with the union of two simple cells, humanity comes into existence. First to form is the so-called Reptilian brain, then the rest of the brain, organs and body parts follow. It's interesting to note the beginning and shaping of human life moves in a spiral path. Not too familiar words, "The movement of the Spiral Arm of a Galaxy." From Macrocosm to Microcosm, the movement is cyclical. I believe the growth and maturity of human emotion moves along the path of a spiral. Countless flat discs stacked together form the spiral with layers and layers of whirling and twirling energy we feel as emotion. Each complete emotional cycle of a spiral is habit forming. Old emotional habits become the resistance to stop new expanding and growing emotional maturity. It's the struggle of the old emotion becoming the new emotion and the new emotion becoming the old, climbing each step of the upward expanding spiral. I believe the greatest challenge to humanity is to find a path towards emotional maturity. The way the world is going we can't afford to be stuck in the lower emotional cycle of Self-Syndrome. Self-centered attachment, together with the intellectual section of the brain, working with the Reptilian, becomes a dangerous combination for emotional disorder and behavior.

The essential Life Force or Absolute Motion, the original cause of structuring the intrinsic and innate nature of the brain which creates a mindset or attitude with the building blocks of thoughts, words and deeds. Electricity seems to work in a similar fashion. It has a power source like Niagara Falls or Nuclear Power Plants with the infrastructure of turbines, generators, transformers, panels, wires, fixtures, etc.   Flip all the switches and it lights up the city. Many times to show that a cartoon character has an idea, the cartoonist will draw a light bulb above the head. Imagine the splendor of the inner brain with light bulbs decorating the emotional spiral stairway like the stars shining in the Galaxy.

Emotional imagery of self-limit creates a box of close-mindedness. The Box becomes filled with self-syndrome that will eventually lead to pain. Opening the emotional box will help to address the pain to gain. Again, the process, pain and gain, gain and pain, pain and gain, climbing each cyclical step following the course of the Spiral Stairway, achieving greater and greater emotional maturity.

Dance of the Ten Worlds

In the Oneness of the mind

    substance of the void

    reside the Ten Worlds

    riding the cycle of birth and death

Consciousness of the senses

    thoughts and feeling

    react and reflect

    the external phenomena

Battle of the boundaries

    limited or unlimited

    casting of attachments

    lesser self to greater self

Constant Change

    wavering attitude

    slipping and falling

    standing and climbing

Thoughts and feeling

    bio network of creativity

    structures and restructures

    the inner state of mind

Path of non regression

    fearless and hopeful

    forever growing

    awareness expanding

    Hell to Harmony

    moment to moment

    the true entity

    dwells in the eternal present

Reg Kimura

Seeking solutions is a positive action that will help to activate more sections of the brain. The book called the "Flow" talks about a man working on an assembly line. Such a boring job; each worker, I think, had something like 28 seconds to put some kind of electrical unit together. The man challenged himself to see how fast he could put the gadget to-gether. He studied in detail all the different parts and which one to start with and thought about eliminating unnecessary movements of his fingers, hand, and arms. He was motivated and became enthusiastic when he was able to assemble the unit in less than 20 seconds. He was not like most of the workers who were clock-watchers. Time went quickly for him. I believe his brain was becoming wired to solutions rather than to stay in an old fashioned comfort zone. He thought of a better position to earn more money by taking a course in electronics. I heard another story about a man who started to work in a small dilapidated hotel in Vegas. His job was to sweep the floors and clean the rooms. The man thought in detail about the best and most efficient way to sweep the floors and keep the rooms nice and clean. He was enthusiastic and enjoyed having a nice clean place. "Cream rises to the top." His alertness and keen awareness of things promoted him to become the manager of the hotel. I believe his brain was structured and wired to having the best serviced hotel in Las Vegas. His passionate emotion motivated him to learn and understand everything and even the smallest detail about Hotel Management and Tourism. Success breeds success and the man built and owns two famous hotels, "The Mirage" and "Treasure Island." I wouldn't be a bit surprised if he goes on to do greater things

In any human undertaking, "To think outside the box" will help to solve and overcome difficulties. Having detailed knowledge of the subject matter and an overview of other subjects that relate to the subject matter, the brain/mindset has much more data and thus better choices to work with and to reason out the best plan possible. Action to implement the plan is the solution. Good example is the New England Patriots football team. The management and coaches are so knowledgeable about the game and players that they see the smallest detail and don't miss a trick. Each player understands everything about the opposing team and knows exactly what they have to do to win. By game time the team is well coached and prepared to play their best game. All of the players picked by the management are team players not into ego-tripping and are able to focus on the solution of winning. Even when the team loses, the players don't cry and complain or make excuses by blaming each other. They learn by their mistakes and help each other to work as a team. Emotionally they are united in spirit and that is a hard combination to beat. It looks like this year, 2005, the Patriots have a good chance to win their third Super Bowl. Of course other teams will watch the films of the Patriots' Games and learn to improve their own game, pushing the game of football to a higher level.

In the reality of the phenomenon, the more we understand the Law of Causality, the greater the reasoning to make out a good game plan. If the plan is reasonable, feasible and believable it could be actualized like the New England Patriots winning attitude. This same procedure will help to overcome almost any problem of self-indulgence and addiction. If one really believes the project is reasonable and feasible, the natural emotion will be generated to reinforce the belief system. Emotional reasoning based on principles will develop a winning attitude.

We can't always win, but we can at least try to structure an emotional box within the mind with a winning attitude. If the box is prone to failure, having a negative attitude, it's best to think "outside of the box" to change things. The Comfort Zone is the result of attachment to habits. Sometimes to change even a negative attitude causes tremendous anxieties and stress and the mindset rather dwells in the emotional box of negativity. For the Comfort Zone of immature emotion to grow towards maturity is not always easy.

What's troubling is the weapon of mass destruction instigated by a mass emotional bureaucratic box. Bureaucracy runs through all organizations, institutions, Governments and even Empires. It's a necessary evil; in fact, I believe the brain itself is structured in a hierarchical bureaucracy. The institution of marriage is the smallest of all institutions. Reasoning and imagining outside of the emotional box networks the pathways of minor or major principles functioning in the brain, synthesizing the symbiotic nature of life to illuminate many of the blind spots to see a greater picture of reality and attain a greater emotional maturity. Snap shots and blind spots produce illusion of thoughts, the main reason for the breakdown in marriage.

Man meets woman

Woman loves man

Man woman marry

Man wakes up

Woman wakes up

"Stranger in the night"

"Bye Bye Black bird" love is blind

Many blind spots

The first step towards self-mastery is to overcome and conquer immaturity. Emotional maturity is the Master of aloneness and togetherness.

The medical profession has such an arterial blockage caused by bureaucracy inside the emotional box that many of the patients end up in a box. How they perform inside of their bureaucratic box is excellent but just surgery and drugs won't be able to handle the ever increasing diseases. They fail to think outside of the box and ignore other methods of healing like Alternative or Natural Medicine, Homeopathy, some helpful Technology, Science of Nutrition, ever improving psychology, etc. With the skyrocketing medical costs and disease on the rampage, they could become victims of their own self-imposed bully bureaucracy. Not too much difference between the Witch Doctors and the smoke of ecclesiasticism of the priesthood. Both are emotional control freaks, having fear of losing power over their followers, which would jeopardize their status and financial security.

They can't stand anybody questioning their emotional bureaucratic box. The age of specialization hinders educators from having an overview of arts and sciences. Educational freedom of thought that crosses the line, in other words, thinking outside the box, is restricted by other powerful institutions such as politics, economics, media, religion, military, unions, etc. The art of politics is balancing all the powerful institutions. Hate to see a theocratic government suppressing the freedom of religion and thought or a military government using force as the only way to govern. Nothing is perfect and I feel the Democratic Constitution of Canada and out neighbor, the U.S. is still the best of the rest. Sometimes it may go too far to the left or to the right but always has a chance to move towards the center. Fortunately, Britain and most of the European nations are stabilized in the Democratic process and unfortunately some countries have to be forced by powerful Democratic Governments to follow their system. The behavior pattern caused by the institutional emotional box is the same today as it was before recorded history. The plus side is we might not have survived without the Box and the future history will depend on thinking outside the box. It's really a dilemma of letting go of the box of emotional immaturity and by stages, climb the slippery slope of maturity.

I guess another way to structure a balanced mindset towards emotional maturity is to have an early start and train babies like puppies. Many wild animals are domesticated and make wonderful pets and companions. It was interesting to watch the people of a village in Guyana. I can't remember whether it was a person that helped a crocodile or a crocodile that helped a person, but the legend says that they made a pact that the villagers would not kill the crocodile for its meat and the crocodile would not eat the villagers. It was amazing to see the men playing with the tail of the crocodile and even sit down on its back. Babies carried in the arms of the men were exposed to the friendliness of the crocodiles as the men walked around and among the big crocs. What was funny was that the baby crocs were very vicious, snapping the big jaws at the trainer, who was an elder that tamed and domesticated the crocodile brain. I hear dolphin trainers have well behaved children. Study the animal kingdom and we could learn a few things about how to rear our own young.

It seemed like a coincidence that I caught part of a TV programme called "The Super Nanny." The Super Nanny goes into homes of families who have dysfunctional kids and observe both the Parents and the kids. She then spells out in detail how to handle and control the kids using the proper approach. She seems to use similar techniques to the ones dog trainers use. What an impact it would have on society if the teachers were taught and trained like the Super Nanny on the TV show. The energy and money should be spent on teachers who teach preschool kids. The classroom would be like on-job training held in the family's home. It would be much more effective in training both parents and kids in communication skills and family responsibility. When the kids grow older, education could continue with a smaller teaching staff to handle the easy to manage students. When these students become adults, I believe they would be well behaved, responsible, social citizens. The high cost of crime and punishment, wars with destruction and weapons of mass destruction would lessen and more money could be spent to develop a wholesome attitude in young children. It wouldn't be a bad idea to make it compulsory to teach

kids at home with their parents. Even immigrant parents and their children could participate in the program. Hopefully, the twenty-first century will be the Renaissance of peace,
education and culture.

Most of the people I have talked with about nutrition make it into a personal matter. Like
religion, it could become very personal. Clinging to partial and personal things make it
impossible to mature emotionally. My Doctor sent me to a hospital to see a nutritionist
who could help me with a diet for high blood sugar. Typical bureaucratic mindset, she
explained about calories, carbs, veggies and protein. She did give me good advice to
change my bad eating habits. The old fashioned food chart that looked like anyone's
guesswork was updated and looked like a common sense scientific chart. Occasionally
someone outside the profession would crossover and make an important contribution to
improve things. Scientists have found Hexagonal water the best water for humans to
drink. The water penetrates the cells more rapidly. The turnover replacement in a baby's
body is much quicker but slows down as the body ages. Might as well consider water as
an essential nutrient. Dehydration speeds up degeneration of the cells of the body. Hexagonal water with friendly minerals makes the body solution slightly alkaline. Alkaline
solution creates an oxygen environment and health professionals know that harmful bac-
teria virus and fungi cannot survive in an oxygen environment. Disease thrives in nitrog-
enous matter, especially animal waste. Many theories "all disease is the result of acid waste
clogging up the body," "lot of disease is the result of dehydration", "dehydration is the
number one cause of stress". I would say a lot of psychological problems created by stress
and distress cause unbalanced brain chemicals that wreak havoc on the body and mind.
The brain/body balance of acid and alkaline, water and salt including all the nutrients and
minerals to balance each other is as complex as the chaos theory. No two brains are
structured in the same way though many brains have similar tendencies.

According to the latest statistics, over thirty percent of the population in the U.S. is obese
and the way junk food is being consumed, it won't be long before we see a lot of fat
Asians, which means I'll have plenty of company. I'm 5'5" and 175 pounds; such a comfort zone to be fat and enjoying Big Macs. Gee whiz, you would think with my knowledge
of nutrition it would be easy to come up with a good fat loss diet and still maintain some
of the junk food and sugar sweet pastries in my diet plan. Gain is pain and my overweight
body is beginning to feel all sorts of painful symptoms of degenerative diseases. I don't
think I could let go of my fat food comfort zone but I would like to replace some of the
junk food with a reasonable, feasible, believable and doable diet plan. The goal is to lose
three to five pounds a year which makes me feel good just thinking about this easy plan
and hopefully, I'll live long enough to have a slim trim body when they lay me down to
sleep. When it comes to thinking about death, I always recall one of my favorite passages
from Eastern thought.

"New born baby utters a cry
Old man gasps and dies"

Sometimes thoughts pop into or out of my mind (life is a quest; death is a rest). Life is a series of breaths and within the breaths are essential elements that sustain life. Not only what we breathe in is important, but what we breathe out is just as important. Also, what we put into the mouth is important and what comes out the other end is just as important. Expansion, contraction, action, reaction, cause and effect, energy in motion, appear to be cyclical and binding separately the small and the big by layers and layers of energy like the blood brain barrier. Most everybody thinks I over generalize in my thinking, which I believe to be true due to my tendency to look for similarities, sameness and common ground rooted in Universal Principles. Filling the gaps with differences between and around and rooted in the symbiotic dynamics of Life and Reality. Just recently a believer in the Bible gave me reading material by a writer who professes to have the true meaning and interpretation of the Bible and that all Christian cults, sects and denominations don't know what they are talking about. It's amazing, the tremendous amount of energy, "Labor of love", the writer puts into his method of thinking and reasoning, going into the smallest and most obscure details to explain passages of the Bible to prove his way of believing was the only way to understand the "Truth of the Bible." Unfortunately, many thinkers, fundamentalists and theologians are attached to looking at the differences rather than the sameness and similarities. They get lost and trapped in the infinite fragmented and partial maze of all phenomena and fail to grasp the Universal Principles of noumena, building a superstructure of theological and philosophical thought on the quick sand of differences. From what little I read of St. Augustine, I believe to some extent he delved into the noumena of infinity and eternity, thinking outside the box of differences and observing and viewing the sameness of Reality based on Universal Principles. Spinoza understood the sameness of Reality using self-evident truth to define metaphysical principles and to validate the inseparability of metaphysical and physical reality, the oneness of body and soul, body and mind, body and spirit. Some Rabbis who could not see past their nose excommunicated him to eternal damnation and a few hundred years later they reinstated him back to the Jewish faith. If Spinoza were a Catholic priest, the Church might have created a new order of the Priesthood and a few hundred years later, canonized him. The Absolute Reality of eternity or infinity cannot be split in two or be separated. This means that immortality of the soul and eternal damnation of hell are nonsense. Even God cannot create something with a beginning that has no ending or create something that has no beginning and yet has an ending. God or human may clone a human but God or human cannot clone an eternal infinite God. Whether it's a critical mass theory or not, more and more people are able to think outside the "box of differences" and view a greater sameness leading one to attain emotional maturity for inner security and peace.

I think Albert Einstein said something like, "To crack the atom is easy. To crack prejudice is difficult." Keep cracking or splitting the finite particles no matter how small they become it's measurable and hence, finite. When the finite particle finally reaches a size that is not measurable it melts and disappears into a monoparticle. Like monotheism, the monoparticle is one infinite particle permeating all of the infinite space. It's only within the mind that the thoughts create division, separation, differences and limitation. Reality or fallacy -- there's no such thing as a finite infinite. Theological thinkers come to a final conclusion of monotheism. The existence of one and same spirit that fills infinite space and the same One Spirit exists in eternity, creator of all finite things both visible and invisible. The rhythm of the universe. The fusion of subjective and objective reality, the finite difference and infinite sameness. Involution: The differences that wrap up and shroud the sameness. Evolution: the unwrapping of the differences to reveal and manifest the sameness. The entity: the true individual is indivisible and undividable. Hence, all individuals have the same inner substance and common resources.

I would like to spell things out a bit more for the thinkers who are emotionally attached to different belief systems. Strong attachment to anything different leads to division and separation. Individuals and groups solely interested in self-service and self-interest sooner or later find themselves tangled up in conflict, chaos and the suffering of hell. Such as believing only and solely in different skin colors as the basis of human worth breeds racism. One bad act by a black skinned person creates an emotional feeling that all black skin is evil, ignoring and deleting other aspects of the human race such as all have red blood, we all have similar bone structure, cranium, spinal cord, two arms, two legs, two eyes, two ears, one mouth, etc. we see but we don't see the common ground overshadowed by negative emotions. Fear is the lack of understanding, transcending selective emotional differences helps to have greater vision and a deeper understanding that lessens fear and hellish suffering. Infidelity in marriage reaps emotional havoc in family relationships. If the couple would hang in and let go or transcend their own self-centered emotional attachment, a greater love is born. My friend Willy is so selective he ignores and deletes everything that is not compatible with his thinking and lifestyle. The only truth is the Bible (the Word of God), the only way to health is fasting (don't eat), the only exercise is outdoor labor (plenty of fresh air), the only music is the Golden Oldies (everything else is garbage), only only only … He finally listened to someone and began to change his tune about regaining health through nutritional diet and supplements, which is helping him to overcome the usual men's problems. If Willy used this same approach in matters of 'other things' instead of 'only things,' he could become one of the wisest men in the world. Once he catches on to both inductive and deductive thinking, he will leave no stone unturned. This flexibility and freedom of thought, like the strings of a violin, not too tight or too loose, will harmonize the middle way, pathway for humanity.

Houses

Father bought a sixteen room junker of a house on Spadina Road just south of Dupont Street. North of Dupont way up on a hill is the famous Casa Loma Castle overlooking downtown Toronto. I don't know how Dad managed to renovate the whole house by himself while working six days a week at his regular job at Lichee Gardens. The only time he asked me to help him was to nail the plywood on to the main floor kitchen. He told me how to do it and really stressed that all the nails should be no more than one half inch apart. When I did part of the floor, the floor looked like it was made of nails instead of wood and it was taking so long to nail a small section of the floor that I did my own thing, hammering the plywood with the nails two inches apart. One evening weeks later after Dad laid the tiles on the floor, he was sitting in the kitchen and as I walked in he said, 'See, the floor squeaks. You didn't hammer enough nails on the plywood. I told you to bang the nails in every one half inch. The reason Dad didn't finish off the job himself was because he thought it was only the furnace room below the kitchen and the people living in the basement apartment wouldn't be disturbed. I felt it was sort of out of character for my Dad to accept a careless sloppy floor job. I remembered that as an eight year old, a handful of rice spilled on the floor. Dad told me to clean it up and put the rice back into the bag. I thought I did a good job of cleaning up the rice but Dad was upset. It was an old house with worn out hardwood flooring full of tiny cracks between the boards. Three or four grains of rice stuck in the dirty old cracks. Dad was uptight and told me to make sure that every grain was removed and put back into the bag. At first I thought he was stupid over three or four grains of rice but then even Mom always made sure that when we ate a bowl of rice, not one little sticky rice was left in the bowl. Mom would stress the fact that poor people died of starvation in Japan. During depression there were never people dying of starvation in Canada. I believe none of the people of Japanese origin ever wasted or threw away one grain of rice. Dad mentioned that I should check the second floor long hallway for squeaks. The squeaking was so bad we all heard the noise from downstairs when people walked along the hallway. I really became aware that Dad did an excellent job. It was like walking on a concrete side walk. Dad built all the kitchen cabinets out of heavy plywood, sanded and varnished them. Many times he told me, 'one nail is holding up the L shape upper cabinets. One nail in the right place could hold up a ton. It didn't seem logical and he never told me where the nail was but I passed it off as 'Father knows best.'

After Father retired, he visited Japan to look up the family genealogy. He told me about 500 years ago one of our ancestors was a psychic monk who helped the police to capture thieves and murderers. Apparently in a trance, like meditation, he would locate where the criminal was and had the power to paralyze the victim until the police arrived. Father gave each of us a beautiful lacquered plate imprinted with three chrysanthemums, the emblem of the Imperial Clan. He said the more chrysanthemums, the higher the status. I chalked it off as our family tree, some women belonging to the concubine of the Imperial Court. I dropped a small heavy object on the lacquer plate and cracked it, so I threw it into a trash can. All my brothers and sisters except Richard were shocked at my careless attitude towards this family heirloom. Dad was disappointed and upset when the family Samurai sword was sold by one of his relatives in Japan. I would have cherished the sword. Anyway, Father not only brought back the recorded family genealogy but also a weak heart, result of having a heart attack in Japan. Bob took Dad to the Shute Clinic in Port Credit. The main Shute Clinic was in London, Ontario.

The Shute brothers belonged to the Royal Surgeon of Ontario and they administered 1600 international units of the brand Webber natural Vitamin E, plus a diuretic in case water accumulated in the lung. At that time they treated over 30,000 heart cases and never lost a patient. It seemed like 1600 Webbers natural Vitamin E was the silver bullet for heart cases. Two months later, Dad built a scaffold to reach the 2nd and 3rd floor and put aluminum siding on the front and side corners of the house. Shortly after, he dug up the front for a front entranceway to the basement apartment. I was surprised to see Dad, nearing 70 years of age, mixing sand, gravel and cement, pouring concrete steps and slabs and laying concrete blocks. He also made a new staircase going from the 2nd floor to the 3rd floor by using a pulley system to lift the stairway from the backyard to the 2nd story flat roof and with the same pulley system guided the staircase through the back door of the 2nd floor, and then put the stairway in place. He did all this work by himself and this was after his heart attack. Fifteen years later Dad died of a broken heart almost to the day a year after Mom passed away. Physically, Mom was a frail person but mentally she was strong willed. No one could deter her opinion or belief. The negative side was she was always nagging somebody who disagreed or didn't do what she wanted. Mom would be upset when Dad got involved in any business. Dad had a hang up about money, causing him anxiety which made him sniffle and edgy and Mom would always say Dad was happiest when he was working with his hands. Mom would always say Dad was stupid to get involved in business or any money matters. When Dad finished renovating the whole house it was a good income property. Mom got tired of tenants so as they left she never bothered to re-rent the apartments and the rooms. It got to the point that only the family lived in the big house. Dad was frustrated losing income from the rest of the house, yet Mom didn't care about lost rent money. She just didn't want any more tenants living in the house. However Mom was a good saver and only bought quality things at bargain prices. Mom didn't want Dad working high in the sky on top of the house so she got many estimates for a new roof and chimney. She finally found someone that did the job for next to nothing.

Thanks to my friend Willie, the Real Estate speculator, Dad bought another house from him on Strachan Avenue. I moved into the house; another junker with roaches and bedbugs. Alex and David, two of my friends moved in also. They were hilarious, like Laurel and Hardy, Abbott and Costello. Alex was tall and thin and David was big and fat. Alex was one of the sharpest, wittiest men around and Dave was just a big frustrated Jehovah's Witness who was a natural straight man for Alex. I was able to get a truck for them to do landscaping and other odd jobs as a business. They never did any job right but were so funny and comical that the customer kept laughing on the way to the bank to pay them. For twenty years they donated to me in billiards. They could never win and yet fantasized that they were better pool players than I was.

In his old age, Dad did a marvelous job in renovating Strachan Avenue. The second floor was designed in a Japanese style decor and Mom seemed content renting to Japanese students. I moved back into Spadina Road until my parents sold the property and fortunately Willie always had a place for me to live. With Willie around, I never had to pay rent most of my life.

Dad was remarkable. I doubt he ever slept more than three to four hours a night. Between his regular job and renovating his own houses, people would ask him to do some work on their properties. People liked Dad and he would go out of his way to help them.

Between times in his busy schedule, Father always participated in activities with the Japanese community. The Kisagari Club was doing theatre and as usual, Dad volunteered to paint all the scenery. At times, Dad worked and painted all night and then went to work in the morning with no sleep. We couldn't go into the cleared living room. Most of the time the whole floor was covered with sections of the painted scenery; there would be a different scene there every time. It looked like a big production. No wonder he spent all those nights working. Once I saw him painting a tree and he said, 'It's going to look like a real tree.' Dad enjoyed painting water color pictures. Two or three times he mentioned a famous Japanese painter who painted humans that looked so real people were fooled. When Dad was a boy he won a competition in painting in his prefecture. He also said that if he'd known at that time that a great artist would become immortalized he would have pursued a career in painting. Dad did beautiful work with wood and made a stool for my Peruvian friend George. He made me a small cabinet 12' x 10' x 8' with no nails. There were secret drawers and compartments which I also gave to George. George has handicraft stores selling mostly items from South America and really knows and appreciates handcrafted artwork. He's still in awe about the stool Dad made for him and says, 'I would not sell it even for $1000.

Mom would be upset when Dad did charity work for the Japanese community. She would say, 'You are killing yourself doing all that work for nothing and people will still criticize and badmouth you. It's not worth it.'

Dad enjoyed politics. He liked working for the Liberal Party. When a Nisei lawyer had trouble trying to get a charter for the Japanese Community Centre Dad went to Ottawa and obtained the Charter right away. Dad was happy Ottawa gave him the red carpet treatment by whisking him immediately into the office of the Prime Minister, Lester Pearson. Dad became friends with Walter Gordon, the Finance Minister. Later, Father tried to help Japanese fishermen on the West Coast.

It had something to do with herring eggs. The Japanese considered herring eggs laid and embedded on seaweed a delicacy. Tons and tons of herring were used to make fertilizers, but as caviar it was much more profitable and beneficial to Canada. Dad lacked the know-how and connections of the feudalistic business institutions of Japan to close the deal and naturally he and his fisherman friend were squeezed out of the picture. Dad did obtain a Federal Charter and Walter Gordon, the Finance Minister, told Dad to go to the East

Coast to see if he could start the herring business. When Dad found an ideal location where herring came to lay eggs, the water was too polluted. None of my brothers knew anything about business or economics, so the Federal Charter was just a waste.

The Sei Cho No I Ye believers needed a charter to build a church. Dad met Senator Croll who okayed the teaching but in those days' people of Japanese descent were the defeated enemies and the government didn't exactly go out of their way to help us out. I feel Dad would have been an excellent ambassador for any country.

Mother was a beautiful, charming and a friendly person who could have easily been popular with the women in the Japanese community. What stopped her was in some issues she was quite outspoken, often had a frank and blunt manner of speaking one of Mom's favorite pastimes was playing Japanese rummy game. The ladies in a Japanese Social Club, knowing Mom loved the rummy game, would keep inviting her but she never bothered going. She didn't like some of the people. Mom would meet a lady friend regularly on a weekly basis to play rummy. They both seemed to hit if off well, chit chatting, laughing and giggling. When they didn't play cards, Mom and her friend would go to a special place for lunch.

To me Mom was one of the most intelligent and wisest persons I knew. She never gave me a bum steer and I think she was seldom wrong. Many things she said, I didn't want to hear and I regret not following her advice. Sure she ragged me but for a good reason. I was out of line. Recently Naomi told me, "Mother thought her father was the most intelligent man in the world." Maybe Mom learned a lot from my Grandpa.

As time went by, my sisters and brothers gradually began to move out of the house on Spadina Rd. rooms became empty and Mom still didn't bother renting them. Dad finally accepted the fact of coming home to an empty house with no tenants except for one man living in the big basement apartment. Mom \couldn't nag or pick on Dad about not having enough money and they actually stopped fighting over money. As a youngster, I saw Mom and Dad fight many times but I can only actually recall four times. Mom would throw things at Dad and Dad would throw Mom on the floor using Judo and then slap her around yelling and screaming. Once Dad pushed Mom out the front door into the cold night wearing only a nightgown. Dad's anger was controlled to where he never really hurt Mother. Dad is the one with all the battle scars. As a child, it was a terrifying experience to see them fight. They argued a lot by screaming and yelling which made me feel like I was living in a war zone. Even when I was older screaming and yelling caused me stress and anxieties.

Their screaming and yelling caused me intense anxieties. Coming home one day in Mount Forest, Mom was laying on the kitchen floor in a fetal position. I thought, "Enough is enough" and confronted Dad on his stupid violent behavior. He swung the back of his hand to the side of my face. For eighteen years, Dad had never hit me and this time I don't know whether his hand touched me or not. It felt like the whiff of a momentary breeze or a mosquito just before landing. If Dad used a samurai sword he would have split a grape in half without drawing blood. Father showed regret and a new fear in his eyes and he begged me to speak to Mom. Before I could put my hand on Mom's shoulder, she said, "I'm okay Reg, I'm okay." I told Dad matter-of-factly, "Mom is okay" and saw the look of relief on his face. I felt good leaving the house, knowing "all is quiet on the home front."

Doreen was the first to leave the family home on Spadina Rd. partly due to the fact she just couldn't get along with Mom. She found a place in housekeeping job which gave her time to take a course in nursing. After graduation, she worked as a nurse at the Toronto St. Michael's Hospital. She got engaged but marriage was not in her cards. Her life was drawn to the Great Rocky Mountains. She ended up living in Calgary, upgraded her nursing career and worked in the cardiac ward at the Foot Hill Hospital. After retirement she still continued to the love of her life, skiing in the winter and golfing in the summer. Even with the rocky relationship with Mother, Doreen still managed to lead a good life. Her recent new adventure is mountain climbing. "Lessening of Karmic Retribution" falling by climbing, only a minor injury. Involved in one of the Buddhist practices, she appeared to have overcome some of her inner demons. Old age is catching up to us and we both hope "Life begins at eighty."

Naomi, the youngest sister, was quite the achiever. Intelligent enough not to argue or disagree with Mom. Had the knack of not rocking the boat. Always friendly to Mom's criticizing or complaining about things. At an early age she went to Boris V Studio to take ballet classes. Mom showed concern about Naomi's bleeding toes, blood soaked shoes and the damaging aches and pains all the athletes in training go through. Mom told me where she finally found the best shoes for Namoi to dance on point. She explained to me all the style and position and movements of ballet that sort of went in one ear and out the other. I didn't have any interest, thinking it was a girl thing. Mom put her heart and soul into encouraging Namoi during the early years but when Naomi became a teenager, I saw her develop confidence and a mature attitude as a ballet trainee. After Mom died, Naomi told me, "Mom always wanted to be an actress." It surprised me; I should have known better. I'm always grateful for Mom who had to drag me to see Naomi dance at her final recital for Volka Studio. I was impressed with her performance and yet had no interest in her dance career. Now I kind of regret it. I believe Naomi was the first girl of Asian background to dance for a Ballet Company in Canada and later the first Canadian girl of Asian origin to dance on Broadway. She was also the first Asian girl to dance on TV specialty shows. When Naomi danced at the palladium in London she received an award from Royalty as the leading dance performer. Not too long ago, she received an award from the late Pope John for being a good active member of the church. Naomi was not a famous dancer but was well known among the professionals. She married a Bostonian Irishman who was not a good dancer but looked like a dancer type. Naomi kept dancing but he quit and, with a friend, started a restaurant in the theatre district. When Naomi stopped dancing she worked in the office of the Metropolitan Opera House. Tragically Jim died of Cancer. Naomi took over the restaurant and made Barrymore's into an institution. Restaurants come and go in New York City and after thirty years, Barrymore's will come to an end. Naomi is a strong believer in prayer and raised a son and daughter who are now both married with their own kids. Naomi is still a cheerful happy person and all the success she had in life was earned and well deserved.

Bob was the average one, a good normal working Canadian. Worked as a postal clerk sorting mail and was quite active with the Postal Union. He married a Nisei girl and had a son and two daughters. They all grew up and got married and Bob has plenty of grand-children. Like all his brothers, he like sports and still plays golf as a senior.

Age-wise, Richard is just over a year younger than Bob. He didn't like academic schooling but managed to take a course in a sheet metal at George Brown College. Richard had the good fortune of having a capable partner who made their sheet metal business a great success. Richard also married a Nisei girl and has a family of one son and a daughter. Both of them are going steady and it looks like they would tie the knot in the near future. Like Bob, Richard enjoys playing golf and recently won the Ontario Senior Golf Cham-pionship. I believe Richard is the first man of Asian background to win that tournament.

Wayne, the youngest, graduated from Central Tech High School and is quite talented in graphics. He won prizes, one of them a design for a candy bar wrapper. He did well as a commercial artist and later as image-maker for corporations until computer graphics took over. It took some time for Wayne to adjust to the new technology. Like his other broth-ers, he loved the game of golf. He played in a foursome for Ontario, playing against the other provinces for the Wellington Cup. The first player of Asian origin to play in the amateur Provincial Tournament, Wayne and I married Caucasians and both our marriages ended in separation. His only son made the PGA. Unfortunately the kid injured his shoul-der in a car accident and Wayne will never know if he would have become a touring Pro. What little it means. I'm surprised my siblings were pioneers.

As for me, like my brothers I played golf but on a snooker table. Sub-cultured, unor-ganized, scrubby, relatively unknown game of Billiard Golf, and yet it's played throughout the U.S. and Canada. Never won a tournament, only money. I believe I was the only person of Asian origin to travel in the United States and Canada to play Billiard Golf. Not quite a legend but on any given day the best in the World.

After leaving Hamilton Mountain Sanatorium, like most young people I didn't know what to do with my life. I took a course by working and studying for a Chartered Accountant Firm and only lasted a year. Partly due to my weakened health, I lacked the mental focus and stamina to grind out a touch C.A. course and besides, at that time I had no interest in accounting and keeping track of other people's money. Had a natural flair for philos-ophy and the ordeal in the Sanatorium, experiencing the nearness of death and the fragility of life, I just couldn't go on living without trying to understand the basic question of life and death and to know the reason why I'm here in the first place. Seeker of the truth, like a sponge my mind soaked up the ancient philosophies and religions of India and incor-porated a framework of Hindu Metaphysics to validate any teaching. Talking and refuting people's religious views using metaphysical principles was like talking to a blank wall. My Yoga teacher warned me that people would think of me as a queer fish so I avoided saying too much. It makes me chuckle when I think I sound a bit like a fundamentalist arguing about any subject.. Mother understood, this trait comes from her side of the family. She told me, "Reg, even if you're wrong, if you believe it to be right, stick to your guns." Non attachment appealed to me but I was not aware of "attachment to nonattachment." Outside of doing odd jobs, I tried to fulfill my ambition of nonattachment aimlessly going nowhere like a floating piece of wood.

To help Dad with the mortgage payment and to avoid Mom's nagging, I listened to brother Bob's advice and worked in the Post Office for a couple of years. Letter sorting was a boring job and if it weren't for a bunch of fun guys, I would have quit after a week. The shift started in late afternoon to 1 o'clock in the morning, not quite the midnight shift. The whole place looked ancient, worn out, shabby, but came alive with the clicking of the stamp machines, guys talking, joking and laughing and always somebody looking for the bookmaker (only bookie I know that went broke). With all the hustle and bustle some of the guys avoided work by killing time in the washroom or walking all over the floor pretending to be busy doing nothing. Others stood around complaining about the work, money and life in general. The P.O. hired an efficiency expert to improve productivity and I presume he didn't do much good. Eventually what helped was hiring women. One tall blonde guy was a workaholic. I thought nobody was faster than me sorting mail. One time the blonde was sorting mail beside me, with his large hand scooped up 3 or 4 times the amount of letters stacked in trays, I held them like a deck of cards, dealing the letters into square pigeon holes specifying the towns for distribution in Ontario. He didn't appear to be moving his arm fast but the timing and the smoothness of rhythm seemed effortless. He also had the advantage of a longer arm to reach the furthest corners of the distribution box without missing a beat and those precious seconds made the difference. If it had been a short furlong horse race he would have beaten me by a nose and if it were a longer race, like a mile and a half, he would have been lengths ahead. Near the end of the night, he would go around helping other clerks to finish sorting the letters.

Years later, no longer with the Post Office, I met one of the old timers who told me the blonde became the head supervisor of the Department. I respected the man's ability and thought he should have been the Attorney General of the Post Office. Every Friday night after work was a full house fun time. We always had 7 to 8 players to go over to the house on Spadina Rd. to play poker. It was an ideal room in the basement of a back addition, separated by a hallway and stairway from the rest of the house. Card games could get pretty loud and rowdy but nobody, including my parents and neighbors, could hear us. We played dealer's choice and most of the guys loved to play high-low split games. Quarter limit with three raises and the last card 50 cents with three raises. It was a miracle. Hershel the hat and I won money every week. Nobody really understood the lowball hands and Hershel was Sitting Bull and would not play a hand unless he had a cinch. Sitting Bull did not have any feathers on his worn out fur hat nor did he smoke a peace pipe, but always had a hand rolled cigarette that never left his mouth and at times burned his lips, making him spit out the sparks. The other Harry, "the Horse" and Abe the rain maker never won and the rest of the guys took turns winning and losing. Winning and losing is a phenomena that makes life interesting.

Mother was getting on my nerves, constantly picking and nagging me to death. Didn't blame her since I never lasted too long on any job. The years at the Post Office was the longest job and even though there were fun times with the guys, I just couldn't see myself sorting mail for the rest of my life. With Mother's temperament there was no way of bumming around until retirement. Meanwhile sneaking in and out of the big house, going to bed in the wee hours of the morning and sleeping in until noon was a great schedule to avoid Mom and it supposedly suited my nonattachment lifestyle. Little did I know, slowly but surely I was beginning to be drawn into the World of Billiards.

Toronto the Good, the good old days. Downtown buildings larger than life made from stone, brick and cemented. When the air was air and the food was food. And ah, the music. Men were men and women were --- things were changing.

Generally speaking women did not swear and did not drink, did not have sex -- well not until they got married -- and did not go into pool rooms.

Pool rooms, the last bastion of male chauvinism. Basement poolrooms were called "Dugouts." Queen and Bay, Bay and Dundas, two Dugouts. Inside it looked dingy. The walls and ceiling were sooted with years of smoke. The air smelled of cigar and cigarette smoke mingled with stale air of yesteryears. Pool tables, benches, chairs, some pillars and well-placed spittoons was the decor.

The sound of clicking and the banging of balls marred occasionally by coughs, hawking and spitting. Friendly fire chewing tobacco stains the floor around the spittoons. From this fertile ground emerged the most fascinating, fabulous games of stick and balls. Round balls in different colors on green tablecloth enhanced by spotted lights.

Like moths consumed by light, gamblers, common thieves, judges, bookmakers, entrepreneurs, artists, laborers gather together to watch or play in the ritual of the only game in life.

The fishes play and enjoy the game. They laugh, they cry, they swear and even pray, you name it. It's the lingo of winning and losing. The pool sharks prey on these fishes. Sometimes a shark will duel with another shark. Some shark will go from poolroom to poolroom; others go from city to city. Few go to another country searching for fishes and sharks. They are like the gunfighters of the old west wanting to be the best or to win the money. From this vast sea of competition come the depth of understanding and the richness of the person and the game.

Enter the Shark Killer. Master of the Game George Chenier. Inducted into the Canadian Sports Hall of Fame.

Cliff Thorburn, the first person outside of England to win the world Snooker Championship and also the first person to have a perfect game in a championship match.

John Bumps Johnson is the Tiger Woods of Billiards.

Paul Thornley is the Guru of Billiards. Knows all the games and all the shots.

Played my first game of pool in Mount Forest. The corner building had a variety store and inside behind the store, separated by a wall, was a pool room with six small tables. To the right of the back wall was an entrance way with the swinging shutter doors you see in western movies and as you walk in to the right was an open archway to a separate room that had two small snooker tables. It was warm in the pool room, an ideal place to hang out during cold weather. I remembered a couple of guys, one was toothless, and both were overly friendly, trying to talk me into playing a game of pool for a nickel. Didn't enjoy playing the game, it wasn't physical enough. Besides, I was a novice and handling the cue stick was awkward, like a guy trying to eat with a chop stick for the first time. However, it was interesting to watch, trying to figure out the overall game of pool.

The next place was in Toronto. After getting to know the guys living on Walton St., the Dugout was just around the corner near Bay and Dundas, a favorite place for the gathering of the clan. One day I went there early and the place was empty except for the owner. In comes this stranger, stomping down the stairs and asked me to play just for table time. Never mind the surprise; he shocked me, making seven red balls and seven blacks. He seldom missed and kept making balls after balls. After the initial shock, it was a fascinating treat to see him clear the table. He knew I was stunned and he had that famous clinched toothed grin with a guttural raspy laugh coming through his teeth. He introduced himself as Donny. Of course years later on I heard most of the fellows say, "Donny Reeves is a Legend."

When we moved to our new family home on Spadina Rd, Walton Street boys and the Dugout became history. I started to go to Bloor and Yonge, a new meeting place called the "Cue Billiards." Met some familiar faces from BC when we lived in the Ghost Town during the war. My Nisei friends weren't exactly pool sharks but were good poker players. Spud and Harry had a suitable place to play cards, only a block away from the "Cue." It was really handy for the guys to meet in the poolroom. Playing poker with my Nisei friends wasn't like playing with the guys from the Post Office where I could win every week. I couldn't win and the losing streak continued week after week. I thought, "Am I this bad or are these guys that good?" Then I caught a guy making a move and realized I was not playing in an honest game. The person who was winning every week, whenever he played a hand, I would fold my cards and drop out. The players that never won eventually stopped coming and the card games broke up after ten weeks or so. Hanging out and playing a bit of snooker, I got to know John Johnson (Bumps). He was black and an alcoholic but what a privilege it was to watch and learn from Bumps. I would sit and watch him play for hours and it took me a long time to know how really good a player Bumps was. I learned the tricks of the trade of a pool hustler from him. What really happens on a pool table with a cue stick and the balls, who knows? Some knowledge of Quantum Mechanics might help.

Win the money, "Win the Bag" was the local pool room near my place on Spadina Rd. had no choice but to win the money in order to buy cigarettes and coffee, hamburgers and fries, rice pudding and pies. Everybody enjoyed the food in the restaurant above the pool room. The place was a fantastic hangout for guys and dolls and sharing food and talking with the local girls and guys was much better than facing Mom although I missed her home cooking.

Willie went broke again and had to go back to work in real estate. He was a type of guy whenever he made big money he would stop working and play around until it was all gone. I remember once he was down to his last thirty dollars, wondering if it was enough to cover the food cost having steaks and Chinese vegetables at Lichee Gardens. The girls were having a fabulous time eating and Willie seemed to be having a good time but I was too nervous to enjoy the food wondering if thirty dollars would cover the cost of the dinner.

When Willie went back to work he always managed to have a brand new Cadillac. Operating without money was always a tough start for Willie. At times he had to hide the Cadillac from the sheriff who was looking to confiscate his car. Sometimes I put fifty cents worth of gasoline in his caddy and split a sandwich with fries for a meal. Willie was an amazing operator in a few weeks he would have money and kept driving himself to make the big dough. Chumming with Willie, the night hawk, made me a night person. He would drop me off at home just before daybreak. I don't know how he did it, keeping irregular hours, and still made big money in Real Estate. Time wise we were predictable, sneaking into the house in the wee hours of the morning and around noon having coffee and breakfast in the restaurant. Then I'd give Willie a wakeup call (he had to work sometimes) and go downstairs to practice or play somebody a game of pool. Steve was a young friendly Hungarian kid about my height who came into the poolroom and wanted to learn to play snooker. He could barely make two balls in a row and at least I made three or four balls. We agreed on a handicap game where he could shoot any ball and I had to shoot according to snooker rules. Altogether seven colored balls, the red is worth one point, yellow – 2, green – 3, brown –4, blue – 5, pink – 6, and the black – 7. Highest score wins so it's a big advantage for players to make blacks, pinks and blues. The 15 reds are stacked in a triangular cluster between the black and the pink ball area. In my case, I had to have the cue ball among the cluster of reds in order to make as many blacks or pinks as possible to score high points. At the beginning it was no contest and Steve didn't seem to mind losing his money. Day after day, week after week and month after month, his game was improving. Since he didn't have to shoot a red ball only worth one point and had the choice of shooting as many blues, pinks and blacks, his score mounted up pretty quick. Once in a while he was able to run up to 50 points. Thank heaven my game improved to a new level to where I was making a lot of points.

One day, walking towards the pool room, Steve came running alongside of me. He was smiling and looked cheerful and then he stopped, stretched his open arms into the air while looking to the sky, "Reg! God and the angels gave me a beautiful hooker to look after me. They blessed me." I felt uncomfortable thinking a nice guy like Steve was a pimp. Principles were clear but morality was vague. I thought, 'Who am I to judge' and passed it off as bad or good Karma.

We usually played for half a dollar or a dollar a game. Now that he latched onto a hooker, he had more than enough money and wanted to play for more money. In those days, playing for ten or twenty dollars was big money. As a kid training in Kendo, I thought of fighting with a real sword to kill or be killed. Even at such a tender age, I realized not to be nervous or scared of dying, otherwise I would choke and not be able to do my best. Gambling for money over a game of snooker wasn't as terrifying. I was now gambling with Steve where he had a chance to win. I couldn't afford to make many mistakes and had to forget that I was playing for big money. I avoided thoughts of losing the rent money or not having money to buy a meal or going into debt or just being branded as a loser. I emptied my mind of negative thoughts to relax and then concentrated a small spot of silent stillness in the mind and then softly, slowly, expanded the concentrated spot to the size of the table. The lights above heightened the vivid clarity of the red and colored balls against the background of the green table cloth. The cushion railing with the six pockets limits and walls in the playing area. In this altered state of mind every little detail, the imperfection, the tiniest flaws, specks of dust, fluffs that cover the miniscule hills and valley of the green terrain are all magnified. In the zone I could do no wrong.

Remarkably, Steve was still improving his game and with the advantage of being able to shoot at any ball he made a lot of points. Amazingly enough, restricted by snooker rules, I began to make bigger runs of 60, 70 and 80 consistently and on rare occasions ran over 100 points. Steve kept smiling even when he lost and once he had a heavy loss he laughed it off saying the money was sent to him by the angels in heaven. A pimp talking like a priest. What kind of karma is that?

Playing Steve every day for hours and hours laid the foundation and development of my ability to control the cue ball. Fifteen red balls and six colored balls clutter up the playing surface of a small snooker table. The area just above the black ball spot is so small and compressed that all the billiard balls look like big bowling balls. Each ball seems to be encroaching on the other's territory, hardly any room to maneuver the cue ball.

A fraction of an inch off with the cue ball and the next shot cannot be made. It was essential to have pin point control to beat Steve. "Master Touch" helped me to make a lot of black balls and sometimes it looked like I was playing a game called "Black Ball Only." Steve's cue ball control improved but still lacked the finesse to overcome my game.

The "Master Touch" is a difficult thing to explain. In a great pressure game the majority of players choke and cannot perform the way they want to. When the player chokes, the brain scrambles and the muscles freeze, ready for fight or flight. The flexibility and smooth movement of arm, hand and fingers that control the cue are lost. It's a must to relax the mind and body. I try not to think about the money, winning or losing, or the consequences. Empty the mind and then focus on the silent stillness and not fight against the pressure of a choked mind and concentrate on allowing the choked mind to release all tension and pressure of dark energy of the muscles piping into a flow towards the elbow. Now all the attention is on the vice like grip of the muscles of the elbow, ready to explode and strangely enough the rest of the arm and body is forgotten, falling into a relaxed state. The first movement of the cue to move forward is the soft and slow, ever so slow, loosening twitch of the elbow muscles, the forearm and hand barely move. The forward motion of the cue is one eight of an inch or less and it's tricky if you want to move the cue the width of a thin sheet of paper. The control of the cue striking the cue ball is dictated by how much, how little, how slow and how quickly the choked elbow muscles loosen and release their tightness. Under extreme pressure, the deliberate choking of the elbow muscles seldom let me down.

Steve told me he was going away with his girl and I never saw him again. All good things come to an end and "Win the Bag" became quiet. I might have been a big fish in a small pond and wondered what it would be like playing in a big pond downtown... Playing on the big table was like playing on the football field. Aiming with the cue on a long shot the object ball looked like it was a mile away. Playing position was much easier, the cue ball seemed to have more room and freedom to move about. In two weeks I'd adjusted to the big tables and felt comfortable playing. The downtown poolrooms had location, location, location and business was much better for the owners and the players. Bumps was right: more money to be made downtown.

Bumps taught me the no, no and yes, yes of poolroom life. Fitting into the downtown scene was gradual. The strength of my billiard game was golf. Touch overcomes putting ability and, as on the golf course, the old saying goes, "Drive for show and put for the dough." Most Snooker golf games are sociable where seven to eight regular players get together to play during the afternoon. The games break up when the players go home to have supper with their families. The game is deceptive, looks simple enough, but playing with a group of guys, it's far more complex than snooker. Good Snooker players lose their shirt not realizing its like going through a mine field. Every evening, the Top Guns in Snooker were having a round robin series. I asked the Hall of Famer, George Chenier what he thought of Billiard Golf. He said he "just didn't like the game." When he was younger he played a bit but he had no patience and had a temper. Golf was just a no no for George. Before they inducted George into the Hall of Fame, he was a legend in the US, UK and Canada. You name it, Snooker, Pea Pool, Skiddles, Number Balls, Billiards on the big table – George was king. Later when I went through the States, the old timers in the pool room would ask me, "How's the King? How's the King?" I was fortunate enough to be able to talk to him and watch him play. Nobody had to tell me he was a Legend. In his old age he was frail but he was still a giant of a man stroking the cue.

When things slowed down at night, I would shoot up to the "Win the Bag." New young faces started to come to the room to play Snooker. They seemed and enthusiastic about the game. The kids were great, educated, articulated, they loved to talk about Snooker and the Hustlers game. Many a night upstairs in the restaurant, I listened to their stories about love life and carefree life style.

Willie would always drop in after work between 10 and 11 o clock at night. Sometimes we played a few games of pool. Other times we talked to the local guys and girls upstairs in the restaurant. Willie, as usual, had a new Cadillac and every so often had to hide it from the Sheriff who was trying to snatch it away from him. Willie thought the whole world was crazy and he loved the freedom of driving around when everybody else was sleeping, having the whole road to himself. The local guys and dolls enjoyed riding in his big caddy hot summer nights along the lakeshore where it was ten degrees cooler. Westhill to Burlington, Willie would turn on the car radio and make everybody listen to Country Western and Golden Oldies.

He hated the new era of Rock and Roll, Elvis, the Beatles and the Hippie Drug movement.

Roy, a Nisei friend, was in the restaurant with a beautiful girl. Roy is a good jazz pianist and introduced Dini, a pop singer. Enigma, dilemma, an alcoholic songstress. Willie, an opinionated perfectionist, thought Dini looked like Elizabeth Taylor. Like most Irishmen, "drinking is the way of life" but was surprised when Dini drank a gallon of homemade Italian wine. Dini never passed out but we had to help her to the car and drive her home. Willie would joke and laugh about "Dini the Lush" saying, not too many women and maybe even his old man could have handled drinking a gallon of wine. Dini lived near the Pool Room and invited me to her house only on Sundays. She never drank on Sundays. "See Reg, I'm only drinking apple juice." She was enamored of a book titled something like, "the Life or Ideals of Radi Krishnan." Since we were both sober on Sundays she liked discussing Yoga and Eastern thought. She appeared to be fascinated by my lifestyle of nonattachment and thought of me as a Golden Buddha with a golden cue. She was way off the mark although I did think I was the man with the golden arm. Her belief was based on emotional intuition and sometimes at a deeper level she strayed away from Universal Principles. If a notion or intuition cannot be validated within the frame work of Universal Principles, for me its fiction. Dini became a vegetarian, having whole grain bread, a variety of nuts, raisins, tofu and other natural foods. She served fresh juices and fresh garden salad with nourishing care and tenderness. I felt her fondness like my Mother's love for me. At that particular time I thought all that good fortune would not help my health because I was smoking like a chimney.

Femme Fatale only on Sunday, her two drinking boyfriends Joe and Al were not allowed to enter her house or see her on Sunday. Sitting in the living room talking to Dini, a person comes through the door without knocking, walks into the living room and without saying a word goes into the back kitchen and out the back door. I thought "this is strange' and before I could ask, Dini explained that the man was a good musician, an old boyfriend a nondrinker. He came over, realized she had company and left. This scenario happened with a few different guys. It was weird.

It was such a nice day, I decided to walk to Bloor Street to meet some friends. On the next block, just around the corner from the poolroom, I bumped into Joe and the first thing he said was, "Not you, Reg. Don't tell me she's got you hooked. You're hooked on Dini." I told him he didn't know what he was talking about. He went on to say Dini cast a spell over guys and at least two dozen guys were hooked on her. Reg, why do you think I'm hanging around here for? I'm waiting for Dini to open the front door so I can be with her. Crying the blues, he mentioned his drinking buddy was in the house having Dini all to himself and was sick and tired of Al always saying, "Dini only loves Al." Joe kept reassuring himself, saying, "Dini only loves me" and warned me, "Dini will devour you Reg, like a black widow spider." When I laughed at his ridiculous comment, Joe got really upset, saying, "You're hanging around here like me. Just to see Dini. You are hooked on her just like me." "Joe, this is the only street that leads to Bloor Street" and I didn't want to argue with him knowing he was too hung up on Dini and just walked away shaking my head, thinking both those drunks were off their rocker. Apparently the Sanskrit word for an insane person is the same as for a drunk person.

Quite often, Willie and I would go to hear Dini sing in a night club. The saving grace for my perfectionist friend was his sense of humor. He laughed and joked about "Dini the boozer" and needled me when Dini sang, saying, "Reg, she's singing this song only for you." Willie became defensive when it was about his life but didn't seem to mind if the brunt of the joke was on him.

Invitation to a jam session. After her performance, we went to an old warehouse off an alleyway between Yonge and Bay, just north of Wellesley Street. Neither proud nor ashamed of music illiterate. The sound was alive, exciting and vibrant. The movement of the musicians, the flashing and the blaring of the brass instruments, the drum beating, the chattering and the clapping seemed to turn each other on, improvising the sound of music. The whole place felt like a free for all paradise. End of the session, Dini invited me to see her new apartment. We hadn't seen each other for a while and had plenty of things to talk about. When we talked ourselves out she asked me to stay for the night. Sex and sorrow for me is not compatible. Whenever I feel sorry for a woman, sex is out of the question. Walking home, just before daybreak, my feelings were mixed. I thought, "Anybody in his right mind would jump at the chance of having sex with a beauty like Dini. Maybe I have ice in my veins and yet the feeling of fondness overwhelmed me and I didn't know if she felt slighted.

The next night I made it a point to see her at the jam session, enjoyed it and went home with her. This time I asked to stay the night. In the morning she appeared to be childlike and apologized that she had to rush off for an appointment. It was the one and only time we had sex and the most natural act I ever experienced. Mutual understanding of giving and taking, no me, me, ego trying to prove something, no faking or pretending, no talking, just the normal sound of love making. Her great wetness overcame the flaw of having no breast. Dini's non existing breast didn't puzzle me as much as the time when I was in

High School where I just couldn't, in the dark, feel or find the girl's breast. Whenever I did think of Dini's flat chest, it made me wonder if she overcompensated to prove her womanhood. One lawyer and his group were investing money into a restaurant and were undecided whether to use a famous football player's name or Dini's name. Dini's love spell won out. We lost touch with each other, she busy with the restaurant and I, doing my own thing.

Willie was on a roll, making a bank roll. It was an unexpected surprise when he gave me some money for helping him off and on during the hard times. Willie, for a change, was going steady with a girl and I thought it was an opportune time to travel through the states and find out how our neighbors do things in the Pool Halls

I was no stranger to the U.S., especially the Big Apple. In the late sixties we went to New York a few times as tourists. My friend really liked Broadway and the Theatres. I stayed at my sister's place which gave him a better chance to schedule his own time to see many of the artists performing my sister was married to a tall Irishman from Boston. He had a sense of humor, liked his beer and put Naomi on a pedestal as a Ballerina Supreme. Their baby son was a beaut and he laughed saying he wouldn't mind if his kid became a pool hustler.

At that time New York was a scary city, so many shootings, stabbings and murders. The day we arrived, a guy bumming a cigarette killed the nonsmoker because he didn't have any cigarettes. A small crowd was gathering around a doorway to a club. I could hear a great solo drumming sound and to the side of the door a sign with the name Gene Krupa. Man! He was my favorite drummer during High School days and to hear him playing in person was fabulous. What ruined it was this guy staggering around in the crowd showed me a large jackknife. Didn't know what he was up to and New York had too many stabbings so I signaled my buddy and we slipped away. One other night, blacks were coming out the back entrance of a club and one of them yelled, "Hey there's Whitey. Let's go get'em. Immediately my friend started moving his fingers and we walked quickly away pretending to be using the deaf and dumb sign language. I heard one of the blacks saying, "Oh they're only dummies" and they all laughed and didn't bother coming after us.

My friend could look stupid but he's sharp, streetwise and a good dresser. He warned me not to play and lose money in the American game of pool, saying "it would take me three years of playing every day for me to compete with some of the good players. Playing snooker we might have a chance to win some money." New York had plenty to offer in the entertainment field but our life belonged to the billiard tables. We had no choice but to check out the pool halls. We didn't bother to play in many of the pool rooms. Biker gangs dressed like pirates were not for us. Once my partner went up to the second floor to check out a room and he came back saying a guy who spoke in broken English with a Spanish accent told him the last time a hustler came in to play he was thrown out the window.

Some pool halls downtown like the "Guys and Dolls" were modern, clean and safe. The only trouble was nobody talked to strangers. Guys would be playing by themselves and if you approached them and asked them to play a game they just ignored you. In pool rooms, if you can't make a game you can't make any money. We went into an old establishment where they had large snooker tables.

Everything about the room was written in class. I felt the atmosphere was filled with the spirit of great players of yesteryear. Someone told me they shot some scenes of the original movie, "The Hustler", with Paul Newman and Jackie Gleason. New York supposedly had the sharpest and the toughest pool hustler in the country. This hotshot, called Fast Eddie, approached me, saying, "Your partner looks like he's loaded with money. He told me to tell my friend that Fast Eddie is a big time gambler with lots of money. Fast Eddie wanted me to act as a shill and I was laughing on the inside, explain the proposition to my partner. Looks are deceiving. Nobody would ever dream that my friend was a sharpie. I went back to Eddie and told him my goofy friend would only play golf on a snooker table and would only play in another pool hall if Eddie could show him big money. The action game was arranged for early evening and sure enough, Eddie showed up with a backer who showed us plenty of money. They started to play a simple form of golf on a small snooker table, each having a shooter and object ball. It was like taking candy from a baby.

The fifth game, Eddie had a chance to win on the last hole but my friend made a routine golf shot to hook Eddie and Eddie started raving what a great shot my buddy made. Even Eddie's backer started muttering away, saying to Eddie, "You are being hustled. Can't you see this guy is no dummy? You're the best player in New York and you can't tell the difference between a shark and a fish. They quit after that game and surprisingly enough, the backer lost over $700 to us. While they were leaving the leaving the room, I could still hear the backer moaning and groaning, telling Eddie, "You're stupid, you're stupid. You are so stupid. How can you blow money to a country bumpkin? Come on. Let's get out of here quick before everybody finds out. We'll be the laughing stock of the Whole World."

Nobody was standing around the table watching the game of golf. After the session some guys came over asking my partner what kind of story he laid down on Eddie to trap him into losing money. Those guys were pros watching the action from afar, knowing a score was going down. They didn't want to interfere or mess up the play so they watched from a distance. They weren't interested in a handout. They just wanted to know the angle of the story in how we beat the well-known Fast Eddie for the money. There was no story; Fast Eddie just put his big foot in his own mouth. To this day those guys will never figure out how a couple of guys from the Boon Docks of Canada hustled Fast Eddie.

One day a nattily dressed stranger came into the pool room with a fancy two piece cue looking to play a game of nine ball. One of the hustlers grabbed him and quickly beat him five straight games. Then the hustler offered to spot the stranger the 8 ball. After a few more games, the hustler offered to spot the 7 and the 8 ball and the hustler kept winning so he spotted him the 6, 7, 8 and the 9 ball, which means that the hustler shot the balls in rotation and could only win when he made the nine ball. The stranger could win if he made any of the balls from 6 to the 9 ball. I wasn't familiar with 9 ball and found it interesting how they handicapped the game. The stranger quit even when he was offered the extra 5 ball as a spot. I thought the Hustler probably could win even if he spotted the guy every ball and all the guy had to do was make only one ball. They were only playing for $2.00 a game and the winner rushed out of the poolroom telling the poor guy to play this other guy saying, "You can beat him." Of course the next Hustler beat the newcomer the same way. Five quickly wins, then spotting him and finally trying to overspot but the guy quit. After the stranger lost to 8 or 9 hustlers, he threw his hands in the air and cried out, "Can't I beat anybody in here?" Every Hustler made about $20 and what I couldn't figure out was why they all rushed out of the poolroom after making such a small score. I thought maybe New York was a busy place. Anyway, the loser ended up playing a 13 year old kid who was a good pool player. Later on, when we came back to the pool room they were playing for $10 a game. The kid had patience, carrying him by letting him win the odd game and then upping the stake to $20 a game. The next day, I heard the kid beat the stranger for over $500.

A big snow storm hit New York and as I walked to my sister's place I saw a guy coming towards me. I thought, "What kind of guy would be walking around in a cold freezing snow storm. Is he a mugger? Plenty of mugging going on in New York." The snow was too deep to cross the street and walk around him. I said to myself, "Mugger or no mugger, I'm walking straight ahead and I'll walk right by him." I broke into a grin and a chuckle when the guy crossed the street and went around me, probably thinking I might be a mugger. The weather was cold but the pool halls downtown were warm.

Talk about cold (I remember taking a train ride in early December to Edmonton Alberta. The train stopped west of Soo St. Marie in the wilderness to pick up two native Indian passengers. Some of the tribe members came to see them off and what a forlorn looking group, living in such a desolate environment, nothing but snow and ice. It reminded me of the time during the war, the nostalgia of living in No Man's Land in the Rockies. I imagine the natives lived in log or wooden cabins, surviving the simple life.

Finally got the feel of Edmonton's cold weather, 40 degrees below zero. It was a good thing the hotel was only three short blocks from the pool room. All the store windows were iced up and the cops wore those big buffalo coats and hats. I came to Edmonton to see John Spencer, the World Snooker Champion, play in an exhibition match and also to play some snooker golf with the locals. John Spencer never disappointed anyone. One game he drilled in the first red ball, a long shot, the ball was close to the rail, a foot past the side pocket on the green ball side. The cue ball was close to the end rail in the black ball area. Sheer power. When the cue ball hit the red ball it paused momentarily and I can't remember if the red ball went into the corner pocket first and then the cue ball zoomed back into the black ball area. It's one of the prettiest sights to see the cue ball at a dead stop. You cannot see the spin or hear the spinning noise on the table cloth and then it pulls back like a yo-yo on an invisible string. Oohing and ahhing after that fabulous shot, Spencer made his first black ball, spreading the pack of red balls and continued on making balls. The tension was mounting and you could hear a pin drop and some guys were sitting on the edge of their seats. When he made the final ball he cleared the table. The roar of the small crowd was so great it sounded like the Oilers had just won the Stanley Cup. Good players occasionally run the table but what impressed me was how Spencer got started with a tremendous power shot. I saw John 'Bumps' Johnson make a shot that belongs in the category of Ripley's "Believe it or Not." Three balls left on the table, blue, pink and black. Easy shot to make the blue into the side pocket, a very slight angler where the cue ball would be further away from the pink. Most professional players will take the easy shot and then make the medium long shot on the pink followed by making the black ball.

Bumps astonished me; he pounded the blue into the side pocket. The force was so great that the cue ball jumped straight up and when it came down, paused momentarily and then drove forward instead of backward, hitting the side rail, then the end rail. Then the cue ball lost its speed. Bumps was excited and raised his cue and arms saying watch this! Watch this! The cue ball was barely moving but when it touched the third rail, the spin was so great it zoomed past the pink ball on the far side. Bumps called the shots "3rd Rail Reverse." I called it, "the sweetest shot this side of heaven." I asked Bumps where he hit the cue ball and he held his cue like a sword and carefully guiding the tip right to the spot of the cue ball, saying, "Right there." It defied all logic; it was slightly below center ball and slightly to the left. Every player knows, below the center spot is to draw the cue ball, not to make it go forward. Let the astrophysicist figure this one out. Whenever Bumps finished playing, the table cloth was scratched up with blue chalk marks. The reason was that after his follow through, the tip hit the table cloth, the stroke going downwards. On that third rail reverse, the follow through, the cue tip was pointing slightly upwards.

Over the years, I thought the one time champ John Spencer, and Bumps, had many things in common. Both had the name John and both drank too much and still played well under the influence of alcohol. They both had the tiniest tip on the cue and the style of play was similar. Rolling the ball, stun the cue ball, juicing the ball with English or powering the cue ball, whatever it took to make the shot the expedient way. The only difference was John Bumps was a hustler, hiding his ability and John Spencer, exposing his game to be the World's best. However hustlers show flashes of their brilliance like Paul Thornley when he beat John Spencer in an exhibition match in Toronto. The professionals or the top gun hustlers on any given day are the best in the world. Let the astro psycho techno scientist figure this one out but I would still bet with a knowledgeable bookmaker to pick the winner.

Talk about a winner, the hustler always wins. I finally found a player to play head on golf that I couldn't beat and broke about even. He was a good player, having the home table advantage and the things I had the most difficult time to adjust to was how the cold weather affected the playing condition of the table. Two days of playing golf and I found the weather too cold to tour the city of Edmonton. I had to go back to the warmer cold city of Toronto the next day.

Bewitched, bothered and bewildered. Before going stateside I went to see Dini managing her restaurant. The chicken dinner was excellent. The décor in the restaurant was a few years ahead of her time, the main stream hippie movement was still not in vogue. She gave it the Hawaiian look. Dini was in one of her bubbly moods and seemed interested in my new adventure traveling abroad. After dinner she wanted a drink and invited me across the street to a nightclub, saying she didn't drink anymore except on rare occasions. We talked like two close friends who hadn't seen each other for ages. Before leaving, Dini said she "missed me and will miss me even more when I'm away." I felt her warm spirit and a touch of sadness in her voice. I hugged her with a great feeling of fondness saying, "I'll miss you too." As I walked up the street the thoughts, "this is the way the cookie crumbles, or, in pool room lingo, that's the way the ball bounces." Our relationship was kiss and goodbye, so I thought. I was planning to go straight to Montreal and then cross the border into the States, but decided to stop off in the quiet town of Oshawa, just east of Toronto. I figured it would give me a chance to regroup my thoughts and a chance to center my being in a quiet environment.

Multiple personality – Dreams of Dini – strange sleep. Stranger still, going early into a poolroom to have a coffee and bang a few balls. Lining up a long shot, lowering my head, chin slightly above the cue, click – a picture of Dini's face appeared on the surface of the red ball. I shook my head and blinked my eyes. Every time I aimed, Dini's face appeared on the ball. I had to stop shooting. This was unbelievable, nonsense, crazy. Is this the voodoo spell Joe warned me about? I had to get to the bottom of this. I went back to my Motel and lay on the bed. Never saw the ceiling, only Dini's face and images. The feeling of care and fondness for her was overwhelming. I felt her presence like the song, "She's under my skin." How the hell is nonattachment going to help me out of this? For two days, most of the time I lay in bed thinking through this hypnotic state; deep awareness, stillness of the mind, obviously all the images of Dini was subjective, created by my own thoughts and feelings within the mind. I was trapped by my own assumption that Dini was everything I wanted in a woman, especially when we had similar ideology of Eastern Thought. Still she lacked the profound understanding of Universal Principals, the soul mate idea was a fantasy whatever that means. Dini could easily be led astray by "the Smoke of Ecclesiasticism", words coined by my Yoga teacher. Memories brought back the vivid imagery of her personality and life style.

Occasionally she would break out spontaneously humming a tune or softly sing a song. Most of the time she was bubbly and enthusiastic, conversing articulately and passionately. At times she would be in a domineering mood, acting like a bossy person. Sometimes she behaved like a child, vulnerable and helpless. Her many personalities had no real substance and yet she was interesting and entertaining and a lot of fun to be with. Enjoying all the time spent with Dini was not it. Only when I became keenly aware of her voice did the spell begin to lift. Hypnotic voice, voicing through her multiple personality, was mesmerizing and controlling. Even the phone was the instrument of her controlling voice; chatting, whispering giggling, laughing, whimpering, etc. seduced my mind. On the third day, I felt my life was back to normal. Only when I consciously thought of Dini, the spell like feeling returned but in a lukewarm way. Today I realize that neither of us had ever heard of Neuro Linguistic Programming and cognitive Psychology and Dini, at that time, used some of the techniques of the NLP to program my mind. Also, without know-ing, I used some of the methods of Cognitive Therapy to deprogram the spell in my mind. Having some useful knowledge of Hatha and Raja Yoga, plus the idea of nonattachment, managed to let go of thoughts of her voice that created the spell within my mind. Epecti-tus, 200 years ago, best explained the ancient psychology of the East and West and the most recent modern psychology of the west by stating, "Men are not disturbed by things but by the views they take of them." In other words, change the negative thoughts to positive thoughts and our pessimistic view will change to an optimistic view that will make all the difference in the world. Just changing the thoughts sounds easy but it is one of the most difficult things to do. The reason is that we do not see our own thoughts that pro-gram our mind and body. Even if we see the thoughts that brainwash our mind, "Is it based on fact or fantasy?"

Many fantasies are based on assumptions and deprogramming and reprogramming into another fantasy is like jumping from the frying pan into the fire. The world is living under a nuclear holocaust. Whether it's going to happen or not is not the question. Rather, than to program our thoughts into doom and gloom we would be better off brain washing our minds to make the world a better place to live before we die.

From Oshawa went straight to Montreal. Had a day to drop into Windsor Pool Room and another one downtown. I bumped into Fast Eddie. It seemed like every city had somebody called Fast Eddie, an offshoot of a movie where Paul Newman played the part of a pool hustler called Fast Eddie Phelpston. I didn't meet Pierre, a very popular name and an old customer of mine. Nobody knew which Pierre I was talking about. A few years before, Pierre was spotting me 40 points in Snooker. The games were going back and forth so I talked him into playing golf with no spot. We played even. For two weeks I beat him every day where Pierre never won a game. Most of the hotshot pool players overestimate their playing ability and act the Prima Donna. He did suggest to cut down the 15 red balls to ten red balls so I continued to beat him for another week. Then he suggested to only have six red balls as obstacles. I kept winning every game until finally he would only play without any red balls on the table. The table looked naked with only his cue ball and object ball and my cue ball and object ball. Even I was surprised to beat him every game under those conditions.

Pierre finally woke up, no matter how superior he was playing pool, his ability and accu-racy couldn't overcome my greater control of my cue ball and object ball.

I went straight to Miami Beach and checked into a tourist home. I browsed around for a week. The weather was hot but the beach was nice. I enjoyed the natural food stand, fresh juices and whole wheat sandwiches. Lying on the beach, the clouds seemed so high I wondered if it was because we were so near the Equator. At night the crescent moon was inverted. I checked out some of the big hotels. I didn't like the heavy drug scene. I enjoyed the vacation atmosphere but did not want to lose the feel of a cue in my hand and decided to drop into a poolroom in Miami. The Billiard Hall was in the same building as the bowling alley, very well air-conditioned and comfortable. I asked the manager if there was any golf game and he said, "Quite often." It didn't take too long before a guy came over and asked to play golf. He knew how we played the game in Canada; 15 red balls and rail golf. Maybe he was a Canadian who knew the strategies and had great touch and feeling for the game. We were both knocking our heads against the wall and after six or seven games we packed it in. I told him, he was a helluva golf player and he said the same thing about me. We patted each other's shoulders and parted as worthy opponents.

Next stop New Orleans. It was very different. I thought it was another country. The French Quarter, its brass band and jazz music, created a constant holiday mood. Food was excellent, from breakfast to Japanese food, and seafood was marvelous. One place, I think it was Clams, after eating the meat everybody threw the shells on the floor. Crunch, crunch, crunch. People kept coming in and out. The dark skinned people were friendly and jovial. I didn't bother playing any pool. Some bars had these dinky tables where you insert a coin to play a game. Always some hustler trying to talk me into a game. I spent two good weeks and left just before the Mardi gras, ending up in San Antonio, a military town with a touch of Mexico. Beautiful hacienda homes. Dropped into a big pool hall. Didn't like it -- too much.

Drinking and too many guys wearing military uniforms. Because of my weak physical condition I didn't want to be involved in any violence although I heard Texans welcomed the Japanese Americans with open arms. Apparently a Texas battalion was trapped, pinned down and being hammered by the German artillery and the 442nd, a group of Japanese American soldiers went in and bailed the Texans out. Would have loved to stay but I didn't like the military presence so I left for a quiet place called Phoenix.

Phoenix looked like a huge crater surrounded by mountains. It was snowing in the mountains and when we came down into the valley the climate was temperate, dry and plenty of sunshine. Unlike San Antonio it was peaceful. People moved to Phoenix to retire. Visited two pool halls downtown which, to my surprise, had mostly big snooker tables and outside of a few stray harmless looking Hippies playing, the whole downtown was dead. Maybe it wasn't the right time of day or the right time of year. Nice change in lifestyle, resting, watching TV and talking to the manager of the Motel about the generalities of Phoenix.

Bored after the third day, I went straight to Los Angeles. The City of Angels was sprawled out and needed a car to get around. I stayed in an Asian community and found a family run restaurant where the food tasted like home cooked Japanese meals. Two days was enough; the city reminded me of Toronto only bigger—"Who needs that?" – And headed north.

San Francisco finally – "My kind of town" Huge china Town, Little Tokyo, Barbary Coast, Fisherman's Wharf and little cable cars going up and down steep hills. I rented a shabby room above a store in Chinatown and spent an exciting week sightseeing. Chinatown was teeming with activities, people shopping, mountains of oranges and fruits displayed on the sidewalk, bake shops, restaurants, clothing stores and an endless variety of shops.

Fresh wonderful seafood dishes at Fisherman's Wharf. Nearby, Joe DiMaggio's Restaurant. What an experience, to drop in to have a meal at Joltin' Joe's Joint. To me he was Mr. Baseball, a true blue Yankee with a record that will never be broken. Silent swing with the bat and smooth as silk playing center field. Nearby my place was a restaurant run by an Italian family and I ate Zucchini for the first time. Another first was having a meal in a Vietnamese restaurant. I avoided tourist traps and found little out of the way eatery where the Chinese meals tasted like home cooking and enjoyed Samurai movies in a little theatre. Breakfast in downtown hotels was reasonable. Steaks and eggs, pancakes with excellent coffee. Natural food restaurants, fresh juice bars. To me Frisco was a gourmet paradise years ahead of Toronto. Today, Toronto is a great place with all the ethnic restaurants and a vibrant Chinatown. Unfortunately there is no Li'l Tokyo but for me Korea town is a good replacement. What prevented me from living life to the fullest was my weak health. When I was staying in Frisco I didn't know I had an overactive thyroid. Occasionally it would really act up and make me feel nervous, jittery and tired. At the edge of Chinatown was a parkette where mostly elderly Chinese people were going through a slow dance. It was relaxing to watch so I sat down on a bench and contemplated their various movements. For a change I was right; their bodies were re-enacting the cosmic movement of the heavenly bodies, something I found out by inquiring after the class was over. It was the first time I'd heard the word 'Tai-Chi'.

After spending a week of leisure time sightseeing, I realized it was time to start playing again. I looked up Billiards in the yellow Pages and found an address of a Pool room on Main Street. I hailed a cab, asked the driver if Main Street was a main drag and it was, so I gave him the address of the Pool Room. The street was deserted which made me feel uncomfortable as it was beginning to turn dark. I said to myself, even in a strange city all poolrooms are the same and walked up to the 2nd floor. It had a short hallway enclosed in glass and a glass door. Before going in, I could see the inside of the poolroom. The place did look like any other big sized pool room, with pool tables and large snooker tables but the people standing and hanging around while others were playing were all blacks. The door wouldn't open but the black person behind the counter came quickly to open the door saying, "Someone got shot in here yesterday so we keep the doors locked." Walking in, I thought, "what the hell am I doing in here?" anyway, I asked for a set of balls and went over to a table and began playing by myself after playing for about five minutes I felt it was safe and I'd survive. Some of the guys were eyeing me but none of them came over to challenge me to a game. Another twenty minutes of banging the balls around and I returned them to the counter and paid for table time. He gave me change and said, "You should go to your brother's place. It just down the street on the other side." I thanked him and left. The street was deserted and it was dark except for streetlights and all the stores were closed. In those days all I heard and read about in a black community was dangerous and life threatening. I walked quickly as possible and after what seemed like ages I found "Palace Billiards." Looking up the flight of stairs to the 2nd floor, the railing was ripped off and only the support hook stuck out from the wall. As I walked up the stairs I thought the place could be another dive. The life of a pool hustler. It's the way the ball bounces or the cookie crumbles, the good, the bad and the ugly.

The entrance had a glass door and I had the nicest shock of my life when I stepped inside, except for the kitchen area, the walls were covered with tiled mirrors and not one mirror was cracked or broken. I thought, with all the violence in pool halls, this place was the safest place in America to play pool. The reason was obvious: to the immediate left was a heavy set judo man who greeted me from behind the counter. He was able to see people coming in and, of course, going out, and looked after everything.

Further on was an open kitchen with a sink, cutting board, fridge, wok, grill, etc. all lined up against the wall. The space between the kitchen equipment and the eating counter was about three feet, plenty of room for the old Chinese man to walk back and forth performing as a cook, waiter and dishwasher. Strictly a one man operation. There must have been about ten swivel stools. I sat down right behind the cook who was stirring something in the wok. I looked up to see the menu board, liked what I saw and ordered beef and vegetables on rice. The wok is a great frying pan for fast cooking. It didn't take too long and the cook turned around and placed a steaming dish in front of me. The meal was delicious but I couldn't enjoy it. The heart was fluttering and I felt a little dizzy.

For a few years these weird symptoms occurred off and on. For months nothing would happen, at times a mild form of jitters and tiredness and once in a while a very severe attack of shaky nerves, rapid heartbeat and overwhelming heaviness. I tried to relax, to slow down my heartbeat but ended up brooding over my predicament. Something was wrong and with this type of physical condition my game would be a wipe out. I started humming a western ditty, words hardly audible, "500 miles away from home, away from home, away from home, away from home, 5000 miles away from home," I changed the mileage to be more realistic. I kept humming and thinking, "what if I had a heart attack?"

"Imagine lying in a hospital with tubes stuck into me."

"Maybe I need an operation"

"I might be better off dead."

I grunted out, "Yeah, the life of a pool hustler." I turned around on the swivel stool and viewed the room. The left area of the room had four large snooker tables and four more directly on the other side. Inside the L shaped of the big tables were maybe eight small pool tables. I still couldn't believe it, three foot wooden panels bordered the room and 5000 mirrors plastered the walls above them. Not one fuckin' mirror was cracked.

Hell, if they'd hung chandeliers this place would look like a palace. I finished off the oolong tea, waved to my newfound friend, the Martial Artist, and took a cab home. I climbed the stairs ever so slowly to avoid a heart attack and stumbled into my old worn out room. I left the clothes on the floor and flopped on the bed, weak, tired, jittery, with a rapid heartbeat, resumed humming the ditty, "5000 miles away from home" and the word 'home' triggered my silent affirmation, "Home is where I hang my hat." "The Universe is my home." I felt a little better but still was concerned with my wellbeing. I drifted off to sleep.

Woke up feeling a little tired but still okay. I was thinking not to do anything strenuous that would make my heart pump like crazy. I decided to do things in slow motion. I really took my time walking up the hill to catch a cable car. Can you imagine taking two steps and resting on the third, another two steps and resting? The resting period became longer when approaching the top of the hill. The cable car ride was all downhill. I decided not to have the usual (famous) steak and egg and walk very slowly to the Palace Billiards.

Next to the Billiard hall was a fruit and vegetable grocery store. At the back of the store and on each side were three little kitchens serving food. I bypassed the Barbecue Chicken place and sat down at a U-shaped counter to order fresh carrot juice and an egg salad sandwich. Then I went to another section and ordered coffee. Dividing the grocery store and those tiny kitchenettes was an area with tables and chairs to sit down and eat. Anyway, it was many years later that Toronto had a similar set up. (It was only a year later in Toronto that I finally went to see a Doctor and all the nutty things happening to my mind and body were symptoms of an overactive thyroid and a fluctuating blood sugar.) After the time consuming way of travelling, I finally made it to the pool room. The guys were playing golf and I felt too weak to play so I sat down and watched them play, giving me a chance to learn the rules and study the strategy of the game. I spent two days feeling out the game by just watching.

Feeling better on the fifth day, I played the first game of American golf in the Palace.

The rules and strategy of Billiard Golf in America is simple enough but it is much more difficult to win the money. The reason is only one player is the winner. The maximum number of players in a group to play a game is seven. It's not like Billiard Golf played in Canada or golf played on a golf course where players come in second, third and so on and still win some money. As soon as a player makes the last hole, the game is over, winner takes all and everybody pays him. The group in the Palace usually played for $2.00 a game and 10 cents a stroke. He collects $2.00 from each player plus the amount of penalty strokes each player made during the game. The strokes are the result of penalties like missing a ball or hitting another ball first and other miscues. The average player makes between 30 to 60 penalty strokes a game. Give or take the average loss for each player is between five and seven dollars a game and the winner collects about $40.00 all told. The game is sociable, entertaining and affordable and most players enjoy the fun outing in the afternoon with the boys.

Most of the money was won by the Texans and I believe some locals never won a game. Sometimes I preferred to sit down and rest watching the guys play golf. If they needed another player in the group they would beg and plead for me to play. I had to laugh to myself thinking, "Imagine the man with the golden arm and these bums twisting my arm to play golf with them." Unfortunately I couldn't play well due to my health condition and it took two months before I won a game. No Texans played in that game which made it a softer touch for me to win. Can you imagine, "Top Canadian Golf hustler never won a game in San Francisco?" Even though my game was not up to par, I was beginning to hold my own, winning the odd game. The snooker tables in the Palace were older than ancient (antiques). Up North we called them trap tables. Shoot the cue ball along the rail the ball will not go into the pocket. The pockets are almost half the size of the regular snooker tables in Canada. Taking dead aim at a ball on the other end of the table with a slow touch shot, it could be missed completely either to the left or right. No rhyme or reason, play the same shot as if there was a nap on the cloth and the cue ball went straight to the target. Recently, talking to P.T. the Guru, he explained, "It didn't matter which siding is used, the cue ball will move in a straight line" and he went on to explain this strange phenomenon that sounded like Quantum Mechanics. My bank roll had dwindled to $300. I figured it might not be too long before I headed back to Toronto. Even as a vacation, the time spent in Frisco was well worth it.

Felt a bit moody over the winter holidays. No white Christmas. As soon as the snow hit the ground it melted. Thought about my separation and the wife living in Ottawa with our two and a half year old son Daniel. I always thought a child should be with the Mother and as for me, I assumed that when he was older we would be able to understand and get along. I started humming again, "5000 miles away from home." I don't know if the nightly silent affirmation was doing me any good or not but I never had any problem falling asleep.

I enjoyed browsing around the palace Billiards watching the golf games and occasionally watched a great game of "one pocket or Nine Ball." These American pool players really play superbly on the small Boston tables. The regular golf games break up in the late afternoon and the place becomes quiet. Its supper hour so I decided to have a Chinese meal in the pool room. After the meal, without thinking, I looked to the left and saw the martial arts manager sitting behind the counter and then I almost fell off the stool. Ike Pauls walked through the door. He might have seen me first through the glass door and without breaking stride came over and sat beside me. I was really glad to see another Canadian pool hustler. "Ike, how the hell are you? How come you're here in Frisco?" he mentioned that he spent a few months in Portland, lost his cue and luggage and came in town with only a quarter. He needed a place to sleep so I offered him my place but he would have to sleep on the floor. It was Okay with him. The linoleum was worn out so much that big patches of the old hardwood flooring showed through. Ike threw the extra woolen blanket I had on the floor and slept on top of it. The situation wasn't that bad. One pool hustler flat broke and the other one on the verge of going broke and even though I couldn't guarantee winning any golf games, I had the Top gun sleeping on the floor.

After a shower and a shave, Ike looked great. I couldn't believe he could sleep so well on the hard floor. It was nice for a change to be able to talk with someone over a late break-fast. Ike was a six footer, slim with athletic build, fair skin and hair, light brown eyes that would look darker at times, soft spoken and had a good demeanor like a regular person, not the type that swaggers into a poolroom like a hotshot. "I like Ike" rated him as a true contender, not a pretender. We seldom talked shop except to get a few laughs talking about the excuses and comedy acts some players go through when losing money. Felt much better with a sharp shooter like Ike around. Moneywise he would not be a burden but an asset and if anything went drastically wrong with my health he would be able to help me. I played golf and he played pool or snooker. Whenever he played, he was able to grind out our meal money. One day I was really into a game of golf when we all heard this loud mouth black yacking away." Anybody wants to gamble for big money? My old lady just left me and I want to blow off some steam. I don't care if I lose money, I wanna forget her." I thought he was a pool hustler trying to make a game. Golf is such an absorbing game most of us ignored his ranting and raving. I wasn't aware of what was happening until Ike came over and asked me to back him against Chico. He explained the game, the seven color balls of snooker to be racked in the shape of a diamond. The snooker balls do not have numbers like the pool balls. Each different color represents a number from 1 to 7 winner breaks and the balls are made in order from 1, 2, 3, to 7. Every ball is worth $10. If a player makes every ball he stands to win 70... If one player makes four balls and the other guy makes three, the winner only makes $10.

In a flash I realized this game was a shoot-out, very little safety play a shot makers game. I noted Ike within the top five sharpshooters of Canada. They may not have the great finesse of pin point control of the cue ball but man do they have the natural ability to make those long difficult shots. Tight pockets or not, no American is going to outplay Ike on the big snooker tables. I practically threw what was left of my bank roll to Ike. Meanwhile, I was still able to concentrate on trying to win a golf game but the thought occurred to me, "It is a good thing Chico is not a golf hustler, I wouldn't be able to win."

Chico and Ike didn't exist in my mind. I was having too much trouble with my own game and completely forgot what was happening on the next table until Chico voiced a loud remark," Jesus, don't you ever miss?" glancing over, I saw Ike whack in a long shot and Chico shaking his head. I guess at the beginning of the match the games must have been going back and forth and now I felt Ike was winning more games than losing. After just shooting a long tricky shot and watching the cue ball slowly move to the other end of the table to hit my ball, I became aware of Ike standing beside me. He was chalking his cue, lowered his head and in a low voice, whispered into my ear. "I'm in dead stroke," which means he's in the zone and can't miss. From then on all I heard was Chico yacking and shouting, "This guy has the eyes of an eagle." "He's threading the needle." "The pockets must look like the Grand Canyon to him." "Is this guy from another planet or what?" "He's not human, he's a machine." "I can't believe you made that shot."

I don't know if Chico was trying to shark Ike or not but I had to give him credit, he played until he went broke. After our golf session ended I sat down on a stool and ordered coffee. Cup in hand, I turned around to see the match but Ike and Chico were shaking hands and I thought, "At least he's a good loser." Chico was still upset as he walked by me towards the door cursing and swearing, "I'll never play a God Damn Canadian again on a big fuckin' table" and stormed out. Ike went over to the front counter to pay for table time and then disappeared into the washroom. Both elbows on the counter, cup cradled in my hands and sipping coffee thinking, "At least there was action and we made a score; that should help the cause." Ike sat down beside me and in a low whispery voice said, "I beat him for $1,800" and slipped me the money. Nobody was near us and I asked Ike, "What do you need?" He said, "Four" so I counted out $400 below the counter where the cook couldn't see and gave Ike the money. I was satisfied in a soft game like that I would gladly have given up half the money. We decided to have dinner in a seafood restaurant, white tablecloth and all the waiters in a black outfit wearing ties gave a formal and relaxing atmosphere. We weren't wearing dress code standard but our waiter showed respect and served us graciously. After we ordered, Ike finally broke into a grin and smiled. "Yeah, Reg, I was in dead stroke." The way Chico was sounding off it seemed like you were making every shot, Ike." "I was in stroke, dead stroke, every open shot the ball was in. it's a great feeling before you shoot the ball you know the ball is in the pocket." "The ball is in, eh."--"The ball is in, eh." I had to laugh and told him the story of Donny Reeves. "The ball is in, eh." Donny, who is so hyper sometimes he just runs around the table shooting making balls after balls with a machine gun type of stroke. Once he needed to make the pink and the black ball to win the game. He shot the pink and ran around to the other side of the table and made the black ball before the pink went into the pocket. Donny was disqualified of the win because his opponent insisted according to the snooker rules the pink ball must be made first before the black ball is made. Donny, insisting the pink ball went into the pocket anyway, kept saying, "the ball is in, eh." "the ball is in, eh." We both laughed, loosened up and celebrated.

As I expected, the next morning Ike said, "I'm going to find a place for myself." It was beyond me how a guy could sleep on the floor and still play a helluva game of pool. I thought the condition was worse than barnstorming baseball players go through. Anyway, we would see each other at the pool hall and if nothing was happening we would go for lunch and even supper. We went quite often to a downtown lunch spot called the "Haven" ad liked the whole grain bread, cheese, sprouts, vegetable sandwiches and the fresh juices. They also had a regular type of restaurant Uptown where they served dinner, so Ike and I decided to try it out. Ike seemed to enjoy the cable car ride and it didn't take too long to get there. The place was easy to find, right on the corner of two main intersections. Natural woody, rustic décor, very relaxing with plenty of outdoor light shining through the large windows on both sides of the street. I believe the glass panels were framed by wooden casing like the colonial style windows. Soup was good served with a small loaf of whole grain bread on a little cutting board where we sliced our own bread and had plenty of butter, salad, roast duck and natural desserts fit for a couple of vagabond kings. Ike thought it was a special treat and I agreed.

Standing on the corner, traffic was heavy with crowds of people coming and going. We were lost for direction and as the light turned green crossing the street, coming towards us was a crowd of people who all seemed to be in a hurry at the edge of the crowd I saw a woman who I thought could be Japanese. I sensed she was a missionary type. Black hair, face expressionless, wearing a dark outfit and stockings not quite up to her knees. "Excuse me, could you tell me where we could catch a cable car to go back downtown?" "Would you like to come to a Buddhist meeting?" she caught me off guard even though I guessed right about her being a missionary, I didn't think Buddhists were evangelical. She kept talking, "It's Buddhism from Japan" and I thought, "What do the Japanese know about Buddhism, after all it came from India." She mentioned chanting and that struck a chord. I thought with my jitteriness and palpitating

I thought humming might help me.

"Ike, do you feel like going?"

"I don't mind but my socks are dirty and smelly. The women said, "Take off your socks and shoes before you go into house, many young people no wear socks." Even though Ike was from a Mormon background, he tagged along so the three of us, "away we went."

In the bus, her face became animated talking about happiness, good fortune, benefits, propagating power, etc. Ike was attentive but I was more into sightseeing. The meeting was in a house near the Haight-Ashbury district. When we entered the house the sound of chanting was vigorous and I didn't like it. Expected something more soothing but then thought, "What's the difference. Chanting is still chanting. We took off our shoes and left them near the pile in the hallway near the front door and a little ways into the hallway was an opening where I saw about a dozen people kneeling on the floor in prayer position chanting. We were seated down on the floor and like most of them kneeled on my legs and a younger girl came beside me showing me the written mantra of the chant and showed me how to hold the beads she gave me. I looked around. Ike and another guest were getting the same treatment. When the recitation started she walked me through with her fingers the strange words written in the sutra book. The chanting was so fast it sounded like a hum but had a definite rhythmic beat. When the chanting ended my knees were killing me so I sat on the floor. Everybody appeared to be energized and hyped up except for the two hippies who seemed to be out of it. They both had long hair and beards and one of them had long finger nails and long toe nails six inches long painted green. The rest of the people were so active they made the place look like a cheerleaders meeting. People constantly jumping up and down giving explanations and testimonials about this great Buddhism. Waving of the arms, clapping of the hands and voices cheering. Two young men, clean shaven with brush cuts, were leading the charge. Both were ex-hippies and now claimed they were happy having a job and practicing Buddhism. The Buddhists would go just around the corner to the hot bed of drug culture and hippie movement and drag some of the strays to this meeting. Later, apparently the media labelled the Buddhist movement, "Hippie to Happy." Whenever there was a meeting, the Japanese women would meet me to make sure I went to the meetings. I had plenty of time to kill so I didn't mind it and learning the recitation of the Sutra was challenging. Ike had a little interest but from a Mormon to a Buddhist was just too much of a "leap of faith."

Meanwhile back at the ranch, the Texas cowboys were acting up and piping, "Come on let's play for some money." "Getting tired of these two-bit golf games." "I feel like having an action game of Golf for a change."

They finally came up with a twenty dollar bill, at $2 a stroke. I had more than enough money thanks to Ike and Chico so I thought maybe I'd donate a couple of hundred dollars just to get the experience. In Boatrace the game was honest, the Texans didn't favor each other, and they fought tooth and nail against everybody.

Beyond the Zone, I couldn't explain what happened. Was it the chanting that caused the mystical experience in playing golf? I hate the word mystical. My playing was not up to par due to my weak health, with the three hot shots from Texas and two best local players, it was not a situation for me to win four straight games. Looking back now, I think relating to the Buddhist folklore and Universal Principles, the nanovibes from the far reaches of the Universe were pulling the strings, demonstrating to me what the rhythm of Life is all about. I was never an accurate shooter with a rake. Using a short rake hit the ball to go three rails, the length of the table and made the ball in the side pocket for the first win. With a long rake, I banked the ball of the end rail at a sharp angle into the side pocket for the second win. The next shot double banked the ball of the two side rails into the side pocket and for the final game, the shooter had to go two rails and cut the ball which was six inches from the side pocket. Unbelievable to win four games in a row. Greatest fluke since the earthquake. I was calm, not elated and maybe a bit stunned. The Texans left immediately, saying, "hey, Pops, pay for the table: and one of them said, "I knew it. I knew it. You been hustling us all along." I would say the feat would be equivalent to a ten handicap golfer shooting two eagles and two birdies in a row. Ike came over and asked, "You win the money eh?" "Yeah, Ike, won four straight games." Ike grinned with a twinkle in his eyes, silently nodding his head as if to acknowledge, "You're the best." This time we went to celebrate in a fancy Chinese restaurant. Counted the money, a little over $1300. I told Ike it was beginner's luck to win four straight. He didn't believe me, I could tell from his tone: "Yeah, sure, Reg." Ike had a fair idea of how well I played golf. Ike and Cliff travelled through Canada in different cities playing pool and when they dropped into Toronto I beat them both in Golf. The last time Bill Warbanick was with them, the big fat man came up to me and said, "Hey, Charlie, after you finish playing you want to play some golf?" My arm was on the table and I looked up and thought, "Must be Big Bill with the big reputation. No matter how good a snooker player he may be, golf is a different game and no matter how well he played Golf, this poolroom was my turf and I knew the tables like the back of my hand. It's an edge so I said, "Sure, why not, we can play." He laughed, saying, "I'm only kidding.

Cliff warned me not to play golf with you." Later he talked to me about a car accident that banged him up so badly he had to have a major operation. The surgery not only affected his nerves but also his pool game. I know exactly how a nervous disorder affects a player. Bill and Cliff went on to England to play in the professional tournaments and I heard Bill started to drink heavily, probably to calm his nerves. Sometimes I wondered if he had never had the accident he might have won the World Snooker Championship just like his fellow Canadian, Cliff Thorburn.

The very next day after my miracle win which I thought was a fluke, a Chinese bookmaker must have thought the same thing and challenged me to play head-on golf. What was interesting and puzzling was that he made an offer to spot me the break and we would play only the last hole. It was easy to realize that the game would be fast and furious, a real action game, and before anybody woke up a lot of money could be won or lost. The bookmaker spent a lot of time in the poolroom, probably taking bets on horses and sports games. I heard he played for big money and always won and I believe that was the reason he didn't bother playing in the penny ante golf games. There is no doubt in my mind that he rated every player that came to play in the Palace. For sure he knew my accuracy was not that good and must have realized my control over the balls was amateurish. He sized me up pretty well but he did not know my off and on touch control was the result of jitters and poor health. Even before we started to play I thought, "Darn it, if I only had the game when I played in Vancouver a few years ago. No sign of jitteriness or tiredness, my golden arm working like a precision clock. In Vancouver, many times I felt I was controlling the destinies of the seven other players, 15 reds, 4 number balls and the white and the 8 ball. Equivalent to controlling the result of a complicated chaos theory. I had the pleasure of playing with John Bear, younger brother of Jimmy Bear and both were well known to be great snooker and pool players. John's shooter would be three to six inches from a rail and he would hit that short rail and the shooter would hit two other long rails going around the table and the cue ball would softly kiss his object ball. Time and time again, he would go three rails hitting the short rail first and his cue ball would softly touch his ball. I thought maybe these native Indians had the eye of an eagle that saw angles clearly and of course, being tall might have helped him. The Bear kept pawing me to play head on Golf for big money. I was a little hesitant to play him.

Finally it happened. A threesome with a hot shot from Toronto to play golf for some decent money. I knew the guy from T.O. was a fairly good snooker player but didn't know he liked playing golf. I won all five games; the Bear came in second every game and won a bit of money and the T.O. player was the big loser. I felt the Bear could have won two or three games and I told him, "Bear, you're the best." I meant it but he snapped back saying, "No, you're the best." He never challenged me again and I detected for the big money the pressure ever so slightly affected his game. I saw John twice in Toronto playing in a snooker tournament. I said, "John Bear if they had a Golf tournament you would win; you're the best Golf player." And he still snapped back, "No, Reg, you're the best." And I would keep saying, "You're the best" and he would reply, "You're the best" and most of the T.O. golfers didn't know what the hell we were talking about although a few who knew John Bear rated him at the Top of the Totem Pole of "the Golf World." In T.O. I was a staller in Golf, nursing and protecting my strawberry patch.

In Frisco I couldn't be a staller playing the Chinese bookmaker. My game was not up to par and I had to try my best, shooting first was the spot he game me so I always tried to bank my ball off the end rail into the side pocket. The trick is, even though the ball didn't go into the side pocket, to leave it as close to the pocket as possible. You can'[t shoot the ball directly into the pocket, either the shooter or the object ball must hit the rail first to make the ball in order to win the game. Occasionally I was able to bank my ball where it stopped near the lip of the side pocket. I tried to do it four in a row but just couldn't do it. When I was playing well I could have done it nine out of ten times. I knew exactly how to stall and how to beat the bookmaker for large money. Unfortunately, with my health I was a has-been and lost the chance to become a legend.

My Japanese lady friend made me promise to meet her at a convenient location so we could go together to the Buddhist meeting. I made up my mind to learn the recitation which motivated me to attend the meetings and eventually was able to go to the meeting by myself. She told me at the beginning she hated the Buddhists when they came knocking on her door trying to drag her to a meeting. She would hide under her bedcover and not answer, or open the door and was glad she didn't have to knock

On my door to take me to a meeting. She had a big health problem that got her started in practicing Buddhism and by talking to people about Buddhism and Chanting she regained her health. Outside of playing Golf in the afternoon, the evening was divided between Buddhist meetings and the poolroom whenever I met Ike, we would still go to our favorite restaurants to eat. Ike spent more time playing cards and we saw less of each other. Later he mentioned he might head on to Los Angeles. A few weeks later, he left a message saying he'd gone south. Without Ike around I had more time to see movies and a chance to go to Lil Tokyo to eat and see a lot of the Japanese flicks. I kind of missed Ike. It was a good relationship while it lasted. I got to know Ike when he came into Toronto a few years ago with his sidekick, Cliff Thorburn. Ike picked his spot hustling pool and Thorburn wanted to be the best and played everybody. It took a while but I finally had the chance to sit down with Cliff and Ike to have coffee in a downtown restaurant. Cliff appeared to be a sharp kid with a real sense of humor and had Ike and I laughing most of the time. He was pleased that Cliff and I finally got together. I'd seen him play snooker and figured he could spot me 20 points. Cliff and Ike stayed in Toronto for a short time and then left for other parts of the country trying to grind out a few bucks playing in poolrooms. A year or so later, Cliff and Ike came back to Toronto and Cliff improved his game by another 20 points. He seemed to have the ability to continuously improve his game. The last time I saw Cliff, he could have easily spotted me 50 to 60 points in a game of snooker. I was beginning to drop out of the poolroom scene and thought about whether Cliff could improve his game at pro-level in England. When he won the World Championship I was surprised and yet not surprised and mostly happy for him. Never met a man more determined to be the best Snooker player in the world than Cliff Thorburn.

Little Shorty from Frisco came into the Palace Billiards and asked me if I came from Canada. "Yeah, I'm Canadian." "You know Cliff Thorburn?" "Yeah, I know Cliff." Shorty said, if you see him, tell him "Shorty said Hello." "Okay." "Every day whenever I met Shorty he would ask, "Talk to Cliff yet?" "Not yet." Later, Shorty told me about when Cliff came into the Palace Billiards flat broke. The owner let Cliff sleep under the tables at night in exchange for him cleaning the tables. A week or so later Cliff got into an action game and beat a guy for about $7,000. Shorty was just raving about how great Cliff played and never realized a Canadian could be such a super player. Shorty was too young to have seen another Canadian snooker player, George Chenier, "the King" who played in The Palace.

Not too long after I left, Paul Thornley another sharp shooter on big snooker tables, dropped into the Palace. Years later, when I met Paul in Toronto he did mention, "No big money game for Canadians on a large snooker table. He also knew about the shooting in Cochran's, the other poolroom down the street. Paul Thornley is an amazing player, give him a cue and he'll play any billiard game at the highest level. Paul could always grind out expense money playing pool but he was always searching for the challenge to gamble for big money.

Playing one golf game a day in the afternoon was good enough for me and I looked forward to attending Buddhist meetings in the evening. One weekend I went with the SGI members to Sacramento, the capital city of California to support and cheer on our brass band, marching in a parade. I believe the Frisco SGI brass band won first prize. Another weekend we all went to see the movie, "Man from La Mancha." "To dream the impossible dream" was the theme song of the movie and all the SGI members related to the song for the goal of establishing a peaceful world.

Within two months I was able to do the recitation of the Sutra and then one early evening after finishing the ritual, I lay on my bed looking at the Buddhist newspapers stacked and piled on the shelf. Members would give me publications and I would just put them on the pile. I never bothered to read them, thinking "what do the Japanese know about Buddhism? After all, it originated in India. I had a belief that the Indian Sages thought of every possible thought possible in Philosophy and Religion. To be bored and "to ignore is ignorance." Ignorance has a fine line that leads to arrogance. Even now I realized my ignorance by ignoring things that restrict my awareness.

Anyway I picked up one issue and started to read. The article wasn't earth shattering. My understanding of the true Universal Principles were buried in a dark cave. Who is this guy, whether he understood it or not, the Highest Universal Principles were brought down to earth and applied to the reality of day to day life. No morality of what was right or wrong but the best possible way for human beings to live and become truly human was to do Buddhist activities. Every evening I would read one of the newspapers and the core message seemed to be all Buddhist practice and activities should be based on Compassion for oneself and others. I realized the activities of SGI were structured within the framework of the Universal Principles which made sense. So I decided to join the lay organization when I returned home to Toronto. Spring in San Francisco was warm and summery. I was swept away by the excitement of the members who wanted me to attend a "Gohonzon Receiving Ceremony" held at the SGI Centre in Daly City, a suburb of Frisco.

Whoever became a member of SGI would receive a paper scroll, a replica of the original Gohonzon enshrined at the head temple in Japan. Nichiren, the 13th century Buddhist sage embodied the Universal Principles by carving the words in Chinese characters inscribed on a plank of wood so his followers could chant to "The object of veneration to observe one's mind" which helps to see the functioning of the inner mind and to become aware of the true entity within. The old saying goes, "Know thyself" to bring forth the best potential. One end of the hall was a big altar with a large Gohonzon enshrined in a beautiful casing. The place was jam packed, people sitting or kneeling on the floor, palms together holding and rubbing beads, chanting vigorously to the Gohonzon. Sitting in the back it felt like summer heat making me feel faint and dizzy. Members kept approaching me, asking and coaxing me to receive the Gohonzon. I kept telling them I'd receive one for sure when I went back to Toronto. When the Ceremony started and people began to receive the Gohonzon, the place was like a madhouse. The loud cheering, the clapping of hands, you would think they were receiving the Gold Medal at the Olympics. The noise and the heat were overwhelming. I just had to go outside for fresh air. The warm humid air outside and the evening breeze made me feel much better. People were leaving the Centre and I thought the ceremony was over and when I went back inside, someone told me the second Ceremony was about to begin. Apparently, 500 people received the Gohonzon earlier and this time 200 more were to receive it. Sitting at the back of the hall, the place looked empty except for the people at the front chanting. The breeze felt nice coming through the side opening and going out the back door. One Japanese lady knelt beside me. Her voice was my Mother's voice. When I was pre-kindergarten age, my Mother was teaching me to count 1, 2, 3 and the ABC's. My mind was just a blank, listening to the caring voice of Mother and I felt the patient, tender, soothing repetitive numbers and alphabets over and over. It must have been a pleasant natural learning process. This lady's voice was caring and comforting and everything she said made sense which appealed to my sense of logistic thinking. I received the Gohonzon that night. The next evening, two Japanese ladies came over to enshrine my Gohonzon. I believe they were so ecstatic and happy

That I became a member that they didn't seem to mind or notice the dump I lived in. I think they felt that once the Gohonzon was enshrined the place became a palace. They explained how to look after my Gohonzon and one of the best ways was to chant a lot. Within a week, I had the strangest experience chanting to the Gohonzon one night. The black Chinese characters on the Gohonzon started to move slowly like a snake and then began to move faster and faster until it looked like whirling smoke. It freaked me out.

"What the hell is happening?"

"Maybe God or Jesus is punishing me for practicing Black Magic."

Then a terrible ugly feeling came over me. All shook up, I didn't know whether to pray to Jesus or keep chanting. I stopped chanting, lowered the cloth to cover the opening of the box to shelter and protect the Gohonzon, went to bed and turned off the light. I asked myself, "Am I hallucinating?" I don't think so. Those words on the Gohonzon actually appeared to move." The thoughts about fasting came to mind. The body protects the vital organs by storing toxins and chemicals in the fat. Whether it's spiritual or not, the practice of fasting increases the oxygen in the body which burns the fat, releasing the toxic chemicals into the blood stream and when the impure blood passes through the brain, it could cause the mind to hallucinate. After all those years of heavy smoking, my body fat must have been saturated with tar, nicotine and other chemicals. The noumenon realm of the mind manifested the two phases of subject and object. Today, I prefer to use the terminology of the Buddhist principle: "Fusion of objective and subjective reality" to explain to myself that weird mystical experience. At that time, satisfied with my own answer, I felt better after a sound sleep. I continued to chant every morning and evening. Time was flying and I started to think about going back home to Toronto. Being involved in Buddhism changed my original plan to go north to Vancouver. I had played my best game of Golf three years before. For a whole year I was in the best of health and it showed in the way I played Golf. The city of the Lions Gates suspension bridge and twin mountain peaks called 'the Lions." The sense of wellbeing enabled me to live in relationship with a wonderful girl, Norma. We lived in a place near Robinson Street, a trendy area in walking distance to the Pool Hall. I was enjoying the food in Frisco and Vancouver in those days was just as good. Seafood restaurants (I'd forgotten how salmon really tasted), Pasta, Japanese meals with sushi, European food, wooden plates filled with a variety of meats, chefs that served breakfast with toasted sourdough bread and a China Town that served great stir-fried menus. I loved the home of my childhood – the mountains – ocean – the fun and games with a bit of violence.

Talk about violence – a native Indian boy in his early teens approached me and said, "If anybody tries to muscle or harm you let me know. I have a Japanese friend, a fisherman who is a good judoman who will protect you." He was referring to John Bear who always threatened me in golf games. I had to laugh and explained to the kid that the Bear was only trying to psych me out and that sort of intimidation happens in all competitive sports. It was hard to believe; here was a kid I didn't know offering me protection. A week later he brought his friend the judoman who was about my weight and wearing a sports jacket that gave him the appearance of a slightly built man. I wasn't fooled. Fisherman's work is tough, plus the hard training in Judo develops knotted muscles with enormous power. He said the same thing the kid told me. It was amazing. I couldn't figure it out – a complete stranger offering to be my bodyguard. Maybe the kid worshipped me like a sports hero. Having enough of these hero worshippers around could create a legend. For twelve months in Vancouver my game of golf was at its peak. Through the years I was always protected from violence. Two bullies who terrorized the city of Vancouver came into the pool room regularly. "One" was a six footer, Anglo-Saxon, built like an athlete and trained in karate. The other was 5'5" with a wrestler type of build, no neck and looked like a fire hydrant. He was of Eastern European background and never walked, just bounced around like a rubber ball, a human dynamo. At least one of them would always pick me up like a baby and rub his stubby beard on my cheek calling me a little monkey. "Everybody loves a winner." They like me and after letting me down they would say out loud "Beat the suckers and take their money" or "grab the money from the assholes" and the Golf players would laugh, thinking it was all a joke. In Toronto a few years later I heard a Japanese judoman joined "the twosome" to form a trio. I wondered if it was the same guy who offered me protection. The last news I heard was about the "fire hydrant" shooting the ex-sparring partner of Marciano and when he heard the guy was still alive he went looking for him in the hospital to finish him off. The judge who was his friend got wind of what he was going to do and talked him out of it. He got a short sentence for the shooting and avoided a life sentence. He was crazy but I guess not that crazy. No crazy or ticking time bomb was allowed in the Palace Billiard – the mirrors proved it. Thank heaven for law and order in the Palace. But outside, Frisco was quite wild and woolly. I couldn't believe an Asian gang went into a Chinese gambling House and shot and killed over twenty men. Always violence and shooting in the downtrodden black neighborhood.

Back in Toronto, as usual Willie had houses for sale. In one of his houses, his brother and relations were staying and I was able to have a bedroom on the second floor at the back. I enshrined my Gohonzon and continued morning and evening ritual of reciting and chanting. The people in the house though I was Okay but were suspicious and fearful of my practice, thinking it was some kind of witchcraft. Considering their traditional Christian background, they lacked the understanding of Buddhism which in many ways is similar to Christianity but who would think that way anyway.

Home sweet home, even sweeter when my wife came back to Toronto saying my son needed a father. She found a place to live in the neighborhood, a convenient place for me to see Daniel. We made an arrangement where I was able to be with Daniel on Saturdays. My son was three years old and seemed like a happy active boy. We did a lot of fun fighting and rolling all over the Mother's bed and floor wrestling and if I felt his balance was good, I'd let him win. Sometimes we would roll up a newspaper and do Kendo style sword fighting. He was energetic, tireless, giggling, laughing and screaming, trying to beat me and never seemed to give up. Once he said, "watch this Dad" and charged head first, banging his head against the wall. His eyes looked okay but I had to tell him, "Daniel, you have to be careful with your head."

I made a new friend in Terry who introduced me to a Macrobiotic diet based on the Yin and Yang philosophy. It came at an opportune time when I finally went to see a doctor who told me that I had an overactive thyroid. Terry convinced me to move into a Macro House where they ate brown rice, grains, miso soup, cooked leafy and root vegetables, beans, nuts, tofu and very little fruit and fish. He explained to me the classification of Yin and Yang foods. Extreme Yin is sugar and drugs and extreme Yang is salt. Taking too many drugs, the Yin becomes Yang. Heat is Yang and cold is Yin. In a hot climate, nature creates a balance by growing fruits that are Yin such as pineapple, lemon, melon, etc. in a cold climate, salt, root vegetables and animal protein will balance the Yin. Terry would say, "Stay away from meats on hot summer days. Big meat eaters have a hard time handling the hot weather; to balance the Yang they drink a lot of beer. Too many bottles of beer make them Yin so they crave Yang like salted peanuts and pretzels. To balance the cold weather drink Miso soup which has plenty of salt to keep you warm. Terry went on to explain human behavior when it came to the military. The Roman army marched on salt (salary). The Japanese and Vietnamese soldiers consumed a lot of salt. The British navy fed the sailors salted pork and if they didn't balance it with lemon, a yin fruit, they died of scurvy. According to Terry, throughout history, the Yang armies were always victorious. I wonder if the modern day terrorists eat a lot of salt. Terry did say that with too many drugs, the spaceyness of Yin will become the uptightness of Yang. Some American troops in Vietnam had the spaceyness and the 'highness' of drugs causing them to question their superiors, think on their own and even desert the army. The Viet Cong soldiers carried a bamboo reed filled with salt, which might have influenced them to become emotionally programmed like robots and willing to die for whatever ideology they believed in. The suicide mission is an extreme Yang condition. Daren from Montreal was passing through to go west and stayed in the house for a week. He said to me, "Reg, the people in this house are much to Yang and uptight. They don't realize miso soup and soy sauce are extremely Yang. They should all be sucking on a lemon or orange to balance the Yang.

My thyroid was acting up, making me uptight, so I began to eat more fruits which helped. Now I think drinking water (Yin) would have helped to balance the salt (Yang). Terry and his young friend were really uptight, going around shouting, "Anti flow, Anti flow. Life is Anti Flow." I told Terry he was too yang and he snapped back "your chanting is very Yang. That's why all you chanters eat Yin fruits to balance the Yang chanting." The ancient Chinese must have been Masters in applying the Yin and Yang system for healing. I heard just by taking the pulse they would know what disease the person had. I guess they might have known the difference of Yin pulse or Yang pulse and relating it to a Yin or Yang disease and again relate the disease to a Yin or Yang diet.

I wouldn't be a bit surprised if the ancient thinkers extrapolated from a simple heartbeat solving the riddle of the most complex life existing in the Universe. Which would be a greater miracle – a simple one celled animal or a complex human animal? I believe there is a fine line to balance the brain chemicals with Yin and Yang. The brain chemicals could go haywire by water torture or a method of continuously dropping a drop of water on top of the head. Bit by bit, if the salt intake is increased on a daily basis, the brain chemicals will become unbalanced and the mind will go berserk. Terry would say, "People who eat Yin food will grow their hair long. Look at all the drug addicts with long hair. Most Yang people will have shaven hair. Terry and his friend shaved off their hair. Terry would say, "Yang people don't like to stay in one place. They like the wide open spaces and travel. Terry and his friend hitchhiked to Ottawa. His buddy went to Europe and Terry moved to Boston, the hotbed of Macro eating. Generally speaking, what Terry said was true but I wouldn't want to put all my eggs in one basket. I believe Terry was too wrapped up in the idea of "food for the body" and was not aware of "food for the mind." I believe Human Spirituality has Yin and Yang thoughts and Yin and Yang emotions. I believe the Law of Causation is a continuous flow, no break or gaps in the series of cause and effect, birth and death, only unawareness on my part, lacking the connections between the flowing principles. The details are too numerous and my brain is not hardwired to go through all the details. Unfortunately Terry's brain chemicals were all too Yang sometimes going over the edge. He spent his time going in and out of the mental hospital.

Meanwhile, SGI gave me the responsibility of looking after members in a District, the smallest cell within the organization. I started to have District meetings in the Macro House where I had a spacious front room on the first floor. Terry and Violet, living in the house received the Gohonzon. At the beginning we only had two or three people attending the meeting. I didn't know what I was doing. Sure, I knew some of the Universal Principles but this was a different ballgame.

Family

Dealing with people and looking after members.

Lightness of Being – a senior member asked me to visit a person in my district who we all knew had a mental problem. Terry, as usual, made a critical comment: "Your friend Arthur has no idea of Yin and Yang foods. Too much drugs, sugar and fruits caused his mind to become Schizoid." It was my responsibility to visit Arthur and encourage him to participate in the meeting to change his life style and Karma. I thought, "It would be just a waste of time. He probably won't be at home anyway. Even if he's home, half the time, with his mental condition, Arthur was in and out of ether. Besides, I didn't feel like going out in the cold subzero weather. It struck me: "Is my attitude negative?" and I thought: "Maybe I'm going against the Universal Principle of Compassion. To care for one person and change "poison into medicine" is an act of compassion. It was not a difficult act like climbing Mount Everest. Why be a hypocrite, believing in Compassion and not doing anything about it? I was in a much better mood after chanting. I bundled myself up and boldly went outside into the stormy snowy day of December. Riding on a street car chanting softly to myself without any particular thought in mind I experienced something out of the ordinary. My chest started to heave up and down as if my lungs were doing deep breathing exercises. Tremendous surge of energy started to course through my body and I felt like a balloon being pumped with air. Suddenly my body lifted just above the seat and I had the sensation of sitting on air. "Is this real or what?" reached down with my hand to feel where the seat was and realized I was not suspended in the air but still seated on a solid surface. I placed my hand on my left chest and it was motionless as it was supposed to be due to the surgery of collapsing the left lung years ago. I didn't try to go into details and analyze this strange but pleasant experience and passed it off as a subjective out-of-the-body-that-didn't-leave-the-body experience. I was still in a state of heightened awareness. Looking through the clear frosted window section of the streetcar, the World was vivid with sharp clarity. … Whirling snow, hovering dark shadows creeping over the houses and buildings decorated with colorful Xmas lights that lined the parade route for my Red Chariot. I recalled the words of a Yoga teacher, "Awareness caused by drugs is a Promethean Spark compared to the awareness of the noonday Sun from a natural high."

Back to the reality of the mundane world. Still feeling good I was able to knock and bang on the front door for a long time. The landlord finally came out and didn't seem to mind my asking to see Arthur. He walked up the stairs to the second floor and I heard him calling, "Arthur, Arthur." I was just inside the door and heard the shuffling of his feet going to the other end of the hallway. He then came back down and said, "Arthur is not home." The thought of "wasting my time and effort" or failure to see Arthur did not enter my mind. I just felt good thinking I'd carried out my responsibility and liked the SGI way of teaching people, "How to fish." While returning home, the words, "Ceremony in the Air" crossed my mind. I know Hindu Scriptures and Buddhist Sutras are loaded with rich imageries, metaphors, similes, parables, etc. I believe the oral teachings of antiquity and ancient texts are authentic in expounding the profound truth in a simple story form. The scribes may distort and interpolate the Scripture but would not have to change the simple stories to suit their own bureaucratic faith. For instance, "Ceremony in the Air" is part of the Lotus Sutra. Why would anyone change the wonderful fairy tale? It's no threat to any ideological belief system. It's about a huge Tower suspended in the Air. When opened, it's bedecked with all sorts of precious gems and jewels. Residing in the Tower are the forces of nature and beings all labelled as Gods and semi Gods. No threat to any teaching for anyone to change the wording of a simple story. I have a sneaky suspicion that Nichiren, an enlightened Buddhist Sage, actualized the "Ceremony in the Air" into the Reality of day to day life. He materialized the Treasure Tower by inscribing words on a scroll representing the Cosmos and the totality of human life. The Treasure Tower was actualized as Gohonzon. The very act of chanting to the Gohonzon is the "Ceremony" and "in the Air" is the bodily breathing of air when chanting. The fairy tale became a reality which threatened other powerful religious institutes and for this Nichiren was persecuted and in constant danger of being killed. Nichiren survived and left his legacy and blueprint for his followers to actualize the simple wonderful stories of the Lotus Sutra to establish peace and happiness in this World.

Over the years, my own idea and understanding about the "Ceremony in the Air" has suited me fine. When I'm really into the chanting and doing SGI activities I do feel at times the "Lightness of Being." When the membership started to grow, SGI rented a larger space for meetings. It was the first SGI Community Centre in Canada. In those days the members would go out on busy corners and spread the word. It happened on a cold snowy day in December. I thought, "Nobody is going to come tonight, not in weather like this." Miracle or not, four people I talked to showed up for the meeting. That great feeling of weightlessness, riding the crest of an unseen wave of energy through vacuum helped me to move about quickly and effortlessly to make sure each guest was looked after by a member. Occasionally my thyroid gland would act up causing a heaviness of body and being. What a difference it was compared to the lightness of being. In that heavy state it felt like I was carrying a couple of hundred pounds walking up the stairs. One member told me she didn't think I had too long to live." I decided once and for all to overcome my thyroid problem and the fear of heights. Now I was really into chanting and I had another one of those subjective experiences. I saw and felt my life and body was a fragmented broken mirror. I had my doubts and thought, "Is this Gohonzon going to put Humpty Dumpty back together again?" the members were all excited to be going to an SGI convention in Akron, Ohio. SGI has a guideline for anybody with a big obstacle to use the big activity as a target date to overcome a specific problem by chanting. A week before the Convention I saw my mirror again. This time the fragmented bits and pieces seemed glued and held together by a putty type of material and smoothed out by sanding and I realized all it needed was more sanding and polishing to become a whole, spotless mirror. This gave me great hope and I wondered if the teaching of the Lotus was the one Supreme Vehicle to attain Buddha hood. Boy did I enjoy the Convention with high spirits. What a Broadway show the Chicago members put on. The Brass Band blaring away in the balcony between curtain calls and intermission. The medley of songs sung by various chorus groups and soloists and the colorful cultural costumes displayed by different dance groups and the pom pom kids captured the Holiday Spirit. Everything was well organized for the 3000 members who attended the theatre show. The words, "this World is for you to enjoy" kept ringing in my ears throughout the years of Buddhist practice.

The SGI conventions in the states were getting bigger and better and the following year in San Diego, the U.S. members put on a great show on ice. The colorful costumes, fancy floats and the graceful skaters performing to the sound of music. I had to give them credit; many of the U.S. members had to learn how to skate and managed to put on a wonderful Icecapade. The members in the arena were cheering, clapping, oo-ing and ah-ing. Ice skating seemed new to a lot of Californians. No wonder some of them were gasping. I believe in those days most of the Californians had never seen a hockey game. Although San Diego was a naval base it was a beautiful city. At the ocean, the endless beach, the famous parkland and the Marine World. I was like a kid seeing the live dolphins for the first time doing tricks and the killer whale putting on a terrific performance. I stayed behind for two days after the Toronto members left for the airport and flew back to Toronto. Next day, a Japanese girl was kind enough to show me around the famous San Diego Parkland. Later we dined and I kept my distance. She was pleasant and very attractive but I was in no position to fall in love. The second day a retired couple staying in the Motel invited me to go boating. Hundreds of yachts anchored to a maze of dock ways, I could not have met a nicer couple. They seemed interested and curious about the organization so I explained what little I knew about Buddhism. They both talked about their life style and seemed to be enjoying life. The man was a retired naval officer and loved the sea. They were looking forward to the coming month to take their annual cruise south along the California-Mexico coastline to their favorite hide-a-way. He kept telling me, "Reg, when you retire, come and live in San Diego. It's like heaven here." Taking the long ride back to Toronto, the foremost thing in my mind was the fear of heights. SGI had already announced the 1975 American Bicentennial Convention would be held in Hawaii and if I wanted to go, I would have to fly. Some members might have thought I was strange going to San Diego by myself. If it hadn't been for my fear I would have gone with them on the plane. My dysfunctional thyroid was improving "lessening of Karmic Retribution" but the phobia about heights was still severe.

One of the reasons I didn't really try to challenge my phobia was I just stayed away from heights so it wasn't a problem. This time there were no shortcuts to Hawaii. I had to fly. I ignored and procrastinated about the challenge for months until I realized there were only eight months to go for the Hawaii Convention. "Fear of failure" of not overcoming my fear of heights spurred me on. I made up my mind to chant five hours straight every night without taking a break or having a glass of water or going to the washroom nor lose focus and intensity chanting to the Gohonzon. All or nothing. I believe it was near the end of the second week that I had another one of those unusual subjective experiences. The Chinese words on the Gohonzon remained black and did not change color or move against the background of red pinkish hue, glowing, pulsating, and emitting some kind of nuclear energy. The Gohonzon appeared to be revealing the core energy that generates the Universe. It was awesome, terrifying and frightening. I had to stop chanting. This time I wasn't "shook up", accepted as a normal subjective paranormal experience. On the final day, I walked across the Broadview Bridge, stopped in the middle, peered over the railing to see the ground below and did not feel the strong gravitational force trying to pull me over the railing and plunge me to the ground. It's weird, even when I was in an apartment or office high above the ground, I would sweat bullets fighting the gravitational force. Those panic anxiety attacks felt so hellish it's a wonder I didn't go overboard. Although not totally comfortable I knew I could handle my phobia of heights.

"Pearly shells A-A-O." What a glorious time in Hawaii. We finally checked into a hotel in the late afternoon and I decided to take a stroll. Walking uphill towards the beach, I couldn't see the bathers but they were shrieking and laughing. Although I was tired after the long flight I said, "The hell with it, I'm going to change and wear my bathing suit." The water was so warm and the waves three or four feet high came splashing onto the beach. The girls were still shrieking and yelling, trying to catch the waves and then doing a belly flop on the incoming waves. Most of the girls from Toronto and Montreal had never seen or been to an ocean beach. The snacks were great, no hot dogs or fries, only packages of sushi rice and noodles sold from the small beach stands. Every day was unbelievable, a real Hawaiian Holiday. Many of us didn't have responsibility to do organizational duties such as being cooped up in the communication room for 24 hours or involved in the Traffic Control Division. Some volunteers were needed to complete the floating platform to stage the biggest theatre show ever in the U.S. I like the Guidelines of SGI; the members come first and for every activity, big or small, they should be looked after, making sure the events go smoothly and harmoniously.

"No accident" was the battle cry.

Having free time every day was paradise. Balmy weather, blue sky and emerald green and blue ocean water. Every chance I had I was swimming in the warm water. They say the temperature of the water is between 72 and 73 degrees all year round. My metabolism went haywire due to my thyroid problem. Even after I stopped surfing, my heart wouldn't stop pounding for quite a while. I guess learning how to lie down and stand up on the surfing board and then going out to catch incoming waves a few times was just too strenuous for my system. Anyway, for the first attempt riding the waves I did well. Some girls from Montreal invited me to go sightseeing. They rented a station wagon and a good natured Japanese man from Montreal was the driver. What a hilarious day. The girls were in high spirits, chatting, joking and laughing all the time. One girl who had low blood sugar had a jar of peanut butter and a loaf of bread and was constantly eating and cracking jokes about herself. No matter where we were Hawaii was a beautiful place. We visited Ikeda Park high above overlooking the ocean, a place named after our President of SGI. The only places that were flat and hot were the pineapple farms. We came across a secluded beach, no food stall, nobody around except for two local guys. We all decided to rest and sunbathe for a while lying on my back, shielding my eyes from the sun, the girls seemed quiet until one of them said, "Those guys look cute." "Yeah, they are." Then one of the girls said, "I'm going over and talk to them about Buddhism." I rolled over on my stomach and the girls were keenly watching the trio. The next one said, "I'm going to help her out. It looks like fun. I'm joining them." I kept rotating my body in order not to get a sunburn. The girls came back and we started preparing to go back to the hotel. Later, the two guys came along carrying bags filled with mangoes and pineapples. The two Hawaiians looked like they were of Japanese origin. I started to get messages and phone calls at all hours of the day. They kept asking where the girls were. Even other strangers would call asking for the girls. Two or three o'clock in the morning, men would wake me up with calls. I had to take the phone off the hook. Some thought I was a chaperone, others thought it was a dating service. Hard to figure out what the Montreal girls were up to.

The night of the big show twenty to thirty thousand people were sitting on the beach watching the panorama of the past 200 year history of the United States the Bicentennial. The movement of SGI is based on Peace, Culture and Education and I thought "what a befitting place for this to happen, right in the middle of the Ocean of Peace (Pacific). This event was made possible by the members who volunteered time and labor of compassion. Many of them went months ahead of schedule to build a huge "Island Stage" offshore. Members did all the designing and sewing of costumes and made hundreds of panels, painted and numbered to be put together like a jig saw puzzle to create the background for different scenes. The music, the dancing, the acting, the medleys, all choreographed, directed and produced by SGI and its members. What can I say: "Fabulous! Fantastic! Breathtaking." In the darkness of the night the brightly lit stage appeared to be suspended in air. It may be farfetched but the magnificent display of the performers on stage re-minded me of the "Ceremony in the Air" as described in the Lotus Sutra. "Could this be the effect of that great Spiritual truth of humanity?" two guys in front of me were making critical comments. "This is unbelievable, greater than anything on Broadway." "Will this be on the National News? It should be." "I like that, maybe we could use it." "I don't think we could use the other part." Obviously they were Broadway Boys making critical comments. They were also curious about SGI. The finale was this Volcanic Mountain built on top at the left side of the island platform erupting and making thunderous noises spewing out fire and smoke. I can't remember if the fireworks started right after the show or another night but it was an awesome work of computer technology releasing rockets after rockets exploding three times, each explosion higher and higher, showing colorful sparks blessing all of us with joy and happiness. The next day I enjoyed myself swimming in the water like a navy seal, checking out the Island Stage while keeping cool in the afternoon sun and listening to the different bands playing onstage. After the SGI activi-ties ended we still had two days of doing nothing but swimming, eating (I got tired of eating pineapples and mangoes) and relaxing. Believe it or not, life became boring and I was happy to board the plane to fly back home.

My thyroid was still a problem, especially when I did anything physical and strenuous. The whole body would feel like a short circuited electrical system. With the jitteriness came the tired heavy feeling of exhaustion. I stayed away from overdoing things and yet, what few Buddhist activities I did seemed to renew my energy. I was off the Macro Diet when I met Michio who came from Boston to give lectures and guidance to the Macro community. He was kind enough to give me a quick consultation about my health. I told him about my thyroid problem and he looked at me carefully saying, "the energy flow is good and your thyroid will be okay in a year." It was uncanny; without knowing my med-ical history he said, "The left side of your body is weak." I had to tell him about the pneumothorax surgery on my left lung and he said, "It is nothing to worry about." I also mentioned I was chanting, "NAM MYO HO RENGE KYO." He simply said, "NAM MYO HO RENGE KYO is good fortune." I didn't have the heart to tell Micho I had quit cooking Macro meals and was only eating in restaurants. I just couldn't see myself spending all that time shopping for Macro foods, cleaning, preparing, cooking and eating my own meals three times a day. It went against my own judgment, knowing that a balanced diet of natural foods was the best way to eat and stay healthy and I made a lame excuse to myself: "At least the chanting will supply adequate oxygen, the element that helps the biochemical balance." It was probably arrogance, a form of ignorance to think I could get away with eating meals in restaurants and still regain my health. For sure, eating certain foods, especially heavy meats speeded up the metabolism, making the heart pound madly out of control and the vicious cycle of jitteriness, weakness, dizziness and put me on the verge of passing out. I think the body uses up a tremendous amount of sugar and oxygen to digest heavy meats. I became addicted to junk food, the bi-polar diet of extremes yin (pastries) and yang (meats). It took a few decades to normalize my thyroid but my blood sugar is much too high. The doctors label it Diabetes II and it comes with all sorts of consequences such as cataracts, nose bleed, dry feet, loss of nerve endings, dementia, poor circulation, etc. Refined sugar is almost like a drug and it wouldn't be a bad idea if the medical profession made it into a prescription drug to regulate how much a person should take. Now in my old age I have two health problems, high blood sugar with side effects and a tumor on my back

Just between and below the shoulder blades. It started as a pimple twenty years ago and now it's grown to the size of a walnut. I figure the way it's growing it will become the size of a plum in another twenty years. If it doesn't bother me I'll wait until it becomes the size of an orange and by that time I'll be at least 120 years old. If I'm still alive then, I'll have it removed by surgery as recommended. The doctor who looked after me thought I had a good attitude. Hopefully, medical science will advance to a point where the treatment will be much more expedient and. Humane.

Health and strength-wise I was just hanging on. For the 1976 Bi-Centennial in New York, my health had to be in better shape. I was not going to be a bystander just watching all the great and enjoyable SGI events as I had the previous year in Hawaii. To be one of the participants I would have to have endurance and stamina. I felt I had no choice but to increase the chanting to energize my body to become healthier. I didn't want my body to fall apart and spoil the fun for myself and other members who would worry about me.

"Knock knock who's there." "Mirror mirror on the wall." While chanting, a mirror again appeared in my mind. Was it a conscious dream? Hallucination? Subjective reality? Who knows? The first time I saw the mirror "It was on the wall and had a great fall" breaking up into fragments after hitting the floor. The second time it was back on the wall, all the pieces glued together by a putty type material. This time the putty was all gone, replaced by a transparent film of the dust. I could see through the smudge that the mirror had no cracks and was in one piece. This encouraged me to chant harder, thinking the mirror would become spotless. I believe the brain is a miniature universe, myriads of mini particles and nano vibes moving in and out of multi-level, sub-level, levels within levels, neuropaths regulating the Brain Body function. Infinitely complex, subtle and subliminal, no section or point in the brain would consciously let me know of everything that was happening simultaneously to my Body Brain function and simplified matters by creating an image of a mirror reflecting my life condition. I sort of felt the mirror was like a thermometer to gauge the temperature of my wellbeing. I heard that researchers who study brain waves claim that chanting creates beneficial alpha waves that harmonize and balance the bio-chemicals in the brain.

The off-key grating and blaring sound of brass instruments would crack any mirror. Most of the members of the band had never played a brass instrument. The U.S. Bi-Centennial was fast approaching. Well? "Practice makes perfect." They began to sound a bit like a marching band. Canada at that time did not have a large SGI membership but still managed to recruit some young men for the Brass section and even fewer girls for the Fife and Drum. Combining the two made up a small but presentable unit, especially when a handful of SGI members from all different parts of Canada volunteered to join the band. Members decided to be very Canadian by wearing Mountie outfits and the women's group did the fitting and sewing of the uniforms.

Sleepless in New York. All through the Bi-Centennial celebration and our SGI Convention, I just couldn't get enough sleep. It all started with the long bus ride from Toronto to New York. This time I was to be a participant, not a bystander. From the get go I attended meeting after meeting. The biggest meeting at the beginning was held in a large Convention Hall with government and city officials to coordinate the movement of the parade and the use of Central Park for all the SGI bands to practice. Some of the floats in the parade were not finished and needed help to be ready for the Parade. One morning a Cargo Van came around and drove some of us to the waterfront. Inside a warehouse was a tractor trailer with a huge stage like a platform where members were building a model of the Golden Gate Suspension Bridge. Some of the guys worked 40 hours without sleeping. I couldn't have been more happy working on the San Francisco float, the city that introduced me to SGI Buddhism. Sitting on the edge of the dock, having lunch, I cringed when I saw the water, ocean water blacker than black ink. I thought that with all the cities in the world it would still take a long time to kill the vast Ocean. The fond memories of the Frisco members and the Japanese lady who took me to my first Buddhist discussion meeting warmed my heart. Is a warm heart a step towards addressing the woes of the world?

The summer heat in New York was hot and humid. Central Park with all its winter green was even hotter, and wearing red T-shirts didn't help, unlike last year when all SGI members wore white T-shirts and it made me think about Hawaii and the cooling effect of bathing in Ocean water. The SGI Traffic Control Division (TCD), the boys in blue wore white officers' caps, blue jackets and white pants. The boys allocated a cleared area of the Park for us to practice our march and to play the band music. The boys in blue looked after us making sure nobody got lost or had any mishaps. Against the green background of the park we began to see other red shirts in the distance, looking like little ants marching to the sound of music. It didn't take too long before the whole park became alive with music and the sound of the drums carried far beyond the park to the surrounding buildings. Many of the apartment dwellers came down to see what the ruckus in their beloved park was all about. None of them knew about our parade that would be on the Avenue of the Americas the next day. I think it could have been the longest parade in New York's history.

Not enough sleep, early to rise, we had our morning planning meeting for the Parade of the Day. Arriving just before 3 o'clock at a designated side street, some of the band units were already assembling. The Boys in Blue were directing and positioning everybody as they arrived. I inquired about Toronto and they gave me a placard, #75. I think five marching bands were on our side street. Just behind us was the last unit of the parade, #76, the New York Brass Brand, and in front of us, #74, a band from the Midwest. At times I find it more tiring to stand in one spot than to walk along. About an hour later, roll call was done by the Blue Boys and everybody was accounted for. Anxious and restless, time drags on and some of the Canadian players started to tinker with their instruments to warm up. When the sound of music is off key and in disharmony it feels uncomfortable and life is no different. Finally the Canadian players played a piece of a marching song and it sounded not too bad. The little sound of music triggered a wave of movement from all the band players and they all started to bring out the instruments. The band somewhere in the front played a marching song and we all stood still, listening. When they finished we all clapped and applauded. Not to be outdone, the Midwest band in front of us played their song and we cheered them on and gave them a big ovation when they finished. The spirit of competition took over and the bands took turns in strutting their stuff. The New York brass band just behind us got a huge ovation. All the other players thought the New York performance was terrific. Stranger than fiction, our tiny little Fife and Drum Corps might have gotten the biggest ovation. A handful of drummers pounded the drums. I don't know how they made such a ferocious thunderous sound. Maybe it was the knack of hitting the drums, or the timing was perfect or it was perfect timing, or the rhythm of the sound waves. Who knows?

The New York Brass Band members were the greatest supporters of our Drumettes. They cheered, whistled, clapped and stomped their feet and smiled in disbelief that such a drum sound could be made by a small handful of girls. Cheered on by each other's applause, everybody played to a higher spirited sound. I couldn't get enough of the music. Everyone was enjoying the blast. Caught in a frenzy, we lost track of time when the shrill whistle from the Boys in Blue woke us up. "Tone it down, keep it quiet, the neighbors are complaining that we're making too much noise." "People coming home from work want peace and quiet." Supper time, it was beginning to get dark and I asked a blue boy, "When are we going to march in the Parade?" "--in about an hour." Two hours later, the Blues blew their whistles, signaling us to move out. Whistle after whistle and the dark side street became deserted and barren.

Even though we were at the tail end, we were now part of the parade. It was almost dark and the city lamps barely lit up the parade route. I could see the people sitting on the curb and the rest of the crowd standing sidewalk deep. Whistles controlled the movement of our unit, when to stop, when to march, when to play music etc. I was closest to the crowd, walking beside our Canadian unit, holding a placard with the number #75. People would come up to me and ask "What group is this?" or "Who are you people?" one person walked with me for a while asking me all kinds of questions about Buddhism. I could hear comments from the crowd, "Wow, this is great!" "Never seen anything like this." "What a fantastic parade." Meanwhile I was glad not to have no severe symptom of thyroid disorder. The shrill burst of whistles was the signal we were approaching the Dignitary Stand. I could see a dozen or so bigwigs in an elevated booth, well lit, sitting and smiling. It was quite dark on the side and behind the stand but I was still able to see the pale outline of faces, thousands of faces. They seemed to be on a hillside or makeshift bleachers.

In front of the Dignitary Stand our Canadian Band made a few fancy steps and the drumettes really pulled it off, making it sound like the full throttle of a large military drum corp. the crowd gave us thumbs up, ovations, we couldn't have asked for more in their cheering, clapping and applauding. I saw the SGI General Director jump up from his seat smiling and clapping, overjoyed by our performance. A month earlier, we had marched in a daytime parade at the Boston Bi-Centennial and he thought our performance was listless and the uniforms too dull and drab for a night parade in New York. We changed the brown Mountie hat into a white trooper's hat and wore silvery white jackets, white pants and shiny white boots. As we were marching away I heard the explosive blast of the New York Brass Band kick in. above the roar of the crowd, the amazing sound of the New York Brass Band was coming through loud and clear. The San Francisco Brass Band was jazzy and did the marching dance. I believe they won first prize and the Lost Angeles Fife and Drum Band had over 300 girls playing the flute. But I still think our Canadian and the New York contingents were the best one-two punch to end the historical parade. The parade ended at the edge of Central Park and the Boys in Blue directed us through the twilight zone of the Park with flashlights, back to our hotel. Too wound up to sleep, some of us went to a nearby coffee shop. We got to sleep in the wee hours of the morning.

Stadium and Baseball, Culture and Convention.

Early morning wakeup call and still sleeping, managed to keep my eyes open. Before breakfast we were given the itinerary for the day. We followed the Boys in Blue into the Subway and everybody seemed to enjoy the fast rackety train ride to Giant Stadium. Even though I was a long time Yankee fan it was still a treat to see the New York Giants and the Chicago Cubs play. We were seated down on the sunny side of the Stadium. I thought, "Now is the time to take a nap." I slouched on the seat, tipped my cap over my eyes and tried to fall asleep. The sun was too hot, the seat was too uncomfortable and the familiar sound of baseball was too distracting. The voice of the Umpire calling Balls and Strikes, the crack of the bat, the chattering of infielders, the cheering and booing of the fans and the vendor shouting 'peanuts, popcorn and cold drinks.' I watched the game in a sleepy numb state, drinking cold colas, hoping to stay cool. Sometimes ballgames drag on and this one finally ended. The Blue Boys ushered us out of the stadium, walked us across the street into another Stadium. Louis Armstrong Stadium was much smaller and probably seated between 10 to 15,000 people. Once inside, the Blue Girls took over and led us to a section to be seated. The place was beginning to fill up with a sea of red shirts. Soon afterwards, everyone was given a small box with chicken, potatoes and cole slaw. Members seemed to be enjoying the meals but I was just going through the motions of chewing the food like a zombie. Eyes were open but the body was asleep. It didn't take long for the Boys and the Girls in Blue to clean up the messy leftovers, putting them into garbage bags and taking them away. As Blue People, it's great to chant and care for others. Through my own experience of caring, my thoughtless mind would cross over to a thoughtful mind. What a beautiful added consciousness of responsibility. "Mindless to the mindful." "Careless to the careful." In this heightened state, many small and little details and other things become clear and obvious. In this way, trouble spots and problem areas are foreseen and the members could be cautioned and guided to avoid mishaps and accidents. Nothing better than to be in rhythm and harmony in day to day life

Plenty of preparation has to be done behind the scenes. Months of preparation, choreography, all the group performances, the making of the costumes, the training and the directing, all done by volunteers. Even though the members are dedicated and united, "ego clashes" make a production a difficult and complex undertaking. Years later the most unbelievable cultural show was held at Tiger Stadium in Japan. Over 30,000 members watched 3,000 SGI performers put on a show, "Culture for Peace."

Let the show begin. When all the high beam lights were turned on, it seemed to be broad daylight in Armstrong Stadium. Fabulous, beautiful costumes, panorama of colors, rhythmic movements of the dances, medleys of songs and music and an array of exciting acts. The cheering and cheering of the people flipped over into cursing and cursing. The thought, "what are all these people so happy about? They must all be nuts." And this terrible unbearable feeling overwhelmed me. I didn't know what to do about this hellish feeling. In sheer desperation I forced out a silent scream. "Nam myo ho ren ge kyo" three times. Like a bolt of lightning", instant transformation of my mind. Gone was that demonic feeling, wide awake, senses clear, renewed energy and immediate ability to empathize and tune in to the joy of all the people. I couldn't help saying to the person beside me, "Isn't this a great show? It's really great!" and he replied, "It's fantastic!" I was so relieved to get rid of the devil possession, I kept muttering 'wonderful, wonderful.' How time flies when I'm in a state of gratefulness. Moment to moment and the show was over and on the other side of the Stadium, there were about 3,000 SGI members from Japan. They gave all of us three cheers. We acknowledged them by cheering and waving our hands. They were relentless, they kept waving and cheering and we kept doing the same.

Then the SGI computerized fireworks started. Rocket after rocket launched into the night sky. Explosions of peace dusting the darkness with colorful sparks. "Big Bangs" and the magical sparks of blessing and then fading into the void. The thunderous sound of a volcano erupted spewing flame and smoke. The man made volcanic mountain used in last year's Hawaii convention had been dismantled and brought to New York .and activated to end the SGI Bicentennial Convention

Now that I'm in my second or third childhood, the days, weeks and months go quickly. Some relatives are proud to be related to Daniel and even friends would ask me how I managed to have a great kid. I believe my wife Nancy has more say in this; after all, she is the one that raised my son.

Saturday was still a day to enjoy. Many times my wife and son and I would go to High Park. Daniel loved running around in the wide open space of the Park. In the fall he gathered autumn leaves to build a fort or hideaway, piling the leaves over and around a picnic table. When we strolled on the grass, Daniel would walk between us holding our hands and doing the somersault like a Ferris wheel going over and over, giggling and laughing like it was the greatest circus act in the world. Like most kids he probably didn't like our separation but at least once in a while he enjoyed the semblance of family life and like most kids he grew up fast. From waist to chest, to eyes and, VOILA, he was taller than me. When Daniel was chin high, he would come to the pool room to meet me and we would go out and do our father and son thing. Most of the time I was busy playing so I would give him a few dollars to play his favorite game of Pac Man.

The game of golf usually broke up around 5 o'clock and I would head on to the nearby arcade to see how my kid was doing. All Daniel could talk about was Packman. He wanted me to learn and play Pac Man. I tried a few times but Pac Man was not for me. I guess I was used to beating humans, not a machine. At least Daniel enjoyed doing things "my way." I liked Swiss Chalet, he liked chicken. I liked action movies, he loved them. Daniel was like a buddy and an easy kid to get along with but whenever he called me "Dad" it reminded me I was still his father. Brought up in a single parent home, I don't think it was always smooth sailing.

Once my wife called and told me to find Daniel; he had run away from home. I was a bit concerned even though she said, "Daniel is not the type of boy who would do anything foolish; he's probably staying at one of his friend's place." Another time she phoned me to say that Daniel and his friends are terrorizing the neighborhood and wanted me to do something about it. Actually, the kids were skateboarding and in a group those skates made a loud irritating grating sound that bothered the neighbors. I know that as kids we put the wheels of a roller skate in the front and back of a two foot 2 by 4 standing on it, going down a steep street was okay and fun while it lasted but eventually the crude skate board would veer off and it was impossible to steer it back on the road. The challenge at that speed was to jump over the curb and do the hop hop on the side walk to retain balance. Otherwise, if we tumbled and fell we were in for a severe abrasion of the skin. As kids we all have creative instinct and I believe we kids were forerunners of inventing many of the sports played today. Skate board is now a major sporting event on snow, water and concrete. We put together a longer piece of 2 by 4 with a wooden fruit crate in front, with V shape wooden handlebars and added roller skates in the front and back of the 2 by 4 and called it the 'box car'.

When a bunch of us rode our box cars down a steep hill, the horrendous scraping, grating, nerve-wracking noise was worse than a bunch of motorcycles. No wonder neighbors complained. I told Daniel to find a street where neighbors tolerated the sound of the skate board. P.T., my friend, saw Daniel and his friends skateboarding on top of a sloped fence and with all the crazy stunts kids do, my son dislocated his left elbow. Karma? "Chip off the old block?" As a boy his age, I dislocated my right elbow. Another thing upsetting the people of the Co-op housing was that Daniel and his friends were running on top of the roofs. My wife was afraid for Daniel's safety. I didn't blame her; the roofs were just too high even for roofers, never mind the kids fooling around on top. Daniel agreed not to run all over the attached roofs, but wanted to sit on top of his roof early in the morning to be by himself. I'm a firm believer that every person should have a moment of solitude in a special place. I respected my son's feeling and could only say, "It's a high roof so be careful when you climb up and down the antennae and also be quiet so nobody knows you are up there." I empathized with his thought and mood, the breaking of dawn, the solar rays skating on top of the trees, the chirping of the birds, the dense underbrush on the hillside, was nature's haven. I recalled some of my own thoughts contemplating, sitting high up on the mountain of North Vancouver overlooking the inlet city, bridge and the ocean.

Later, as a young teenager in the heart of the Rockies, observing at the bottom and the top of the mountainous ranges, the stars that seem so close, the lakes, rivers, streams and forever the green trees, inspired me to seek and try to understand the invisible moving behind the curtain of creation. Just imagining the immense power of the invisible and visible reality made my own power and problems insignificant. I assumed Daniel had lofty thoughts and that touched me. Recent hearsay relating to the science of the brain – I suspect the brain has the ability to observe the observer. Without the brain, no thoughts originate in the finite mind. The mind is one entity but has two aspects, the finite and the infinite.

Daniel was chest high when he started asking me about hell and after life. This upset me when I heard he was learning all this in Sunday school. I told my wife to get him out of there and she already suspected it was not the right thing for Daniel and agreed. My wife received the Gohonzon and chanted for a while but preferred to get involved in Native Indian Spirituality. She insisted that I go to the Wandering Spirit Public School to see the projects on display by the eighth graders. I was taken back by a scenic painting and a poem done by Daniel. My English is not that good but I thought the poem could have been written by any of the great English poets. Just prior to this my wife told me, "Daniel gave a lecture on

Spirituality at the Native Indian Centre and got a standing ovation. A Peruvian friend, George had a South American Handicraft store next to my Natural Food restaurant and Daniel would come over on weekends. Most of the time I would be busy cooking and looking after the restaurant so my son spent a lot of time playing with George's son, making up games and their favorite was romping, jumping and tumbling over layers of Peruvian carpet at the back of the store. George had talks with Daniel and was amazed at his awareness of North and South American Indian Spiritual Culture. Daniel's grandparents on his mother's side were both educators in Ontario and after retiring they moved to Victoria B.C. Later, his Grand Pa came to visit his relatives, the MacLeans, near Chatham and on his way back stayed for a few days at Daniel's. We all went to see a movie and I think it was, "The Last of the Mohicans."

In the car on our way home were a friend of mine, Ned, who was the driver, Daniel, his sister LaToya and her friend (both native Indian), Grand Pa and myself. They were discussing the pros and cons of the movie when Grand Pa innocently blurted out, "Well, the Indians were savages." Slight pause; the remark didn't mean anything to me until Daniel said, "Savages, Grand Pa?" And that was it. Ned was surprised. Daniel was so tactful. I thought it was funny and realized my son was much better in his approach towards people than I was. Daniel was well liked, bright and hyper and women thought he was a good looking boy.

After a snowfall Daniel would come to the restaurant, take my shovel and clean the sidewalk. One regular customer in the restaurant told me, "Daniel is sharp as a whip." He said my son was charging 25 to 50 cents to shovel snow away from storefronts. The guy laughed, saying one shopkeeper didn't have the money and Daniel said, "Its okay, I'll do it for free." I had to laugh, wondering if it could be the Japanese-Scottish blood in him.

Sometimes I wonder if prayers are answered. Due to our difference in lifestyle, when Nancy was pregnant she would be sleeping when I came home late. One night, I crawled into bed around 2 AM and she was lying on her back sleeping peacefully. I felt her large tummy and rubbed it gently in a circular motion and prayed for an avatar to be reincarnated. I believe the baby's body is the extension of the Parent's body but the spirit belongs to the Universal. I also believe in the Divinity within all humanity and like most people my own is wrapped up and shrouded by misdirected emotional hang-ups. I could talk the talk but was not a good walker. I prayed for my son to be a Spiritual Warrior that could walk the walk,

The day Daniel was born, Jim and I went to St. Michael's Hospital. Looking through the glass partition, Diamond Jim was overjoyed saying, "Reg, look at your son's face and the movements of his hands. He looks like an Emperor." Jim was more excited than I was. Whenever I beat a good golf player, Jim would call me the Emperor. Jim kept an eye on Daniel while he was growing up and often made comments about my son having eyes of compassion.

As a boy, I played a lot of team sports but Daniel seemed to prefer individual sport. While in public school he took lessons in judo and karate. He also liked going up to the Northern Wilderness with the Native Indians to learn how to hunt deer and moose and enjoyed fishing. He surprised me when he chose Eastern Commerce, a high school that taught business courses. I could only think, "Well maybe the Scottish blood in him likes business." Daniel's lips couldn't adjust to blowing the trumpet so he ended up playing the piano. He did some acting and appeared in a couple of films with the Native Group. Of course, in high school he started going out with girls but that's not my story. Daniel's academic standing was not good so he didn't qualify to attend the top universities for business courses. He realized the importance of having good grades, studied hard, and managed to hit the Honor Roll at Ryerson. For Physical Education he took up fencing and played squash and tennis. After graduating, Daniel did not seem to have any problem finding work in the Corporate World. What can I say: "He doesn't smoke, drink or take drugs and it just occurred to me that I never heard him swear, at least not in my presence." He seems to have a head on his shoulders and we don't always agree but it's nice to learn from my son. Daniel has empathy and communicates with people far better than yours truly. Nobody is perfect and he married a wonderful girl two years ago and that's why I'm writing this story as a delayed wedding present. My son is very supportive of his Mom and Sister and my relationship with him is depicted in two Father's day cards he sent me.

Father's Day Card:

"There never seems to be enough time to visit as much as we like or to call as often as we want -- But Father's Day seems to be the perfect time to express the love that's in my heart for you ALL the time"

Father's Day Card:

"The more I see of life, the more I realize how precious you are to me"

Dear Dad, Happy Father's Day!

I wanted to send you a little card to remind you how much I appreciate you.

The older I get the more I see, and all the experiences I go through show me that you are right -- the proper attitude is so important. Thank you for sharing this lesson with me.

I miss you and I love you.

Daniel

August 1st 1999

Dear Daniel,

I decided to prolong my sojourn on this planet by looking after my health. I will begin by drinking bottled water instead of eating junk food and sweets at the movies. Also, I will eat more fruits in this hot weather and cut down on pastries, especially at night.

Throughout the limitless space and time and among all the countless human beings past, present and future, you became our son. The wiser I become the more I appreciate you as a wonderful person. What good fortune for myself, Nancy and the kids!

Whenever an occasion arises, chant NAM-MYO-HO-REN-GE-KYO to feel good and manifest your great Life Force for your happiness.

Love as ever,

Dad

Dear Dad,

Although every day is special and unique, Dad's Day is a good opportunity to express the deep affection and gratitude that I have for you.

I am proud to be your son -- thank you for everything that you have shared with me.

Love,

Daniel

July 1, 2000

Dear Daniel,

What a happy occasion it was to spend some time with you on Father's Day weekend. Thanks for the card.

It was nice to hear that you are doing so well work-wise in Halifax. I noticed you seem much empowered. It's great to experience empowerment because in troubled times it helps to maintain confidence. Of course you know chanting always helps me to feel good.

Remember, Daniel, when you are empowered you are like a great ship. Stay on course by avoiding going too far one way or the other and you will weather all storms. What a great way to live!

I'm glad you're having a training course soon in Toronto. Looking forward to seeing you again.

Love,

Dad

The last worthwhile money game of Golf I played was with Bruce. For years we played either within a group or just the two of us. I had Bruce's number and whenever we locked horns head on I always managed to win the money. Bruce was one of the best Billiard Golf players in the city, soft spoken and a clean competitor. We were our own referee and we trusted each other's judgment call. Never did I think I was taken advantage of in penalty calls. The light reflecting on the surface of a ball would ever so slightly flicker, which means, in fact, that some contact was made between two balls, and depending on the shot it could be either a foul or fair shot. Major League sports with professional referees, using playback films, still make mistakes and with all the games Bruce and I played, it's remarkable we never had a disputed penalty call.

Downtown the Big O was the largest pool hall in the city and the Big "C" was the first pool room with a modern décor and only a city block separated the two. In the earlier years, the Big O had golf games every afternoon, seven days a week. That's where I met Bruce and it didn't take me too long to realize Bruce was one of the best players in the city. Good players are transient, especially a player like Bruce who would disappear for a while playing in a bigger action golf game in some other Pool Hall. The only time I wasn't around is when I went out of town. The action in the Big O slowed down, making the Big C my hangout. When the Towne Billiards went out of business due to demolition, the golf players came up to the Big C and played Towne Style Golf. I have to admit it was probably the toughest style golf game played in the city of Toronto. Most types of golf games were based on tic tic ticky ticky games but the Towne boys blasted the shots, making the 6x12 snooker table with 31 balls moving in all directions resemble a pin ball machine. Even if a person shapes up to go into a pocket, if seven players blast their shot before him his two balls would be out of position. In this sense, it was like the golf game played in the U.S., VERY tough to win a hole. I believe a miniscule malfunction of my thyroid caused me to lose 10 to 15 percent of my skill and ability and I was just hanging on not to lose money playing Towne Golf with the boys. One afternoon when the session was over, I decided to eat nearby and check out the Big O. the place was almost empty. I noticed Bruce sitting near the counter on the other side of the room. I went over, we shook hands and started our usual shop talk.

I sensed it was coming; he finally asked me to play golf. My game was slightly off but I thought "what the hell, why not?" for old time's sake. And besides, we weren't playing for big dough. Like all championship sports, the player or team that has the momentum wins. I couldn't break his momentum and Bruce played flawlessly. He was that good. The next evening he beat me again. Bruce knew he had me and kept bugging me to raise the stakes and I kept refusing. The third evening was the same. I had no chance of winning so I quit, making it a short session. Bruce was disappointed. For years, he consistently lost money to me and now when he had a chance to get even, I quit. He was razzing, needling and even goading me to play for big money. Sure, I reacted a bit, saying, "Yeah, we can play for big dough but up the street in the evening at the Big C. Bruce jumped at the chance and we made arrangements to play the next week. Bruce mentioned he was going to have a money man as a backer so one way or another I had to show him some decent money to play.

I went looking for Cal, hoping he would bankroll me. During the Good Ole Days of Towne Billiards, Cal was top gun, winning the city championship one year in Snooker and he even beat Donny Reeves, the legend, in a money match. The Towne boys had their own golf games and in the beginning, Cal played with them. His insight into the group game of golf was so great he almost controlled the outcome of the game. He explained to me one strategic shot that helped my group game of golf. Towne Billiards went out of business when the Developers demolished the building so all the players and friends came up to the Big C to play golf and hang out. It was a bad break for Cal when he got hepatitis, weakening his body and nerves and he lost the desire to play. He told me, "If I can't play to the best of my ability, it takes all the joy out of playing." I related to what he said but kept playing for a few years more and finally quit the game altogether. Many times we sat down in a food court and talked about golf. He understood some of the symptoms of a thyroid disorder and how it affected my game but was happy I kept playing. He loved the style and the way I played golf. He laughed when a couple of Towne players who only played at night challenged me to play head on golf, saying, "They got such a big ego, they actually think they could win. It's a joke." Cal knew I was just toying with them. It was always a pleasure to sit down with Cal and talk. Whenever we met he greeted me with warm feeling like we were blood brothers and the feeling was mutual.

Very few golf players reached the level of Cal's caliber and even fewer had the toughness of Cal's heart.

After a day or so, I finally found Cal. I asked him about backing me against Bruce. He was a bit hesitant, knowing Bruce was a great player, and asked me, "How's the thyroid behaving?" I answered, "I'm only playing up to 90 percent of my game and Bruce was just edging me out playing down the street in the Big O. I explained that the action game would be played at night in the Big C on the table where I played regularly with the Towne boys in the afternoon. Cal knew if I played on that table I would have the advantage of overcoming the ten percent handicap. I explained a bit more of my detailed game plan and he quickly realized I had the upper hand. No problem, he said, "I'll back you, go ahead and play."

Bruce and his money man showed up on time almost to the exact second at 7 o'clock. Without giving them a chance to catch their breath, I said, "We'll play for $20 a game and $2.00 a stroke and we play on a table at the back, away from the entranceway, counter and people. They were full of confidence and they both agreed to what I said. Cal had things to do but watched the first two games and then left. Each game went according to Hoyle, and Bruce was not able to gain any momentum to win a game. When his backer dropped over a $1,000 he pulled up and said, "Enough is enough" and the session was over. I believe Bruce got carried away with the feeling of confidence and lost touch with reality. I had experienced the same thing once before. The top gun in Snooker from the Cue Billiards and his money man challenged me to play head on golf. They picked a neutral pool room which was fair enough. I knew them both and the money man will never make a bad bet. I did not bother to go ahead of time to practice and learn the conditions of the table we would be playing on.

I was just brimming with too much confidence and thought all I had to do was to watch him play a couple of shots, including a few of my own shots and I would pick up all I needed to know about the table's condition. Everybody thought $10 a stroke was big money, which it was, but they put a cap of $100 loss on each game. I was disappointed because it took away the pressure of a money game. What threw me off stride was that the table was located in the corner and was not in line and parallel with two walls.

To catch imaginary lines of an angle on a table is very important in playing golf. The walls were too close to the railing and every time I sighted the correct angle on the cushion railing it would shift and skip around when I blinked or moved my head. It seemed like I was looking through a powerful bifocal or trifocal lens, giving me a mild eye ache. I lost the first game, which could have gone either way, and in the second game, victory was in my grasp but it slipped through my fingers. My ball was over the lip of the last pocket and all I had to do was make it for the win. But no, I had to be the Big Shot. The shot was fairly long and I decided to play the touch game, all I had to do was shoot and just touch the ball that was over the pocket without making it.

Of course the next shot would be to plug and obstruct the pocket, which means the other player would take a penalty to remove my ball. Anyway, the touch shot never touched the other ball. It was short by an eighth of an inch. No table is absolutely level. I would like to think my touch was perfect but the ball had to go ever so slightly uphill towards the last hole. My backer wanted me to keep playing but I quit. I didn't like the shifting tricky angles that gave me a headache and they didn't want to change tables. The money man from the Cue couldn't get out of there fast enough. He probably lost faith in his player; after all, his man made a mental error of going into the wrong hole which is unheard of among the golf players and also, I believe he knew I would adjust to another table much more quickly.

I waited for Cal after the session with Bruce and when he came back, he showed a tinge of emotion when I gave him half of the winnings. Money wasn't the question; it was the way I played according to the game plan that moved him emotionally.

Moneyman, bookmaker, handicapper, however Cal was hooked on horses. He would go early to the racetrack with a stopwatch and clock the horses working out. If he liked the running time of the horse he would check the racing form and do his due diligence and when things fit into the formula the money went into the ticket wicket. Visualizing the running of the race, all the horses jockeying for position and when his horse won by a neck or by a length, exactly as he foresaw the outcome of the race, he got the greatest kick and satisfaction. It's impossible to handicap every race and Cal had no patience to bet only on choice races. He might have beaten the track. Unfortunately, as most horse players say, "You can't win betting every race." Nobody is perfect but Cal was still a cut above the crowd. Later when I heard he went south of the border with Paul Thornley looking for pool action, he couldn't have picked a better top gun sharp shooter and I also thought, "P.T. couldn't have picked a better moneyman." What else? They did well.

P.T. wanted to take Bumps to the U.S. mainly to play the action game of "One Pocket" but Bumps didn't like the racial things in those days. Too bad, what a combination, for sure it would have been a legend in the making. When Bumps was fifteen years old he played pool on a small Boston Table and told me, "I got tired of making ball after ball and running table after table" so he switched to the larger snooker table. He enjoyed playing the "cat and mouse, hit and run" game which means making a few balls and then playing safe. This way, neither Bumps nor any pool hustler had to show their true worth. It's difficult to rate a pool hustler. Bumps never bothered to win Tournaments or championships. He always insisted that someone else was the best player in the room where he hustled. He just played well enough to win the money. Having a likeable personality to entertain, he cultivated guys who enjoyed playing with him. His philosophy was, "Take only a half a loaf, never a whole loaf." That way none of his customers went to the poor house. Enigma dilemma. Here's a man with black skin, a boozer, a prime candidate for skid row who made the Pool Room his stage to perform as a Master of Ceremonial Art. Bumps had a steady glow regulating his booze intake. Handsome six footer, graceful athletic body with plenty of animal magnetism.

Like a black panther, he would gracefully stalk around the pool table and zero in behind the cue ball; his leg stance, body leaning over the table, the arm movement holding the cue going back and forth, a perfect natural balance of a pool player. Even his life seldom went off balance. He kept a bottle of whiskey hidden in the toilet tank and he would frequent the washroom to take a swig or rush out to the nearby bar and down a shot or two of whiskey and then hurry back to continue playing. Bumps always had a pleasant glow maintaining and regulating his booze intake. Whether playing snooker one on one or playing with a group Pea Pool or Poker Pool. Once in a while if the games continued on longer than usual, the booze would catch up to Bumps. He would begin to stagger, slur his speech and squint his bleary eyes. In that short interval of time, in a drunken state, he forgot himself and threw caution to the winds trying to make every difficult wild crazy shot. "Boom", the balls kept going into the pocket. It's a miracle to find order in the chaotic movement of the Billiard Balls. When he finally missed a shot or two he'd hang up the cue saying, "I quit. I can't see anymore."

Loyalty among thieves. Bumps was straightforward, honest and would never cheat anybody. He would never throw a game or double-cross his friends. I trusted Bumps. Ross, another good pool player talked about the time he was scared stiff when he and Bumps went into a Black Bar in Buffalo. The blacks didn't like any whitey stepping into their domain and were on the verge of beating the crap out of Ross. Bumps stepped in front of Ross and told the blacks, "You'll have to get me first before you lay a hand on my friend." Whatever Bumps did must have worked. They quickly got out safely. Later Ross moved to California and Bumps lost the taste for going stateside. Violence in Pool Halls is rare but it happens. Bumps was great as a peacemaker. He saved my ass once or twice. One wacko had a handful of billiard balls waiting for Bumps to come out from the washroom and, at point black range, throw the balls at his head. Limey, standing beside the screwball with a cue in his hand, yelled at him, "Put those balls down or I'll beat your head into a bloody pulp." Bumps appreciated Limey and for sure Bumps would protect anybody against the act of senseless violence.

Willie often said, "Bumps sure made a lot of shots in a drunken state." Bumps and I first met Willie in the Cue Billiards. The idea of a good hustler is "keep the game close and win by a nose." Willie didn't know how good the master was and they played for days. Bumps was super in making the last two balls the pink or black as game ball. That's how pool sharks string along the fishes. Playing every day for over a week, Willie never won a game. Finally Bumps had to spot Willie ten points and they continued to play for another week. The games still went down to pink or black and Bumps always made the game ball which was of course either the pink or black ball. After another week, Bumps was spotting Willie 20 points. Willie loves the game and has a competitive spirit and thought he had a chance to win.

Billy told him, Bumps was a hustler who was too good for him. But Willie wouldn't listen to his younger brother's advice. It was still the same old story; the games were going down to the wire and the pink or black decided the winner. Willie still hadn't won a game in almost a month of playing every day. "It's still the same old story, a fight for love and glory." Willie was getting a 30 point spot and still losing by pink or black. Billy relayed a message to Willie, saying he had to be at the lawyer's office to close a deal but Willie didn't care; he wanted to beat Bumps one game even if it meant blowing a Real Estate deal. I love that song, "Time goes by." And Willie's spot went up to 40 points and "Still the same old story", pink or black, pink or black.

Willie still couldn't win a game. Willie was not that bad a player but Bumps wouldn't give him more than 40 points. Willie quit, realizing that Bumps didn't miss and had great control over the cue ball to play safe. My educated guess was to make a fair, even game, Willie needed 80 points from Bumps. As a hustler, Bumps would never over spot and always made sure he had plenty in reserve in case he needed it. Bumps was content playing for $2.00 a game which was enough to supply his daily booze for over a month. The three of us became good friends and whenever we had a chance we sat in a Tavern swapping stories, me with my coke and them with their whiskey cokes.

Harvey was a gentleman, scholar of the Snooker World, and learned the advance skill from George Chenier, the Hall of Famer. For years he played with George for $2 a game, the cost of taking lessons. Harvey invited me into his house. He was a foreman and looked after the machines of a large company. Half the basement was filled with tools and the other half was a special space for half of a snooker table that he had made. He practiced just making black balls off the spot. No wonder he made a lot of points making the black.

Harvey was an excellent person to represent the corporate world of Billiards. He played an exhibition match on a small snooker table with the great American pool player, Willie Masconi. No American is going to beat Harvey in a snooker game except maybe a hustler in hiding. Whenever George came back to Toronto they would play at the Uptown I pool hall on Yonge Street just north of the Cue Billiard on Bloor. The other Uptown II was on Yonge Street close to St. Claire Avenue. Wherever George played, he attracted people interested in Billiards, the aura of the Master was exciting. Seasoned players, novices and thrill seekers all hoping to catch the magical moment, a performance that surpasses expectation. Like the time George ran five hundred runs in a roll or a single shot that makes a spinning cue ball act like it has a mind of its own.

Harvey was a square John who didn't really gamble but wanted to experience the big action game of a hustler. He told me he put aside $500 to gamble in Snooker. Harvey had a reputation as a good Snooker player and Bumps managed to get a ten point spot from him. The deal was if Harvey wins the game, the spot is still ten points. If Bumps wins a game, the spot is taken away. The first game, Harvey ran 70 odd points and won easily. The second game he ran over 80 points, not even a contest. I had to pull Bumps aside and tell him, "The guy is freewheeling and making every ball in sight. You'll have to cool him off by playing tougher safeties. Besides, the well is running dry." Bumps quietly said, "Safeties. No. I'll run a few balls this game." Bumps ran 75 points and I believed he stalled missing a pup, the red ball over the side pocket.

Willie was tickled pink when Harvey said to him, "Your man showed too much; even George Chenier couldn't have done it any better." Harvey was unnerved and started to miss a few shots and Bumps, as usual, played his cat and mouse game and eventually took a big chunk of Harvey's gambling money. Bumps disappeared with his share of the money won. Later I realized that whenever Bumps had big money, he'd go out on a binge and we wouldn't see him for a while. The Uptown II boys were under the impression that Willie was the big moneyman for Bumps. It wasn't too long afterwards that they backed Don Reeves the Legend to play Bumps. Of course Bumps got a 16 point spot playing "Black Ball Only." Bumps, with his superior safety play, made a good player look bad. Reeves played like a cripple and Bumps told me it was psychological. Apparently, in his young days when Reeves was a hot shot, he went to the West End Parkdale Billiards to challenge Bumps. Reeves couldn't win playing even.

Leo Levitt from Montreal might have been a worthy opponent to play George Chenier. Leo was the First Canadian to run a perfect game in Snooker, 147 points and for whatever reason, the same year he dropped into Parkdale Billiards to play Bumps. Each won one game and the gang in Parkdale were betting on Bumps and wanted him to keep playing, but for his own reasons, Bumps quit after playing two games. Unfortunately, I never saw Bumps play in his earlier years in Parkdale and he later started to play in the Cue Billiards when he was in his thirties and I watched him play for thirty years at midtown "Cue Billiards", downtown "Big O" and "Big C" and Uptown 1 and 11.

I often thought that if Bumps hadn't had a drinking problem, he would have been a real contender to win the World Snooker Championship held in England and also to win the American Pool Championship in the U.S. George Chenier, the Hall of Famer, came close. The only time the Great George played for the championship overseas. In 1951-52 he lost to Walter Donaldson who went on to become the Champ. If it weren't for that loss, George would have won the championship. George had the high run in the tournament of 144 and it caused some bitterness because the table was declared non-standard and they didn't recognize his feat.

The high run was 142, co-held by an English pro, Rex William, and a Canadian player, Bill Werbenick, until much later Doug Mount Joy, an English pro ran a 145 in the 80s and then a Canadian, Cliff Thorburn, was the first foreigner to win the World Pro Snooker Championship. Also, Thorburn eventually became the first player to have the high run of 147, a perfect score in a championship tournament George played Fred Davis in Vancouver for the World Championship and lost 31-28.

My friend Willie said, "George was ahead by eight games and his brother died, otherwise George might have beaten Fred Davis. I saw George and Fred play an exhibition match at the Midtown Billiards. George was not his usual self and Fred Davis was brilliant. My youngest brother put together a ProSnooker Tournament using a quick and shorter format. After Fred Davis won the Tournament, he told everybody that he respected George Chenier very much and thought George was the greatest." He told me, "I played over my head to beat George." Fred was a gentleman and I only heard good words about him. George was also an excellent pool player, competing against the best US. Players. He was the first to run 150 points in a straight pool championship against a famous player, Irving Crane.

Talent wise I think Bumps was as good as or better than the top players in the world. I don't know if I'm qualified to say this but I spent thirty years in Pool Halls watching the Master play. Hustlers hide their game well but once in a while Bumper showed world class brilliance and class. Bumper had customers who played a game called "Follow." It's the same game as snooker except the money won or lost is based on a point system. Usually Bumps played for 25 cents a point. If a player wins by a point he wins 25 cents. If he wins by 100 it's a 25 dollar win. At times Bumps would be penniless when he started the day with a "Follow" game. Bumps would never ask me for money but wanted me to be around in case he lost a game by too many points. That never happened. Even at the beginning of the session he hustled, winning by a small margin or letting the other guy win by a few points. Some of his customers were capable of running 100 points. Bumps was a master with the "cat and mouse" game and he couldn't have done it any better if the games were fixed. Bumps needed me just in case the guy fluked a ball and ran a lot of points. I never had to dip into my wallet and give him money, which meant he was on his own and didn't have to share his winnings with me. Besides, Bumps only wanted to win enough money to pay for the drinks, the table time and the meals after the session, and, if he was lucky enough, to have money left over to buy a bottle of whiskey the next day. Remarkable, when you considered how he controlled the billiard balls that controlled the other guys' money to control his own life.

Occasionally, while he was playing "Follow", I would signal to him that I was leaving. He would come up to me and ask, "Reg, could you wait until the next game? I'm going to run some balls." He wanted to win enough money just in case the other guy got lucky. This situation happened countless times and each time he said, "I'm going to run some balls," he ran between 70 to 80 points. What is amazing is, he never let himself down. He didn't have to come up with an excuse like "I'm having an off day" or "I had bad luck" or "the balls were laying awkward", etc. he never had to take two or three shots to be ahead by 70 points. He always did it in one shot, running more than 70 points. Remarkable, considering that some players would say, "I'm going to make this one ball" and miss.

The story was going around that a hotshot from Uptown II was playing as good as or better than Reeves the Legend. The hotshot and his money man challenged Bumps to play at Uptown I. they knew Bumps beat Harvey and Reeves with a handicap spot and wanted to play Bumps even without a spot. They thought playing even, they had the advantage and wanted to win some decent money.

Willie was Bumps money man. Willie was always short on money during the Winter Festive Season, living the life of Feast or Famine and with little money acted like he had plenty. Bumps lost the first two games and I was surprised that the Uptowner played so well. Bumps might have been under the weather and mentioned he needed a bowl of soup to settle his stomach. Willie told the Uptowners, "Bumps isn't feeling good. We are taking a lunch break." Uptowners were smiling and snickering a bit and the backer said, "Make sure you guys come back." The Bumper pounded his chest like a gorilla and hollered out, "I'll be back and I'm going to grab the bread." The soup must have helped Bumps a bit and he showed his professionalism, not for one game but nine straight games. The first game was a "cat and mouse" win. Bumps won each of the remaining eight games in two shots; never missed a shot and never ran more than 40 points. He did this by running close to 40 points and played such a tough lock up safety that the other guy was forced to leave Bumps a shot, giving him a chance to run 30 points or so. It takes 75 points to win a game.

The money man was stunned and his player looked sheepish. They were used to winning and couldn't believe they'd lost. I believe that one reason the guy played great was that the Uptown I and II tables had bigger pockets and the rail shots were much easier to make. I believe he wouldn't have as good playing downtown with the tighter pockets. Bumps went on a binge with his share of the money and disappeared for a while.

Bumper's idea of a perfect game was based on the cat and mouse. He talked about the special game he played at the Westend Parkdale Billiards. It was the other guys' break and he only loosened two red balls from the pack, playing safe, leaving Bumps a long shot. Bumps made the red and a color and another red with a color and without disturbing the pack of red balls, he just feathered the outside red and let the cue ball run downtable for a safety. The guy had no loose red ball to make so he played safe by nicking the pack of reds and going back downtable with the cue ball. Bumps was left with only one open red which he pocketed and made a color and then brushed the cluster of reds to play safe sending the cue ball down table again. The guy didn't have an open shot on the red and played safe; meanwhile he might leave one or two reds open and every time Bumps would make the open shot and play safe, so the guy never saw an open red ball to shoot at. Even though the guy lost the game, he couldn't believe Bumps was making those long shots after his safety and wanted to play out the game. Bumps told me he played a complete perfect game of cat and mouse. I don't know enough about Snooker to say which would be harder: to play an all-out offensive game and run 147 points or an all-out defensive game where the other guy never has an open ball to shoot, plus making every open red ball. I guess it would depend on variables and circumstances.

Once I walked into the Cue Billiards and stopped just inside the doorway. Bumps was playing on the front table closest to the door. He'd just made the black ball to win the game but the cue ball came towards me and fell into the corner pocket. The scratch cost Bumps the game. He was ticked off, saying, "You know Reg, this is the second time in my life that I scratched. Didn't think the roll was so bad on this table." This told me he knew at all times where the cue ball was going.

Players who bragged about their game rubbed Bumps the wrong way. Some guys would boast about being great shot makers. Others would talk about controlling the shooter for position. Some players like to show off how much spin they put on the cue ball or a long power shot to draw the ball.

In the Big C Billiard Hall, everybody was impressed with a player who used extreme English (spin) on the cue ball. He thought he was the King of the English. Bumps played him once and made a couple of shots that made the English King's head spin. He actually went to the cushion railing with his fingers traced the angle of the cue ball and said, "I could never put that much running siding on the cue ball. Another guy from Parkdale liked gambling with short reds instead of the 15 red game. He would make a game with either three or six red balls. This gave him a great advantage because of his skill making long difficult long shots. He did say to me, "I couldn't pot or make long shots as good as Bumps and could not shoot harder than Bumps," but he also added, "I beat Bumps playing Snooker." Most of the good players say, "Bumps is a good hustler but I beat him."

Jackel, like Harvey, had George Chenier as a mentor. Like Harvey, he was well dressed and the nicest person you could meet except when it came to talking or playing Snooker he became obnoxious. Jackel and Hyde personality. Quite often he would practice by himself making the balls. If somebody was watching, he would talk to him about what shots to make and explain the correct sequence of running the balls. He was a good student of the game but study alone is not going to make a great player. Jackel was an intelligent, passionate, argumentative, egotist and I kind of enjoyed his antics. I thought he brought color and character to the Pool room scene.

Jackel played Bumps quite often at the Big C Billiards. They played for hours on end for $5.00 a game. The games went back and forth and at the end of the session they would break even or Bumps would be ahead by one or two games. Jackel must have gotten antsy and said, "Let's play for some money. We'll put up fifty dollars each and whoever goes ahead three games win the money." They played for two days and nobody could be up three games. Jackel would lose a game and win a game back and forth and he lost his patience, saying, "This is crazy, we could play all year and nobody would be a winner. Let's make it two out of three and get this thing over with." They both won a game apiece, so the winner of the third game would win the money. In fact, it went to the last ball to decide the winner. Bumps played not quite an end to end safety. The black ball, a bit off the side rail, maybe a quarter of an inch and two feet away from the corner pocket. Jackel was standing at the other end of the table, the cue ball a few inches away from the end rail.

He was shaking his head, saying, "How the hell can a guy play a safety of this shot." He couldn't figure a way to play safe with a hope and a prayer, tried to make the ball. He stroked the cue well and almost made it. The ball caught the corner of the pocket and ricocheted to the other outer edge corner doing a quick quake (shake, rattle and roll) and rolled away from the pocket. Bumps was left with a long shot and I wondered if he would make the ball. After all it was my $50 riding on the game, and when he took four or five extra strokes, at least he was trying. Sweet "Boom" when the game ball goes into the pocket. Game over and the first thing Jackel said was, "How can a guy play a safety of that trap shot." I was going to tell him but Bumps showed him by placing the black ball and the cue ball as they were and made Jackel shoot it, explaining how to play a safety. Sometimes the most obvious is the most profound. Jackel played a great safety end to end, the cue ball resting on the top rail and the black ball almost touching the bottom rail. He couldn't believe how simple a shot it was and had that look like he discovered the mystery of the Universe.

Bumps wasn't fond of Jackel's mouthiness. Jackel made me laugh when he called Bumps a chicken. He kept saying Bumps is gutless; every time he makes a red ball in the black area he doesn't stay there to make the black ball but plays it safe by drawing or bringing back the cue ball for position on the blue or the Mickey Mouse colors on the Diamond. Bumps is afraid that if he missed he'll leave me among the open reds where I can win the game. George and all the good players stay in the black ball area to win the game. Bumps is a chicken. He'd rather play safe in case he misses." When we left the room, Bumps matter of factly said, "Ah, one of these days I'll show Jackel how the game is played." A few weeks later they were at it again. The games were going back and forth until Bumps made three or four reds and the colors and then said, "I have a chance to run the table. " Jackel, with a big cigar in his mouth, shot back, "Yeah, go ahead." Bumps' tempo of play slowed down. His face appeared to relax, his eyes intense, focusing on one ball at a time. One tricky shot, a red ball at a sharp angle to make in the side pocket, played good close position and nursed the ball in. After that shot, Bumps had no choice but to make the blue ball into the other side pocket and I believe it was the only time the cue ball went to the other half of the table hitting the bottom rail and coming all the way back to the top where the reds were bunched up. At times Bumps would pause to look over the reds

To see a pattern of sequence in making the balls. I've seen some of the top English pros and George Chenier after making the black ball, the cue ball gently breaking some reds away from the pack and continue making the balls. For me it was the first time Bumper showed me he had the ability to loosen a few red balls from the cluster. His positioning of the cue ball was flawless, always, always having a ball to make. The few shots he made brought back memories and familiarities of when I played on small snooker tables needing crucial pinpoint control in making black balls.

Only a handful of guys watching and nobody was moving or making a sound. The balls kept disappearing until no reds were left. It was just the matter of mopping up the six remaining color balls. Two balls to go with an easy shot to make the pink and then the black for a complete runoff. It might have been a very awkward angle on the pink. I think on a follow through the shooter could hit the black or be too close to it, which means on the other side of the table. Bumps would have to use a long rake to thin cut the black into the corner. If he had a bit more angle, the cue ball would naturally slide down for an easy shot to make the black. Bumps powered the shot, the hit sounding like a sharp, shrill, splintering of glass or ceramic. "Psssst!" the cue ball shot forward about ten inches towards the black and stopped.

It reminded me of a golfer's wedge shot, the golf ball moving like a low flying missile hits the green, skims about then feet and stops cold turkey. If the golfer doesn't hit it right, "Bye Bye Birdie, I could die." At least Bumps didn't have to use a long rake or walk around to the other side of the table to shoot the last ball. It was not a 90 degree cut but pretty close to it, a very difficult thin cut for anybody to make. Left leg straight, feet or toe on the floor, lifted his right leg over the railing, laid it on the table, leaned his upper body towards the middle of the table, head turned facing the black ball. Bumps looked like a contortionist but his eyes, head, chin, neck shoulders arms and hands were in alignment with the stroking cue. Thoughts flash through my mind, "For years, I've see Bumps stall, missing a shot. Deliberately missing a shot is a Hustler's "trade mark." Bumps took five or six extra strokes which meant he was trying. The black ball went into the center of the pocket. Bumps was exuberant but showed constraint ... 139 points and the highest run in "The Big C" Billiards was the loud voice of the score keeper. The other guys were happy witnessing "

A helluva game" as one guy put it. My young friend P.T. watched.

And probably thought, "I'm going to do that." Jackel had that amazed blank look and said to me, "See what I mean, everybody plays like a champion when they play me."

I could honestly say over the years in separate occasions in different time periods whenever Bumper said, "I'm going to run a few balls," he always ran over 70 points. This must have happened many times. When he said, "I'm going to grab the bread." He never missed a shot and never left the other guy a shot." Bumps ran 75 points on a do or die game on Harvey who said, "Even George Chenier couldn't have done it any better." Bumps never had an off day when he said, "I'm going to make a few balls." He was able to do it. Now I wish he had failed just once so I could say, "At least he was human." I hate to put anybody on a pedestal of divinity.

Players and everybody would say all sorts of conflicting and controversial things about Bumps. "He can't play when he's sober." "He has to drink, otherwise he chokes." "He just plays good enough to win the money." "He's no George Chenier or Cliff Thornburn." "I've seen him drunk as a skunk making all kinds of balls." "He makes balls and plays good when he's sober." "He's not good enough to win a tournament." Etc. etc. etc. everybody who played Bumps would say, "I beat Bumps." There is a reason and most of them won the battle but lost the war. Bumps was fun to be around with, always up beat, my kind of guy. Even after a binge, looking like a downtrodden derelict, probably depressed, didn't take him long to be back on track. What lifted his spirit? "Flick of the wrist, stroke of the cue, Lord of the Game."

Everything is motion, even the most solid looking object is vibrating. The big planet to the smallest particle is just a density of concentrated motion. The space between them has less density with less concentrated motion. Relating to Human motion is a precursor to emotion, feeling, thoughts, etc. the multi-dimensional functioning of the powerful invisible emotion creates a force field bounded and insulated by an emotional Ozone Layer. Like all spatial substance, the layer protects its singularity and uniqueness by trying to prevent things from entering or leaving. Everybody lives in their own World of Reality and Delusions and they think and feel they have a greater life or a lesser one. The strength or weakness of everyone's emotional force field depends on the quality and quantity of awakening awareness. Bits and pieces of information knowledge and experience has limited awareness that leads to mistakes, mishaps and misfortune. The emotional ozone layer is like the skin that bruises, ruptures and tears apart and wreaking havoc on the emotional Ego World. If the wound does not heal, the Ego World could go the way of the dinosaurs. In my case, I was guaranteed to fail in the business world. Without due diligence and a solid business plan and very little awareness of running a business, my emotional box had too many blind spots that blindsided any success. Now in my old age, I realize the importance of understanding things and to be careful in making emotional choices that lead to failure.

The World of Billiards has the same emotional causal pattern. Some guy goes to a local poolroom and learns how to make a few balls and then begins to beat the local players. Emotionally, he feels like he's living in the world of billiards, thinking he's the best, and goes to a big time Pool Hall. It all depends on the capacity of his awareness. Very few go on to better and greater things. Most of them are trapped, emotionally attached to a small time mentality of a local pool room and never have an awakening. They make mistakes, assuming partial facts, rumors and hearsay as the only Reality. Lacking understanding of the real Billiard World, they get swallowed up by pool sharks and get labeled as "Born Losers." Fact or fallacy, the real story goes around and around the pool halls and eventually turns out to be a fantasy story. Even in the great respected institutions, many leaders make emotional choices based on fallacies to control the group. Bully bureaucracy and the army of control freaks. They don't see anything outside of their own Reality and lose touch with the real World. I guess it's a necessary evil. I don't know which institutional group would be the worst.

No wonder that when I say "Talent wise, Bumps was the best", many pool players would think I was nuts.

Almost everybody who hung out in the Downtown pool halls thought another friend of mine was a nut case. Diamond Jim was a gem of a man. He lived life to the fullest and talked about his escapades, making outrageous claims, and they all thought Jim was full of bull but enjoyed his stories, jokes and antics.

Sublime to the ridiculous. Jim lived the life of James Bond without the violence. During WWII he was an officer in the Canadian Army and successfully defended four Canadian soldiers who were court-martialed. Jim was not a lawyer and I agreed with him when he said, "you either know law or you don't." he was invited to a lot of Socialite parties and the media made him out to be another Oscar Wilde. Even in the limelight, Jim mentioned that the English still looked down on him as a Colonial. It reminded me of Grandfather's Island country. If a Japanese lived outside of Japan for a year or two and went back to Japan, they would consider him worse than a Colonial and out and out Gai-jin, a foreigner.

After the war, Jim had a dual role, having an affair with a beautiful Communist Countess and spying on Communist activities. He was also a good investigative reporter and communicated directly with President Eisenhower and Secretary of State Dulles. Washington was in a stalemate with the two Communist countries, Russia and China. Jim mapped out the policy and coined the word, "Cold War."

Jim must have been a great reporter, otherwise why would he have had access to the wire service? In his younger days he worked for the Toronto Star and the Winnipeg Press. Later he went to the U.S. and worked for the Hurst Newspaper in Los Angeles. He might have broken a rule by taking a photo of a condemned man on death row inside the prison and sent the guy's picture around the world via wire service. Jim was handsome and had no problem dating beautiful actresses and even dated the famous Fontaine sisters from Canada. As I said, Jim was a good investigative reporter and rubbed the Mafia Bosses the wrong way. They both feared each other and met a couple of times to work things out. Jim went to New York and worked for Arthur Rank in the film industry. World War II broke out and he came back to Canada to join the army.

After the smoke in Europe, Jim finally settled down in Toronto.

I first met Jim in the Big C Billiard. Due to the demolition of the building, Towne Billiards went out of business and the Towne players came up the street to the "Big C" where I hung out and played mostly Billiard Golf. Jim introduced himself to me saying, "I hear you play a pretty good game of Golf, but that's not my game. I'll play you a game of "Pink ball only". For an elderly gentleman, he played pretty well, not too bad as a shot maker, but lacked the finesse of controlling the cue ball. He was different and interesting and I felt he was not the type of man to hustle. He probably sized me up pretty well and after two sessions we quit playing and became good friends. Jim had a way with the females. Grey hair, blue eyes, handsome, slim, built and tall at 6'3". He never ran out of words of flattery and the girls loved it. I never heard Jim swear and maybe he had such a wealth of vocabulary he didn't need to. If it weren't for the shabby dark blue pin striped suit, Big Jim would have looked out of place in a pool room. Paul Rimstead, a popular newspaper columnist, wrote an article about Jim. Jim didn't mind that the article mentioned his shabby suit but was upset that his name was printed incorrectly. I had to laugh when Jim wrote an article and the newspaper printed Paul Rimstead's name as Bill Bumstead, in reference to the famous old cartoon character.

It took a while for it to dawn on me that Jim's biggest interest was the Criminal Justice System. Almost daily, he would go to the Courthouse and watch what was going on. Once he did something unheard of, removing a senior court judge from the bench. He told me he used an underhanded method to do so. Apparently, Jim was convicted of defrauding a woman in the stock market. A couple of the guys in the know told me, "Jim didn't have to go to jail or have a criminal record. Jim told me, "The big boss didn't help me out." I like to believe it was a setup and Jim wanted a criminal record that would help him to further his investigation and research in the Criminal Justice System.

For whatever reason, Jim was always dropping into Carlton Street office to see the Boss of the Blue Machine. One drug dealer, who liked playing Golf with me, said, "Jim is a high class stool pigeon." Everybody in the downtown Pool Halls was laughing at Jim, dressed up in a white Panama hat, red and white striped jacket and white pants, barking away at the crowd on Yonge Street, using a cane to steer them up the flight of stairs to Starvin' Marvin's Strip Club. Of course he casually mentioned to me that he was doing research on the Mob's operation of the Girlie Club. Much later, when he married a girl from a wealthy family, he was flashing thirty purple $1,000 bills downtown. Everybody thought he was a nutcase, saying, "He's going to get mugged and even get killed." He told me, "Don't worry, Reg, I have a couple of plainclothes men nearby to protect me and they will nail anybody who tries to rob me." They didn't catch any criminals and I think Jim himself, with his steely blue eyes, looked like a copper. In fact, he looked like a high ranking RCMP Officer that would scare away anybody. Jim was well connected, coming from a family of Empire Loyalists. Married a girl from across the tracks, believing generation after generation of the bloodline was not healthy.

Jim's mother was a brilliant bridge player and a powerhouse. She told Jim to make sure his father's name was on the list to be the Cabinet Minister of Health. At that time, Jim was working for the Toronto Star and his father's name was not on the list. He phoned Mom and all she said was, "Well, we will have to see about this." She had many lady friends in the right places and her husband, a medical doctor, became the Liberal Health Minister of Ontario. Both the family daughters married into corporate wealth and a nephew became Secretary of State under Pierre Trudeau.

Jim told me about the family gathering for a party: while he was sitting at the bottom of the staircase, one of his sisters came over and said, "Jamie boy, don't look so glum, this party is for you, be happy you're out of the Can, you're free." Jim said to me, "the rich have no shame."

Jim always had flowers and small gifts for the secretary at the Carleton Street office. He also had a way with words to charm the ladies. She liked him and gave Jim the VIP treatment. Once a back bencher was ahead of Jim, but the secretary told Jim to go in first to see the Boss. The guy might have been ticked off and said, "Faulkner, you're nothing but a name dropper." Jim snapped back, "You – just dropped my name." She thought it was hilarious.   Once I saw the Blue Machine Boss running up the stairs of the Big C Pool Room calling out, "Farley, Farley." Jim was just at the top of the stairway and they both rushed down and in a hurry to go somewhere. They didn't see me standing on the side at the bottom of the stairs. Whenever Jim had something important to do, he would drop into a small house-like building on 10 Toronto Street or a large Insurance building on Bloor just east of Yonge Street. I don't think Jim would do anything important without talking things over with men of influence.

When Pierre Trudeau said some negative things about Royalty to the Press, Jim said, "I'm going to straighten out the Prime Minister." Jim was a one-man boiler room working the phones. It didn't take too long before all the newspapers in Canada were carrying the story about Trudeau's comment about the Royal Family. If the story was big enough, Jim would use the wire service to take it down into the U.S. Jim knew the power of the Fourth Estate and whether promoting a pool player, billiard tournament, actor, singer, guitarist or any political issue, he would make the press dance to his tune.

Jim, for years, lived on a meager Army Pension but finally married a lady from a wealthy family. I don't know if he really meant it when he said, "I just wanted to prove to one or two guys it's easy to have big money." Whenever we were in a restaurant, he would talk to babies, little children, Mothers, and always bought sweets for the kids. Jim talked to a lot of people which helped him to feel the pulse of society. He would slip five or ten dollars to some of the down trodden bums that hung out in pool rooms, found jobs for the unemployed, helped people to become Canadian Citizens, helped lawbreakers to get a new start, the list goes on.

When the President of SGI came to Toronto, I invited Jim to our General Meeting. Jim always talked like he was the greatest and I was taken aback when he said, "Your President moves in International Circles and I'm not in that league. I won't be going." I was so happy when he changed his mind and showed up at the meeting. Later he told me, "We don't know enough about your President but will have to keep an eye on him."

Jim was frustrated knowing the democratic process was not always perfect. He worked with passion behind the scenes for our freedom, protecting and preserving the Criminal Justice system. Jim was a true blue Canadian and Canada owes him.

We the people only have partial awareness of the whole truth. How much do I know about the truth of Bumps, Big Jim and even my own life? Not much but more than most people who think they know. The less they know, the greater the half-truths and fallacies. Hardly anybody agrees. One friend read a book about brain Science and said, "The brain chemicals could play tricks and your own brain could deceive and betray you." Where is the truth when you can't trust your own brain? No wonder the World rotates around like a big Nut House. I believe there are ways to train the brain to become loyal and trusting. It must be good fortune to have beneficial alpha waves in the brain to harmonize and balance the brain chemicals which could help to have a clearer awareness of awakening. I may not become the Teacher of the Law but hopefully become a bit wiser in my old age? Who knows?

CPSIA information can be obtained at www.ICGtesting.com
Printed in the USA
LVOW04s1328290615

444281LV00028B/1449/P

9 781491 084915